AF508092

SHABD YOGA

AND

SANT MAT ©

The Path to God Realization

Thomas J Douglass

Thomas J Douglass Publications

2009 U.S. Copyright #1-6342317481

2020 U.S. Copyright #1-9002811921

ISBN: 979-8-9894871-4-1

Author's Introduction

While attending college in Colorado in 1969, I learned about Kirpal Singh from a friend purely by chance. I wasn't particularly interested in religion and I wasn't shopping for a guru. But it sounded interesting so I obtained Kirpal's book, "Naam or Word", and read it all the way through in one sitting.

The book had a profound effect on me in two ways. First, as a peace activist, I came away frustrated after learning that the teachings of all the world's major religious institutions were based on the same esoteric truths. These were the same institutions which had battled, both intellectually and with the spilling of blood, for thousands of years over their perceived differences. I thought that if people knew this; if they could understand this common esoteric thread the way I had just come to understand it, maybe it could lead to a climate of religious tolerance and mutual respect. Perhaps it would even lead to peace on earth. I was a young man inspired by hopeful possibilities.

I also came away with a desire to experience the mysteries which I had just read about. Later that year, I received initiation instructions and began practicing Shabd Yoga. About a month later, I arose at 3:00 A.M. to meditate and experienced samadhi for the first time.

In 1972, while on tour with Kirpal, I met with him privately and he instructed me to continue to spread the teachings of Sant Mat and Shabd Yoga. At that time, he gazed into my eyes intently and I experienced overwhelming blissful intoxication when his spirit entered into my body and merged with my own spirit.

Meeting up with Kirpal and his teachings profoundly transformed me and altered my life's trajectory. It gave me a truer understanding of myself and my existence. I therefore dedicate this book to the memory of my spiritual mentor, Sant Kirpal Singh.

Introduction to Shabd Yoga

Shabd Yoga, also known as Dharana Nada Yoga, the discipline of listening to the inner sound current, is an effective means of fostering the development of one's consciousness, a valid method for achieving evolutionary spiritual growth, an effective means of tapping into and experiencing a person's innate inner bliss, and a certain means of achieving self-realization. When practiced regularly and accurately; Shabd yoga works!

Shabd Yoga has been practiced throughout the millennia, and throughout the world, by many philosophers and mystics, hailing from numerous cultural and religious backgrounds. These philosophers and mystics have subsequently become associated with certain ideological traditions. Evidence for the practice of Shabd Yoga is found in many places within the world's sacred literature, stemming from the writings of these teachers and others who wrote about them. Mostly for these reasons, the practice of this ancient method has taken on a religious veneer, including theological explanations and codes.

In this context, one should understand that a person's ability to tap into the subtle realms of human consciousness through the practice of these methods is universal, being an evolutionary feature common to everyone. The innate ability of a person to tap into the subtle aspects of their higher inner self existed prior to the practice of shabd yoga itself. The technique's simplicity belies the often-complex theological associations it is often burdened with.

This publication goes to great lengths in order to present the background and history behind the practice of these methods, including references found within religious literature stemming from numerous traditions. Presenting these references is necessary, in part, in order to make the case for the widespread phenomenon of the practice itself. However, these religious associations are not necessary in order to understand, practice or benefit from Shabd Yoga.

In fact, these religious associations can be cumbersome. They can create a roadblock for someone who is in search of the benefits which can be derived from the practice of shabd yoga, but who is reluctant, for whatever reason, to want to associate with any kind of religiosity or theological codes. A person can entirely throw out; disregard all associations with religion and theological references, and achieve precisely the same results as another person who practices the techniques while simultaneously embracing these same theological associations. Shabd Yoga, as an effective yogic, metaphysical practice, stands on its own.

Regarding organizations involved in the teaching and training of people in the methods of practice, some have adopted a somewhat elitist, guru-centric viewpoint. They suggest that anyone who initiates the practice of Shabd Yoga and who wants to achieve the greatest benefit from said practice, must first become associated with a particular teacher or group. In their view, anyone who receives instructions elsewhere has a kind of diminished status and is unlikely to benefit from the practice. In their view, their teacher, and/or their particular organization, is a necessary intermediary for achieving success on the spiritual path.

In this context, there are two important factors to bear in mind;

1. Anyone can benefit from the practice of Shabd Yoga, regardless of how they come to learn the methods for practicing the techniques.

2. Choosing a teacher from which to learn these methods is still an important decision, the same way it is important to choose a competent teacher for any field of endeavor. It is always beneficial to have someone instructing you who has either mastered the process himself or who has a significant amount of personal experience with it.

In this regard, an experienced teacher is also advisable because Shabd Yoga, when practiced accurately and regularly, will very likely lead to changes in a person's consciousness. A practitioner of Shabd Yoga will experience a more highly developed spirit body, resulting from the activation of the spiritual senses of seeing and hearing. A practitioner will have new experiences, both mundane and subtle, which may at times benefit from explanation or clarification. Having a seasoned, experienced teacher to consult with to help support one's ongoing development is a valuable asset.

The milieu of spiritual and religious traditions and teachers is replete with tales of successorship-related dramas and controversies. It comes with the territory. It's a given. Debates over who is a rightful successor and who is not, has given rise to guru politics; my guru is superior to your guru, etc.

In the case of my own teacher, Kirpal Singh, he did not publicly name a particular individual to replace him. There are contrary opinions about his succession which are held by some, but this unavoidable fact remains; had Kirpal wanted to name a single individual as a successor, he could have done so in a public and unambiguous way. He did not.

This ambiguity has led to a proliferation of numerous teachers and unique groups, each devoted to teaching some form of Shabd Yoga. Swami Ji's original Radha Soami group in Agra has experienced a similar branching of groups and proliferation of teachers. In the world today, there are now over a hundred teachers of Shabd Yoga. In fact, over the course of the 160 years of the Radha Soami movement, since Swami Ji began his public teaching, the pattern of succession has been multiple successors accompanied by opinions and arguments about who is valid and who is not. The model of openly appointing a single guru as a successor to a living teacher hasn't been the norm within Radha Soami. It's been the exception.

Personally, I'm in favor of presenting this practice to a broader segment of the population. For that reason, I'm inclined to view proliferation in a favorable light. Of course, any new aspirant would be advised to be prudent in his selection of a teacher. The integrity and spiritual development of any prospective teacher should be taken into account.

To my way of thinking, there are two critical factors regarding anyone's choice of a spiritual mentor.

1. the motives and sincerity of the student

2. the motives and sincerity of the teacher

The teacher also needs to have a significant degree of inner spiritual development, but I include this in the motives and sincerity of the teacher.

Up until the mid-twentieth century, if one was to find a teacher of this spiritual science, he had to go to India. India is, and has been, planet earth's primary (although not exclusive) womb for spirituality and teachers of yoga for a very long time. But even though we are fortunate for India's role and grateful for the contribution that India and its teachers have made to the spiritual evolution of humanity, spirituality is not the monopoly of any race or sect of people or any geographic locale. Spirituality is universal and its teachers need not hail from any particular place or bloodline. Spiritually speaking, there is one race; the human race.

Indian teachers teach through the prism of Hindu culture. Hindu culture is an age-old component of the collective knowledge of humanity. It is replete with sound wisdom and philosophy. However, for someone new to this yoga, especially a Westerner, when it is presented through the prism of Hindu culture, a person can confuse the practice itself with the culturally-oriented presentation; which is the husk, not the kernel. It is important to draw attention to the fact that this yoga is not a 'Hindu or Indian phenomenon'; it is a universal, human phenomenon.

Swami Ji Shiv Dayal Singh is the foundational teacher of Radha Soami. The term 'Radha Soami' is used generally in reference to the organizational entity that provides spiritual training. Swami Ji and his mentor, Tulsi Sahib, used the term 'Sant Mat' to describe the practice of Shabd Yoga, the theoretical teachings associated with it and the spiritual lifestyle which is prescribed by teachers and adopted by students. Sant Mat translated means "teachings of the Saints".

Today, Swami Ji's purely spiritual movement; 'Radha Soami', aka 'Sant Mat', is now 160 years old and generations of teachers and students have come and gone. What has happened historically to purely spiritual movements, is that over time, they devolve away from their focus on the inner spiritual development of the individual and become religious movements, with emphasis shifting to theoretical teachings and organizational allegiances and biases.

Regrettably, the devolution within Sant Mat and Radha Soami appears to be underway. Some scholars of religion have begun to classify Radha Soami as a new religion, having now the component parts and characteristics which define what a religion is. My hope is that this publication will help to refocus attention on the spiritual development and enlightenment of the individual practitioner, rather than emphasizing theoretical teachings and organizational politics.

I have also introduced the term; 'Dharana Nada Yoga', because it describes the ancient practice in a literal way, using the terminology of the language of yoga. Our popular twenty-first century contemporary yoga is a marvelous component to Western culture. But contemporary yoga is missing something; a vital link to its past. It is missing the practice of Shabd Yoga, or Dharana Nada Yoga, the practice of listening to and being consumed by the audible harmonic current of life. Now, the time has come to reintroduce it to yogis and yogic practitioners, everywhere.

Shabd Yoga and Sant Mat
Table of Contents

PART I

The Yogic Science

CHAPTER 1

CHARTING THE WAY

Everything is music. Everything. And this music is alive and conscious.

All of creation including human beings, plants and animals, the entire physical universe, and all of the mental and spiritual planes of consciousness are all essentially music. This fundamental truth, that everything is music, can be realized - experienced by anyone. Looking back in time, many souls have realized this truth through personal experience and anyone who wishes to, and who is willing to devote the time and attention required to realize this truth now, or any time in the future, can do so.

Creation is not music in a literal sense, at least not in the way the word 'music' is commonly used. Music is an art form invented by people, created by people, for the enjoyment of people.   It utilizes sound vibrations which coexist in strict mathematical relationships, known as harmonic ratios, and changes in those vibrations measured in time.

The essence of life is also a wave structure, or structures. And like music, these waves are configured harmonically. But these waves are not measured in time. They allow for the structure of time itself. They also form the basis of mass. Their simple harmonic relationships; the ratios between their various frequencies and wavelengths are not only fundamental to everything in the universe. They establish the archetype for mathematics itself.

These waves, however, were not created by a human. This 'unstruck' harmony was present at the moment of creation, was the cause of creation, and sustains everything in creation. It is the essence of being. It is the essence of life. It is the essence of us. Why does this art form we call music so appeal to us, have such an attraction over our attention and our senses? Because it mirrors the essence of our own being. If you yourself ever come to know this reality by experiencing it firsthand, you will probably describe the experience in terms of music. When a person experiences the 'music of the spheres', he comes face-to-face with the essence of the mystery of life and creation.

> *"Harmony is the source of manifestation, the cause of its existence, and the medium between God and humans…Eternal harmony is the harmony of consciousness which, being in itself eternal, all things and beings live and move in it – yet it remains remote, undisturbed and peaceful…All vibrations from the finest to the most gross are held together by this harmony, as well as each atom of manifestation – and both creation and destruction take place in order to uphold it."*
>
> Hazrat Inayat Khan

The world's sacred literature contains references to this truth in statements made by masters and sages regarding their own mystical experiences. Some of these written accounts have been preserved in a lyrical or poetic style while others are more direct and literate. These sages tell us that this harmonic essence can be heard and communed with. Further, it emits light and has the innate qualities of love and bliss. But without our own experience as a reference, these words from the past sages have been misunderstood and misinterpreted. As a result, this mystery of life has, for most of humanity, remained a mystery.

In the Vedas, this unstruck, vibratory, harmonic primordial essence is referred to as 'Nada'. Nada is a Sanskrit word. It is not only found in the Vedas, it also appears in other religious literature originating from Hindu culture, including the Buddhist sutras. Nada is just one of many terms that have been utilized over the millennia to refer to the primordial, harmonic essence of life.

The "Nada Bindu Upanishad", written some time before the Christian era, is devoted to a discussion of the practice of Dharana Nada Yoga (Shabd Yoga) and to the transcendental experiences of inner divine sounds that can accrue to an ardent practitioner as he becomes more adept it its practice.

> *"31. The Yogin being in the Siddhasana (yogic posture) and practicing the Vaishnavi-Mudra, should always hear the internal sound through the right ear (right side).*
>
> *"32. The sound which he thus practices, makes him deaf to all external sounds. Having overcome all obstacles, he enters the Turya (higher conscious) state within a fortnight.*
>
> *"33. In the beginning of his practice, he hears many loud sounds. They gradually increase in pitch and are heard more and more subtly.*
>
> *"34. At first, the sounds are like those proceeding from the ocean, kettle-drum, waterfalls and rapids; in the middle (stage), those proceeding from Mardala (deep double-drum), bell and horn.*
>
> *"35. At the last stage, those proceeding from tinkling bells, flute, vina (an Indian instrument played like a slide guitar) and buzzing of bees. Thus, he hears many such sounds more and more subtle.*
>
> *"36. When he comes to that stage when the sound of the great kettle-drum is being heard, he should try to distinguish only sounds which are increasingly more subtle.*
>
> *"37. He may change his concentration from the gross sound to the subtle, or from the subtle to*

the gross, but he should not allow his mind to be diverted from his concentrated attention.

"38. The mind having at first concentrated itself on any one sound, fixes firmly to that and is absorbed in it.

"39. The mind, becoming insensible to the external impressions, becomes one with the sound as milk with water, and then becomes rapidly absorbed in Chidakasa (the field of consciousness where mind prevails).

"40. Being indifferent towards all objects, the Yogin, having controlled his passions, should by continual practice, concentrate his attention upon the sound which subjugates the mind.

"41. Having abandoned all thoughts and being freed from all actions, he should concentrate his attention on the sound continually and allow his Chitta (mind) to become absorbed in it.

"42-43(a). Just as the bee drinks the honey, not caring for the fragrance, so the Chitta which is always absorbed in sound, does not yearn for sensual objects, as it is bound by the sweet smell of Nada (Amrit or divine fragrance) and has abandoned its restless nature.

"43(b)-44(a). The serpent Chitta, through listening to the Nada, is entirely absorbed in it, and becoming unconscious of everything else, concentrates itself only on the sound."

Nada Bindu Upanishad

Communion with the Nada is similarly referenced in other Vedic texts.

"Even if karmas (sin) should accumulate to a mountain extending over many miles, it is destroyed by meditation on the Nada. At no

time has there been found a destroyer of karmas like this.

"Bījākshara (holy mantra) is the supreme bindu (means of unification). Nāḍa is above it. When that Nāḍa sound ceases, then the Nāḍa-less is the supreme state. That yogin who discovers as the highest, that which is above Nāda, which is anāhaṭa, has all of his questions resolved."

Dhyanabindu Upanishad of Samaveda

"When hearing is absorbed in the Nāḍa, the highest state is reached. Nāḍa is like a pure crystal extending from the root chakra to the third eye. It is that which is spoken of as Brahma and Paramāṭmā.

"One hears Nāḍa after the repetition of this manṭra, thousands of times. This Nāḍa is of ten kinds. The first sounds like 'chini'. The second sounds like 'chini-chini'. The third resembles the sound of bell; the fourth, that of conch. The fifth is that of ṭanṭri (archaic string instrument with one or more strings). The sixth is that sound of ṭāla (hand cymbals); the seventh is that of flute; the eighth is that of bheri (kettle drum); the ninth is that of mṛḍanga (double-drum); and the tenth is that of thunder. He may experience the tenth without the first nine sounds, through the grace of the guru."

Hamsa Upanishad of Sukla-Yajurveda

"The person who desires all the wealth of yoga should, after having given up all thoughts, practice with a subdued mind, concentration on the Nāḍa, alone."

Varaha Upanishad of Krshan-Yajurveda

"Now, the light which shines above this heaven, above all the worlds, above everything, in the highest worlds, not excelled by any other worlds; that is the same light which is within man. This heavenly light is visible. And of it, we have this audible proof, when we thus hear, by plugging the ears; what is like the rumbling of a carriage, or the bellowing of an ox, or the sound of a blazing fire. One should worship as Brahman that inner light which is seen and heard. He who knows, becomes conspicuous and celebrated. Yea, he becomes celebrated!"

Chandogya Upanishad

Another, later description of the nature of the experience of concentration on the Nada is described similarly in the standard fifteenth-century yogic text, 'Hatha Yoga Pradipika'. The author, Svātmārāma, first describes the practice, then explains what sounds are heard by novices, and those heard by more experienced adepts.

"I will describe now the practice of anâhata Nâda, as propounded by Gorakshnath, for the benefit of those who are unable to understand the principles of knowledge—a method, which is favored by the uneducated also.

"Those desirous of the kingdom of Yoga, should take up the practice of hearing the anâhata Nâda, with mind collected and free from all cares.

"Âdinâth propounded millions of methods of trance, and they are all valid. Of these, the hearing of the anâhata Nâda is the only method, the best, in my opinion.

"A Yogî should determine to practice constantly in the hearing of the Nâda sounds. Sitting in Mukta Âsana and with his attention,

the Yogî should hear the sound inside his right ear, with collected mind.

"The sound which a yogi hears by closing his ears with his thumbs, should be heard attentively, till the mind becomes steady in it. By practicing with this Nâda, all other external sounds are stopped.

"The ears, the eyes, the nose, and the mouth should be closed and then the clear sound is heard in the passage of the Sushmana, which has been cleansed of all its impurities. In the beginning, the sounds heard are of great variety and very loud; but, as the practice increases, they become more and more subtle.

"In the first stage, the sounds are surging, thundering like the beating of kettle drums and jingling bells. In the intermediate stage, they are like those produced by conch, Mridanga (deep drum), big bells, etc. In the last stage, the sounds resemble those from tinkling bells, flute, Vîṇâ, and buzzing bees. These various kinds of sounds are heard as being produced in the body. Though hearing loud sounds like those of thunder, kettle drums, etc., one should practice with the subtle sounds also. Leaving the loudest, taking up the subtle one, and leaving the subtle one, taking up the loudest; thus practicing, the distracted mind does not wander elsewhere.

"The mind, like an elephant habituated to wander in the garden of enjoyments, is controlled under the hypnotic attraction of anâhata Nâda.

Hatha Yoga Pradipika

It should be noted that this time-honored yogic practice has also been referred to simply as 'Nada Yoga', a term many centuries-old. Originally, Nada Yoga referred exclusively to the practice of listening to the inner transcendental sounds. However, Nada Yoga has now come to be associated with yogic practices which incorporate physical sound-making devices, such as musical instruments and Tibetan bowls. By contrast, 'Dharana Nada Yoga', or Shabd Yoga, refers exclusively to the practice of listening to the inner transcendent sounds of the Nada. Outer physical sounds are not incorporated into its practice.

Historically, the practice of Shabd Yoga is universal with respect to place and time. One excellent example of this is the Chinese master Lao Tzu, who referred to these same essential truths in his great gift to humanity, the 'Tao Te Ching'.

"The Great Music has the faintest notes...

To understand such harmony is to know the Always So.

To know the Always So is to be illumined."

In the first line of the couplet, Lao Tzu first establishes that the Great Music is faint. Therefore, to catch it, one must listen carefully and attentively. He goes on to reference the music's radiant characteristics by telling us that to know it is to be illumined. He knew that few in his generation, and in later generations would be able to comprehend and appreciate his words.

"True words are not fine sounding,

Fine sounding words are not true."

With these memorable words, Lao Tzu opens the 81st and final chapter of his remarkable book. These two lines are taken from a well-read translation by a 20th century scholar, Arthur Waley. Another translation, by Dwight Goddard and his partner, Bhikshu Wai-tao, characterizes the idea differently.

"Faithful words are often not pleasant;

Pleasant words are often not faithful."

These translators present Lao Tzu's idea a bit more gently. But regardless of which translation we prefer, Lao Tzu's message comes through. When we encounter new ideas that contrast with our established beliefs or notions of truth, we are likely to resist them at first. At best, we will consider them in terms of how they do or do not agree with what we currently believe. Our resistance is a function of two things;

1. Human beings place a very high value on ideas and beliefs. We are more likely to associate with someone who thinks the way we do than for any other reason, including family and ethnicity.
2. We also have an inherent insecurity about the major questions concerning God and creation, the meaning of life and death, and of our spiritual identity and fate because we really don't know the

answers to these questions, and when we establish a set of beliefs to address them, it unnerves us to contemplate alternatives which may ultimately prove us to be wrong.

These same fundamental questions are faced by every single person who comes into this world, and the day we set out to find answers to them is a lucky day for us because they will continue to nag at us until we discover a way to satisfactorily resolve them.

Competition for the hearts and minds of people through spiritual, religious, and philosophical ideas is a dynamic and highly contentious component to the history of civilization. Ideological differences are one of the principal factors dividing the peoples of the world into cultures, nations and social bodies. It is not necessary to enumerate the many challenges and conflicts which the world faces today, and has faced throughout history, which stem in whole or in part from conflicting ideologies. One need only refer to a newspaper or a history book to find examples of this sad reality. In the twenty-first century, our ideological labels are more likely to be one of many components to our conflicts, which make them more complex and difficult to resolve.

What is ironic about this dilemma is that there are many parallels and common themes which can be found by comparing the world's great religious traditions and texts. While most of these texts, especially the ancient ones, have been compromised over time for various reasons, they still provide the core teachings for us in a fairly reliable format. One example of a common theme is the question of creation. Nearly all of the world's religious and cultural traditions have an explanation or myth regarding creation. This includes not only traditions stemming from Europe, Africa, and Asia, which could have experienced some cross-pollination of ideas, but also from America and the Pacific Islands. Each explanation is different, but the fact that all of these groups concluded that there was a point or moment of creation is remarkable.

We also find a unity of ideas in principles of moral conduct. The 'Golden Rule', for example, is a universally recognized precept.

> *All things whatsoever ye would have, that men should do to you, do ye even so to them.*
>
> **Christian**
>
> *Whatever thou hatest thyself, that do not to another.*
>
> **Jewish**
>
> *No one of you is a believer until he desires for his brother that which he desires for himself.*
>
> **Islamic**
>
> *Hurt not others in ways that you would find hurtful.*
>
> **Buddhist**
>
> *This is the sum of duty; do naught unto others which if done to thee would cause thee pain.*
>
> **Hindu**
>
> *Regard your neighbor's gain as your own gain, and your neighbor's loss as your own loss.*
>
> **Taoist**
>
> *As thy deemest thyself, so deem others.*
>
> **Sikh**
>
> *In happiness and suffering, in joy and grief, we should regard all creatures as we regard our own self.*
>
> **Jain**
>
> *Do not unto others what you would not have them do unto you.*
>
> **Confucian**

One taking a pointed stick to poke a baby bird should first try it on himself to feel how it hurts.

West African

That nature alone is good which refrains from doing unto another whatsoever is not good for itself.

Zoroastrian

All things are our relatives; what we do to everything, we do to ourselves.

Native American

The fact that there are many parallels to be found by comparing the theoretical teachings of the past masters and religious traditions is a subject which has been explored by scholars extensively, and there have been many authoritative books published on the subject.

"Every religion emphasizes human improvement, love, respect for others, sharing other people's suffering. On these lines every religion had more or less the same viewpoint and the same goal."

The 14th Dalai Lama

One of the earliest-known comparative studies of religious principles originates out of seventeenth-century India. The Risāla-yi Haqq Numāon ("Compass of Truth") is a revealing pamphlet written by the Sufi mystic, Dara Shukoh. Dara Shukoh was the eldest son of Shah Jahan, the famous Mogul emperor who built the marvelous Taj Mahal in Agra, India.

Dara Shukoh became the disciple of the great Sufi master Mulla Shah Badakhsi of Kashmir. Within his introduction to the text of 'Compass of Truth', Dara Shukoh discusses the underlying divine unity inherent in all religious traditions. Dara, who was raised and educated by Persian Islamic scholars, became keenly interested in Hindu philosophy, especially the parallels he observed between Islamic and

Hindu theology. He rejected the dogmatic, parochial approach to the acquisition of knowledge and truth inherent within Islam. His text goes into some length comparing the two religious schools, concluding that the same inherent truths were present in both.

What is perhaps most significant about Dara Shukoh and his 'Compass of Truth' is that he was an accomplished practitioner of Dharana Nada Yoga. Within the text, he discusses the details of the practice itself along with various attainments associated with its practice; knowledge which had previously been closely-guarded by Sufi mystics for centuries. The Compass of Truth stands out, even today, as one of the most specifically-detailed descriptions of the practice of Dharana Nada Yoga ever published. Dara Shukoh called the practice of Dharana Nada Yoga; *'Sultan-ul-Azkar'*. Along with concentration on the Nada, his method included breathing exercises (pranayama) and repetition of a mantra. (His technique will be further examined in Part V.)

Regarding the practice, he states;

> *"Oh friend! When thou desirest to commence the practice of meditation, devote yourself to Sultan-ul-Azkar, called the 'king of*

meditation'. To master this noble practice, thou must do as follows. Thou must go either by day or by night to some desert place, which is free from the haunts of men, or to a cloister where no sound can reach, and sitting there, direct thy attention to thy hearing. And in this attention, thou must fix thy mind so long as thou canst, because in the beginning, a very subtle sound will become audible, to perceive which would require thy utmost attention of concentration. When thou hast once caught it, that sound will become so powerful and overwhelming, that it will draw thy mind away from all other attractions, and it will absorb into it."

Ultimately, and sadly for India, Dara Shukoh was executed by one of his younger brothers, who challenged him to his rightful succession as emperor. Charged with apostasy and heresy by his younger brothers, he was imprisoned and subsequently beheaded in 1659.

There are two distinct components to a spiritual master's teachings; the practical or theoretical portions, and the esoteric portion. The theoretical portions, the teacher's theological exegesis and principles of moral conduct, have been preserved over time through a combination of written and oral traditions. The esoteric portions, for the most part, have not been preserved because in order to properly train someone in the practice of the spiritual disciplines, or sadhanas, the teacher must be someone who is himself an adept in those disciplines. A living teacher is also required to provide guidance to those who are embarking on the inner spiritual path, a teacher who has himself already journeyed successfully on that path himself. It is also beneficial to have a living guide who embodies the energy of a soul who has crossed into the higher spiritual planes so that those around him can bask in his spiritual radiation.

What has happened throughout history, with respect to the esoteric portion, is that each tradition eventually finds itself depleted of competent spiritual adepts who can effectively carry on with the esoteric training and the group devolves from a spiritual body into a religious body with emphasis placed on the theoretical teachings alone. You can track this devolutionary process in the history of every major religious institution.

While scholars have identified the various theoretical parallels, it is not generally understood that there is also a common esoteric thread. That thread is Shabd Yoga. Nearly all of the world's great spiritual masters were practitioners and teachers of Shabd Yoga.

The term, 'Dharana Nada Yoga', is a new term, even though all three words derive from ancient Sanskrit origins. Many past mystics and masters have practiced the ancient spiritual science and they all had their own terms to refer to its practice. Examples include:

- Sant Mat
- Surat Shabd Yoga
- The practice of the Word
- Path of the Masters
- Radha Soami
- Sehaj Yoga
- The Science of the Soul
- The Science of the Beyond
- Para Vidya
- The Yoga of the Sound Current
- Tao
- Sultan-ul-Azkar

The twentieth-century master, Kirpal Singh, used the term 'Surat Shabd Yoga, which had also been used by the nineteenth-century Radha Soami masters Swami Ji and Rai Saligram. Many scholars and others have streamlined this term, calling it simply; 'Shabd Yoga'.

Surat Shabd Yoga literally means the yoga of absorbing the attention (surat) into the sound current (shabd). Dharana Nada Yoga means precisely the same thing. Dharana is the sixth limb of Patanjali's Ashtanga Yoga. Dharana is the focused concentration of the attention. Nada is the traditional Sanskrit term referring to the primordial, harmonic sound-principal at the core of all creation. So, Dharana and Nada taken together mean the state of having one's attention absorbed into the audible essence of life. Adding the term 'yoga' to 'dharana nada' denotes the active practice of sadhanas intended to result in union of the soul with the oversoul through the process of absorbing the attention into the primordial sound principal. This yoga also entails absorption of the concentrated attention in the celestial light, radiating off of the vibrating Nada.

The spiritual path has two distinct stages: self-realization and God realization. Self-realization is the process which prepares a soul for his initiation onto the path of God Realization. Self-realization is not a singular process but rather a multi-faceted process unique to every individual, taking many forms and involving many distinct endeavors and disciplines. These endeavors may include religious and philosophical study, yoga, selfless service, and religious, mystical and life experience. A self-realized person sees himself as a spiritual entity and is conscious of the interconnectedness and interdependence of all life forms. To say that there are many paths which lead to self-realization is a valid statement.

However, to say that there are many paths to God realization is not an accurate statement. There is a specific, natural mechanism integrated into the architecture of the human consciousness which provides a means for each soul to contact the Nada, the harmonic essence of life. Once this harmonic essence is contacted, a soul may travel to its source through Dharana, the concentration of the attention and Dhyana, the sustained concentration of the attention. This process is essentially a linear one and there are many stages of development along the way.

Successful employment of this natural process necessitates the development of our spiritual senses, especially seeing and hearing. In the physical world, we process information gained from our conscious experience from impressions which come to us by way of our five senses. Of these senses, seeing and hearing are the most vital. But our physical senses are only capable of processing information in the physical world. They are of no use in the spiritual realms. However, our spirit bodies have been similarly fashioned with spiritual senses, and again, the two most vital are spiritual seeing and spiritual hearing. One may rightly argue that it is in fact our physical bodies which have been fashioned after the image of our spirit bodies.

So, cognitive experience in spiritual realms begins with the development of these subtle senses. The awakening, development, and utilization of the spiritual senses is the natural, universal method employed by mystics and saints throughout the millennia as the means for furthering their spiritual development and for treading the path toward God realization.

The Buddha (master) who authored the Surangama Sutra, one of Buddhism's most sacred texts, after devoting one third of the sutra to a narrative comparing inferior methods of spiritual practice to 'transcendental hearing', concludes his remarks by declaring; "This is the only way to Nirvana."[1]

It is important to note that our religious and cultural identities have no bearing on the path of God realization either way. One need not make any changes with respect to beliefs, social labels or mode of livelihood. Historically, souls who have found success on the spiritual path have come from every conceivable cultural and religious background.

---

[1] Dwight Goddard, A Buddhist Bible, P. 260, Beacon Press, 1994

Lao Tzu said that there was a Tao or 'way'. That way is Shabd Yoga. Like all masters, Lao Tzu encountered a good bit of resistance from the people he attempted to teach during his life. He was an idealist and would have preferred to have his students come to him as blank slates so that he could write his knowledge directly into their minds.

> *"In the days of old, those who practiced Tao with success did not, by means of it, educate the people, but on the contrary, sought to make them ignorant. The more knowledge people have, the harder they are to teach..."*

But people are not blank slates, which is why we need teachers.

A careful study of Lao Tzu's writing leaves little doubt that he was a practitioner and teacher of Shabd Yoga, one of many to have walked the earth over the millennia. To appreciate this most ancient form of yoga, it is best to consider it, not just within its historic context, but also in light of the great scientific discoveries which have taken place over the last hundred years or so, which have been profound.

The following pages will explore;

1. The classical and esoteric basis of yoga.
2. The phenomena of life itself from the perspective of both science and mysticism.
3. An exploration of the world's sacred literature in search of references to the practice of Shabd Yoga and some of the challenges we face when trying to use these texts as authoritative sources.
4. The colorful relationship between science and religion.
5. A study of the life and teachings of some of the historic masters who have practiced and taught Shabd Yoga, especially over the past 500 years.
6. Instructions for seekers after truth.

CHAPTER 2

THE WAVEFORM –
ARCHETYPE OF DUALITY

"The difference between science and mysticism is very slight: science is bound within the physical world and mysticism is not. Considering the idea of creation from a material point of view, a scientist can go so far as to realize that there are certain factors which were created and which formed matter. He can recognize molecules, atoms and electrons, and then he comes to vibrations; but from here he stands still. He concludes that the basis of the whole of creation must be movement, and that the finest aspect of movement is what is called vibration.

The Vedanta speaks of Nada Brahma, or Sound-God, meaning that the Word or Sound or Vibration was the creative aspect of God, which shows that the mystic does not differ much from the scientist who says that movement is the basis of the whole of creation. When one considers this similarity, one must agree with Solomon that there is nothing new under the sun. The difference is that the mystics of ancient times did not end with the recognition of movement and vibration, but went on to trace it back to its source in the Divine Spirit."

Hazrat Inayat Khan

The entirety of creation; physical, astral and causal planes are all comprised of vibrations or wave structures. The most elemental of these waves, the smallest common denominator of all being, is spirit, or what saints and masters have referred to as 'the Word'. In ancient Hindu philosophical writings, it is referred to as 'Nada'. It is the essence of all life and cause and sustainer of all creation.

In the physical universe, wave structures comprise the basis of everything. Wave structures are the archetype of physical and mental existence; of being.

Wave structures form the foundation for duality. Existence, or 'being', requires duality. Without duality, the physical universe would not, could not exist.

Wave structures form the basis of spacetime. Waveforms have two distinct features; wavelength and vibrational frequency. The length of waves provides for space and the frequency provides for the phenomenon of time.

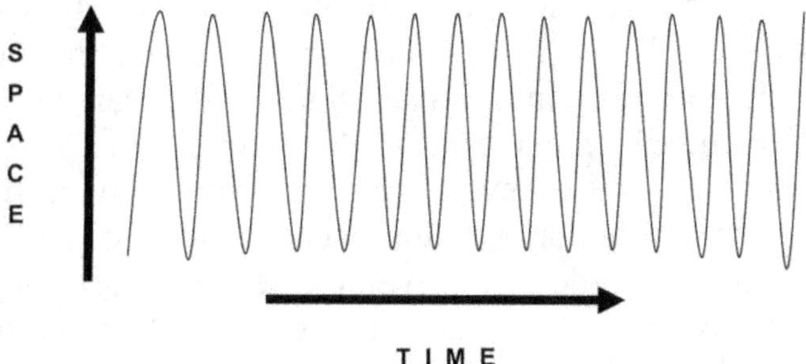

Atomic structure is comprised of waveforms and empty space. Atoms have protons, which are positively charged waves. Electrons are negatively charged waves and neutrons are waves with no electromagnetic charge. Subatomic particles are also waveforms, some with a positive charge, some with a negative charge and some with no charge.

Electromagnetism is another essential component to physical duality. Electromagnetic charges are either positive or negative. Without electromagnetism, and its functionality to either attract or repel, the atom could not exist.

Dual-structured waveforms exist throughout the universe. Examples include the background radiation from the so-called 'big bang' and gravity waves caused from exploding and imploding stars. The universe is full of photons of starlight; waves that possess both a positive and negative charge.

All of these dualistic waveforms that provide the building blocks for everything that exists in the physical universe are patterned after spirit, the essence of existence, which is the power of life or the power of God. Spirit is God's life-power infused into manifested creation. That spirit-power is the canvas upon which the physical and mental planes are painted. That canvas, referred to by saints as Nada or Naam or The Word, is comprised of subtle waveforms that exist in harmonic relationships. Human beings have the capacity to witness this harmonic essence within the depths of their own beings, in the recesses of human consciousness. Those with favorable spiritual development and background can discover and experience this 'music of the spheres', and the light that accompanies it, spontaneously. Souls who incarnate with this level of development from birth are rare. Most people who choose to seek the revelations of spiritual divine light and sound must adopt spiritual/metaphysical disciplines, or sadhanas, in order to develop the necessary degree of receptivity. Shabd Yoga is the sadhana that masters and mystics have adopted throughout the ages to achieve this.

The universe, and everything in it, is alive. The universe is itself a living entity. Life is generally assumed to exist where we see motion; such as a living animal or within a dynamic living cell. Scientists tell us that the universe has no center and that everything in the universe is in motion. The universe is not only expanding, it is accelerating. Within the tiny atom, there is an enormous amount of motion. Electrons orbit nucleuses at astoundingly high speeds near 600 miles per second. The nucleus of the atom, the proton and neutron, are spinning on a mutual axis at a speed of roughly 40,000 miles per second, which is 22% the speed of light.

Science claims that there is only one constant in the physical universe: the speed of light. But there is another constant: the law of cause and effect. Isaac Newton was the first scientist to observe and expound upon the law of cause and effect. His understanding and his explanation of this universal truth was rudimentary, limited to the standards of knowledge of his time. But he saw it and he articulated it in a manner appropriate to his era. Cause and effect is at work in all mental and physical activity in the created universe, from the macroscopic to the microscopic.

In the field of quantum mechanics, scientists conduct experiments on subatomic particles. They cannot see these particles but they have devised means of detecting them. They have discovered that (given the current limitations of their understanding of the laws of physics) it is impossible for them to determine where a particular particle will be at any given moment. They can only say there is a certain probability it will be here or there. They have also learned that the interaction of the experimenter or observer with the experiment itself influences the outcome of the experiment. In other words, it is impossible for an experimenter to have a purely objective observation of these experiments because once he introduces his consciousness as an observer, he himself becomes a component of the experiment.

Most physicists, including John Archibald Wheeler, have now concluded that this phenomenon is true on all levels; micro and macro. Anton Zeilinger, a leading experimental physicist, has reflected on Wheeler's views saying, "The outstanding feature of Professor Wheeler's viewpoint is his realization that the implications of quantum mechanics are so far-reaching that they require a completely novel approach in our view of reality and in the way we see our role in the universe. This distinguishes him from many others, who in one way or another, tried to save pre-quantum viewpoints, particularly the obviously wrong notion of a reality independent of us."[2]

Human beings are intricately tied to everything in the natural world with an ongoing flow of causation connecting everything and everyone. The Native American version of the golden rule; "All things are our relatives; what we do to everything, we do to ourselves", appears profound in view of this scientific paradigm. We cannot think of ourselves as objective, non-participant observers regarding anything we think or do in our lives. Instead, we are causally tied to everything. Peering into the world of the quantum provides us a means of verifying this truth, but just because we don't see it on macro levels does not mean that the law of cause and effect is not at work.

The law of cause and effect operates at all times, under all conditions, in every aspect of creation including the affairs of human beings. Ancient Indian philosophers recognized cause and effect long ago. They gave it a name; the 'Law of Karma'. They saw it in terms of a person's interplay with all things in the natural world, including the earth itself and all of its life forms. The Law of Karma (cause and effect) is the mother of all human laws. It is the reason why we need to have socially-based laws. It is the foundation for all of the laws of the universe, including gravity and relativity.

The fact that particles, planets, and people move according to cause and effect, suggests a universal consciousness of the law. This in turn would suggest the presence of consciousness in all features of creation, large and small, animate and inanimate. One could conclude from this that everything is living and everything is conscious.

One of Galileo's most profound contributions to science, later championed by Newton, was his realization that the underlying truths of the natural world could all be explained

---

[2] Anton Zeilinger, Why the Quantum?, 2004, Cambridge University Press

and demonstrated in terms of mathematics. The relationship between a certain thing and everything else could be described mathematically. Einstein and subsequent scientists have essentially adopted this view as a given.

Viewing creation through the lens of mathematics reveals an orderly world that is tied together in abstract, yet organized and rational relationships. Everything we observe and explore in the natural world can be viewed in terms of mathematical relationships.

One of nature's most curious phenomena is the presence of reoccurring ratios. One example of these ratios is harmonic ratios. Since we ourselves at our spiritual core are comprised of harmonic vibrations, we recognize harmonic relationships when we hear them. We also know dissonance when we hear dissonance. This principle of harmonics is ubiquitous, built into the fabric of creation. Harmonic ratios are specific mathematical relationships between two or more wave frequencies. The most common, the 2:1 ratio, is the octave. The ratio of a perfect fifth is 3:2; a major third is 5:4, and a perfect fourth is 4:3.

Some scientists have discovered examples of these ratios in their research. One example comes from the field of astrophysics. Dr. Omer Blaes, professor of physics at the University of California, Santa Barbara, is part of a research team which has been studying light at the event horizons of black holes, also known as accretion disks. Dr. Blaes has also been looking into the nature of the complex radiation magnetohydrodynamical (MHD) turbulence in the form of energy waves which radiate off of the event horizons. These energy waves have pronounced peaks and valleys. By measuring the varying wavelengths at each of these extremes, and comparing the numbers, all of these points form perfect harmonic ratios with each other, particularly octaves and fifths. Dr. Blaes was not expecting to find this and has stated that the exploration into the phenomenon of harmonic ratios in nature begs further inquiry.

CHAPTER 3

RELIGION SCIENCE AND SPIRITUALITY

Baba Sawan Singh, a twentieth century shabd yoga master, was the first to point out that there was an underlying esoteric thread which tied all of the world's great religious traditions together. After a careful study of the sacred texts of the past masters, he concluded that they all apparently practiced the same sadhana; shabd yoga. He reached this conclusion primarily because he was a realized soul himself and he could see that even though the accounts differed in some ways, they all described the same general process; ingress into the higher spiritual planes by way contemplation of the inner light and sound current.

Sawan's insight was also supported by his religious training as a Sikh. In the course of his own study as a young man, he learned that the Sikh sacred scripture, The Adi Granth, was not only a compilation of writings from the masters who had appeared in his own tradition, but it also contained nearly 800 hymns from 25 mystics outside of the Sikh lineage. But most of these 25 mystics were Indian saints who lived between the 13th and 17th centuries. Sawan's investigation into the world's great sacred literature included accounts going as far back as 1000 B.C. From this, he concluded that the practice of Shabd Yoga was indeed universal and timeless and was not exclusive to any faith, ethnicity or tradition, including the Sikh faith.

Sawan's 50-year spiritual mission began around the dawn of the twentieth century and coincided with the great revolution in science led by Albert Einstein. During this period, there was enormous public attention throughout the world directed toward science and the new discoveries as people began to look more and more in that direction for answers to questions concerning life and the natural world. What set science apart from religion in people's minds was that the new knowledge was empirically-based and verifiable.

Sawan saw an important correlation between science and Sant Mat because unlike mainstream religious ideologies and practices, the practice of Shabd Nada was empirically-based and verifiable. In an attempt to draw attention to this, he coined the term; 'Science of the Soul'. Sawan also used other terms to describe the spiritual science including 'the practice of the Word', and 'the practice of the sound current'. The term 'Word' has been used by many masters in describing the essential power of life (spirit) including Jesus, Guru Nanak and Kabir. 'Sant Mat' was a term used by Sawan's own spiritual mentor, Baba Jaimal Singh. 'Sound current' was a term used by Jaimal Singh's guru, Swami Ji. The spiritual organizations in India that have spawned out of Swami Ji's original Agra group use the term 'Radha Soami'. By interchanging terminology, it serves to help remind people that all of these terms refer to the same thing.

The relationship between the fields of science and religion is a complex and intriguing one and continues to play itself out as science marches on toward greater and greater discoveries and religion attempts to hold her ground and maintain her relevancy. Today, we find an area of common interest in the moral arguments concerning the use of advanced genetics and stem cells. Another popular area of discussion centers on comparisons between metaphysical ideas originating primarily from Eastern traditions and recent discoveries in physics and astrophysics.

Historically, the religion vs science drama involves Christianity more than any other faith because it is principally in the West that science has undergone its dramatic awakening and evolution. At the core of the dispute between these two camps is the contrasting methods by which each seeks to acquire knowledge. Science utilizes a process of empirical observation and verification; aka the 'scientific method'. Religion, on the other hand, employs a combination of religious experience, belief, and reliance on sacred texts which require interpretation.

Both of these institutions could actually benefit from the other's approach. Science could benefit by broadening its scope to include inquiries outside of the physical universe and the natural world; questions that probe the nature of consciousness and the essence of life. Religion could benefit by adopting a more empirical approach in its quest for answers to life's most challenging questions rather than relying so much on the interpretation of ancient sacred texts, many hundreds of years after their writing.

St. Augustine was the embodiment of the theology/science confluence. Augustine was a clergyman, a natural philosopher and is one of Christianity's church fathers. According to Augustine, there are two means of making knowledge statements, through faith and reason, stemming from the two books, the book of nature and the book of scripture. Inquiry into both books requires the application of logic and reason. He also maintained that the two books had to agree, that there was unity of truth. He further asserted that the interpretation of biblical passages should be held provisionally because scripture could only be fully understood in light of our current state of sure rational knowledge. He sums up the science/theology question with the statement; "I believe so that I may understand, and I understand so that I may believe".

Perhaps the most memorable saga in the colorful history of science and religion is the story of Galileo who challenged the church-accepted belief that the earth was the center of the world. He, along with Nicolas Copernicus and other natural philosophers, took the position that the sun was the center of the world. Galileo, with his telescope, found actual evidence to back up the notion. But the church, in a post-reformation era, was not receptive to new ideas, especially ones that did not conform to the strictest literal interpretation of scripture. The scripture, in this case, was the story of Joshua fighting the battle of Jericho. According to the Old Testament account, God halted the movement of the sun long enough for the Israelites to complete the battle victoriously. The church applied the logic that if it was the earth that traveled around the sun, then God would have stopped the movement of the earth, not the sun.

But in the end, what this affair really came down to was a battle of egos; Galileo's, versus all of his opponents in established academia, including Pope Urban VIII. Galileo published his ideas in a narrative with three characters, one of which, Simplicio, was a dunce. Galileo placed some of the Pope's ideas into the mouth of the dunce, his enemies used it as an opportunity to defame him to the Pope, and the ultimate outcome was that Galileo was sentenced to house arrest for the rest of his life. But the story does illustrate the two different approaches to acquiring knowledge that these two sides have traditionally clung to; empirical evidence, in Galileo's (science's) case and the interpretation of ancient religious texts in the church's case.

Religious practice does, of course, involve experience, including such activities as prayer, recitations, pilgrimages, fasting, service to the needy, participation in rituals and events, and other observances. All of these activities are beneficial and can play an important role in the development of self-realization.

Mystical experience is the highest form of religious experience. It involves the direct communion with the power of God, or Nada. This communion takes primarily two forms. Through the practice of Shabd Yoga, one comes into contact with the power of God through meditation on the two attributes of this power that manifest within human beings; the inner light and sound. But there are other forms of mystical experience and one does need to be a practitioner of Shabd Yoga, or any spiritual sadhana for that matter, in order to experience them.

For instance, during sleep, people sometimes have spiritual dreams or visions. While asleep, our body is in a state of repose and the racing mind has time to settle down which allows for the soul to take charge of perception. These experiences may have a precognitive element. A person may have some vision of an event which is about to take place in his life, or perhaps he sees something which has some profound meaning for him, something which if rightly interpreted can help guide him in some useful way. These visionary dreams are usually very vivid and they are easy to remember the next day. Often, after experiencing a visionary dream, a person wakes up in the night before falling back to sleep. Experiences like these can happen to anyone.

We find accounts of mystical experiences in all of the great religious texts. Paul, for example, while traveling to Damascus in a wakeful state, had a vision of the ascended Christ in which he saw the radiant form of Jesus and also heard his voice. In the Torah, we have the famous vision of Moses witnessing a bush all aglow with celestial light and a voice which gave him instructions pertaining to the Ten Commandments. The prophet Mohammed reported that while meditating in his cave, he was visited by the archangel Gabriel who appeared out of the reverberation of bells and gave instructions regarding his mission and some of the text of the Koran.

Religious and mystical experience is, of course, highly personal and subjective. For this reason, many intellectuals do not take these types of experiences seriously. They cannot be readily repeated and therefore are impossible to verify and analyze. Scientists and psychologists prefer more materially-oriented areas of inquiry.

Baba Sawan Singh wanted the spiritual path associated more with the sciences because he wanted it to be viewed as an empirical path of first-hand experience and verification. But at its core, spirituality is about love, humility and desire; the desire to know God and to find answers to life's thorniest questions. Along with investing the necessary time and attention into spiritual practices, these three things; love, humility and desire are essential for success on the spiritual path.

Blind faith does not do justice to any intelligent, rational person. On this, scientists and mystics can agree. Those who engage in disciplined spiritual practices, or any other type of religious or devotional practice, should walk the path of experience.

Yoga is the path of experience devised by ancient Indian philosophers, designed to unite the soul with its source. Patanjali, the author of "The Yoga Sutras", is considered to be the progenitor of the modern yoga science and his original Ashtanga Yoga sought to achieve that end. Shabd Yoga, as taught by saints and masters, like all forms of yoga, is patterned after Ashtanga Yoga and is the easiest and most direct means to the goal of unification of the soul with the oversoul, or God.

CHAPTER 4

CLASSICAL YOGA

(This chapter has been condensed from the book, "The Crown of Life" by Kirpal Singh. It represents approximately 15% of the content of Part One of that book, and has been edited. Kirpal Singh intentionally left all of his writings in the public domain so that they could be utilized by anyone engaged in presenting information regarding Shabd Yoga to the public. This author felt that rather than use "The Crown of Life" as a source book, it would be better to condense the relevant portions of the book down into a chapter.

The Crown of Life

This study of comparative yoga was initially inspired by the various queries on the subject which kept pouring in from seekers and disciples in the West. As it has now evolved it may, I hope, be of service not only to those whose questions first led to its writing, but to all seekers in general who wish to understand what classical yoga is, the varieties of its basic forms, and their respective modes and spiritual efficacy.

In this age of publishing there is no dearth of books on yoga. However, if one scrutinizes them carefully, one finds that the majority fall short in one direction or another. They either treat it as primarily a system of asanas and physical exercises, or as an abstract and highly monistic system of thought, positing the unity of all existence and the ultimate oneness of the individual soul and the Oversoul. In either case, the view of yoga that we gather is an incomplete one, reducing it from a practical mode of spiritual transcendence and union with the Absolute, to a system of physical culture or school of philosophy.

To avoid the possibility of such error, the ultimate aim of all yoga, at-one-ment with the Supreme Lord, has been kept as a focusing point for all discussions in this study. All the important forms, ancient and modern, are taken up in turn, their practices explained and discussed, and the extent to which each can lead us toward the final goal evaluated. This last is perhaps the most easily misunderstood and the most widely confused aspect of a comparative study of yoga. It is a characteristic of mystic experience that the soul as it ascends to a plane higher than the one to which it is accustomed, tends (in the absence of superior guidance) to mistake the higher plane as the very highest, the Absolute Realm. And so, we find that most yogic systems, while taking us partway up to a certain point on the inner journey, mistake this for journey's end.

KIRPAL SINGH, Sawan Ashram, Delhi, June 6, 1961

YOGA: AN INTRODUCTION

All the great teachers of humanity, at all times and in all climes – the Vedic Rishis, Zoroaster, Mahavira, Buddha, Christ, Mohammed, Nanak, Kabir, Baba Farid, Hazrat Bahu, Shamas Tabrez, Maulana Rumi, Tulsi Sahib, Swamiji, and many others – gave to the world but one sadhana or spiritual discipline. As God is one, the God-way too cannot but be one. The true religion or the way back to God is of God's own making and hence it is the most ancient as well as the most natural way, with no artifice or artificiality about it. In its practical working, the system needs the guidance of an adept or a teacher well versed in the theory and practice of Para Vidya, the Science of the Beyond, as it is called, for it lies beyond the grasp of the mind and the sense faculties. Where the world's philosophies end, there the true religion starts. The scriptural texts give us, at best, some account of the Path so far as it can be put into imperfect words, but cannot take us to the Path nor can they guide us on the Path.

How to remove the veil of ignorance is the problem of problems. We have allowed it to grow into an impervious rock too hard to be blasted. Still, the sages have provided various means to rend the otherwise impenetrable veil, such as Jnana Yoga, Bhakti Yoga, and Karma Yoga and other methods. The light of true knowledge, as visualized by Jnana Yoga, may be able to dispel the darkness of ignorance, just as a lit candle may dispel darkness from a dark room. By Bhakti Yoga one may be able to change the course of hatred, separateness and duality into that of love for all, at-one-ment and oneness with all living creatures and thereby be established in the all-embracing love for all. Finally, by means of Karma Yoga, one may be able to root out feelings of selfishness, ego-centricity, self-aggrandizement and self-love and engage in charitable deeds of philanthropy and similar activities. These are, in the main, the three paths, or rather three aspects of an integrated path of head, heart, and hand, whereby one may achieve the desired end, the union of the soul with the Oversoul. They may for convenience be briefly termed the process of self-mastery, self-sublimation and self-sacrifice, leading ultimately to 'Cosmic Consciousness', or awareness of the all-pervading Reality as the basis of all that exists.

The term 'yoga' is derived from the Sanskrit root 'yug' which means meeting, union, communion, consummation, abstraction, realization, absorption or metaphysical philosophizing of the highest type, that promises to bring close proximity between the soul and the Oversoul. Patanjali, the reputed father of the yoga system, after the fashion of his progenitor Nandinath, defines yoga as elimination of the 'vritis' or modulations that always keep surging in the mind-stuff or 'chit' in the form of ripples. He calls it Chit vriti nirodha or the suppression of the vritis, i.e., clearing the mind of the mental oscillations. According to Yajnavalkya, yoga means to effect, or to bring about, at-one-ment of the individual soul with Ishwar or Brahman. The yogins generally define it as the unfoldment of the spirit from, and disrobing it of the numerous enshrouding sheaths in which it is enveloped in its physical existence.

Vritis: What They Are

When a current emanating from the spirit strikes any object, such as a physical thing, a mental feeling, an idea, or a sensory sensation, and returns to its source, it is called a 'vriti'. The vriti produces a modulation in the mind-stuff. All our knowledge of the world without and within comes from vritis or the rays of thought. A ray of light, reflected from or originating from an object, passes through the eyes to the brain, where it is converted into thought impressions making us aware of the object.

The vritis constitute so many hurdles in the way of the soul seeking to understand its true and essential nature, which in reality is nothing but that of God. Kabir therefore says: "Soul is of the same essence as that of God". Muslim saints speak of the soul as the 'fiat of God'.

If one could but clear the chit of the vritis, nothing would be left except the pure essence of Godhead. Hence, we have the oft-repeated famous dicta on Yoga, as in the following:

> *"Clearing the mind of the mental oscillations (vritis) is the essence of yoga"*
>
> Patanjali
>
> *"Union of the soul and the Oversoul is yoga."*
>
> Yajnavalkya
>
> *"Extraction of the soul from the materials of life by disrobing it of the enshrouding sheaths is yoga".*
>
> Machendra Nath and Goraksh Nath

<u>**Soul and Oversoul**</u>

Soul is the Reality and the Essence. It is one as well as a totality. In one there is always the delusion of many, and the totality does signify the existence therein of so many parts. The ideas of a part and of the whole go cheek by jowl, and both the part as well as the whole are characterized by the similarity of the essential nature they share.

The essence of a thing is its Johar, its very life breath. It is the only primal principle that pervades everywhere and is the reality behind all forms and colors. This active life principle is the very source of creation and goes variously by the names of Prakriti in the subtle, Pradhan in the causal, and Maya or matter in the physical world.

In nature itself, both in the subtle and causal planes, these two principles are always at work: God and Prakriti in the subtle, God and Pradhan in the causal, and soul and matter in the physical universe. The creation everywhere is but the outcome of the impact of the one on the other.

Soul then is the life-principle and the root cause at the core of everything, for nothing can come into manifestation without it. It has a quickening effect, and imparts its life-impulse to the seemingly inert matter by contact with it. It is by the life and light of the quickening impulse of the soul that matter assumes so many forms and colors with their variety of patterns and designs which we see in the universe.

This life current or soul is extremely subtle, a self-effulgent spark of Divine Light, a drop from the Ocean of Consciousness, with no beginning and no end, and eternally the same, an unchangeable permanence, boundless, complete in Itself, an ever-existent and all-sentient entity, immanent in every form visible and invisible, for all things manifest themselves because of It. Nothing is made that is not made by It.

<h1 style="text-align:center"><u>Prakriti or Matter</u></h1>

The term 'Prakriti' is a compound term and is derived from the Sanskrit root 'pra' meaning first, and 'kar' signifying to act, and thus Prakriti stands for 'original matter' (latent energy) which, when acted upon by positive spirit force, brings into being the many forms, patterns and designs in the vast creation of the Great Creator. This is called 'Maya'. The process from passivity into activity of energy leads to creation, or manifestation of the hitherto unmanifested spirit force. Prakriti by itself can neither be felt by the senses nor has it any existence of itself, but comes into manifestation only when acted upon by the spirit force.

Brahman or spirit force comes into being only through a gross covering (kaya). The yogins have taken into account the five koshas or the enshrouding sheaths that have come to cover up the spirit current in its downward descent, and have devised and formulated ways and means to remove them. These koshas or coverings may briefly be described as:

1. *Anand-mai Kosh (Bliss):* This is the first and the foremost of these koshas or coverings. This is almost an integral part of the soul itself. It is the most subtle sheath, like that of a thin covering over a lit candelabra. One experiences it a little when in deep and dreamless slumber (sushupti), for on waking up he retains a hazy idea of the anand or bliss that he experienced in that completely undisturbed state of rest.

2. *Vigyan-mai Kosh:* This kosh covers the mental apparatus or intellect with its two phases: one concerned with knowledge (gyan) on the physical plane and the other with enlightenment (vigyan) on the spiritual planes.

3. *Man-o-mai Kosh:* This is the next covering or sheath that the intellectualized or the cognitive soul wraps around itself by further intensive contact with Prakriti (matter), which now begins to reflect

the mind-stuff as well; and with this added faculty the soul becomes inclined toward the mind and gradually gets mind-ridden.

4. *Pran-mai Kosh:* The covering of the 'pranas' (the vital airs) constitutes the fourth sheath around the soul. As the thinking (cognitive) and mind-bound soul presses still further upon matter, it begins to vibrate with pranas, which are of ten types according to their functions.

5. *Anna-mai Kosh:* When the cognitive, mind-bound and impulsive soul works upon the Prakriti, it forges therein yet another type of covering, that of anna-mai. This is the last of the five sheaths, and for its maintenance it begins to feel a continuing need for anna or foodstuff, and other sense objects. This anna-mai covering is just an inner lining of the physical body (gross matter), which in fact is its outer manifestation; and it continues to wrap the soul even when its outer form, i.e., body, declines, decays and disintegrates. The existence of this coarse physical body depends upon the healthy condition of the Anna-mai kosh.

The aim or purpose of all yogas is to gradually disentangle the soul from these coverings one by one, until it is finally disengaged from all of them and is restored to its original and pristine glorious state of self-luminosity, which is no less than that of several suns put together. Most of the yoga systems take this to be the be-all and end-all of all spiritual endeavors. This in fact is the highest and the last stage of self-realization, but is yet a halfway house on the spiritual journey – a stage of no mean consequence, for it is from here that a rare soul starts toward the much-coveted goal of complete realization of God, since it is knowledge of self that gradually leads on to knowledge of God.

<u>**The Three Bodies and the Five Koshas**</u>

The human body consists of three raiments: physical, astral or subtle, and the causal or seed-body. In the physical body we have all the five koshas or coverings, and this is why we, in our waking state, get some knowledge and experience of all the five things: bliss, cognition (inner and outer), mindfulness (chit and its vritis or mental modulations), pranic vibrations and the physical system.

As one rises into the astral or the subtle body, one loses consciousness of the physical existence, while the soul mentally experiences the rest of the four states, viz., bliss, cognition, mindfulness and pranic vibrations. As the spirit travels higher on into the causal body, even the mental apparatus itself drops off and only the power of remembrance remains, and it witnesses and gives an account of the bliss experienced in that state. Blissfulness, being the essential and inseparable quality of the soul, inheres in its very nature. This is why the searching soul ever feels restless, and feels terribly the loss of its essence in the mighty swirl of the world.

THE BASIS OF ANCIENT YOGA
<u>**Yog Vidya and Yog Sadhana**</u>

From the 'Yajnavalkya Smriti', we hear that Brahma was the original teacher of yoga. But the yoga system, as a system, was first expounded by Patanjali, the great thinker and philosopher, in his Yoga Sutras, sometime before the Christian era. The yogic system is one of the six schools of Indian philosophy (Khat Shastras) that were systematized and developed to set in order Indian thought concerning the cosmos, the individual soul, and their interrelation. These philosophies resulted from an attempt at reformation and restoration of the ancient and time-honored concepts on psychological and metaphysical matters.

The word 'yoga' in common parlance means 'method'. In its technical sense, it connotes 'yoking' or 'union' of the individual soul with the Oversoul or God. In this context, the yoga system denotes a 'methodical discipline', which aims on the one hand at 'unyoking', or separation of the individualized soul from mind and matter, and on the other hand, 'yoking' it with Brahman. It therefore, means and implies the search for the transcendental and the divine in man.

The word 'yoga' is however not to be confused with 'yogmaya' and 'yogic powers' which denote respectively, the supreme Power of God per se (creating, controlling and sustaining the entire creation), and the psychic powers (Rihis and Siddhis) that one may acquire on the path of yoga. Again, yog Vidya, or the science of yoga, has a two-fold aspect; the physical as well as the spiritual.

The term 'yoga' in this context is, therefore, to be strictly confined to one of the systems of philosophic thought as derived from the Vedas, and is concerned with the sole object of regaining the soul, through spiritual discipline, now lost in the activity of mind and matter, with which it has come to identify itself by long and constant association for aeons upon aeons. The soul, conditioned as it is in the time-space-cause world, has but an imperfect perception and cannot see the reality, the 'atman' or the Divine Ground, in which it rests and from where it gets its luminosity.

To free the individual soul from the shackles of mind and matter, yoga insists on (1) concentration, and (2) active effort or striving, which involves the performance of devotional exercises and mental discipline. Self-realization is the highest aim of yoga.

Plexuses and Chakras

Whenever several nerves, arteries or veins interlace each other, that point or center is called a plexus. Similarly, there are plexuses or centers of vital forces in the 'Suksham' or subtle 'nadis' and these are called 'chakras' or 'padmas'. The nadis are the astral tubes made up of astral matter, and serve as passages for subtle pranas through which they operate in the subtle body as do the nerves, arteries and veins in the gross physical body. These subtle tubes or nadis spring from 'Kanda', or the center where the 'Sushmana Nadi' meets the 'Muladhana Chakra' at the base of the spine.

Of these nadis, Ida, Pingala, and Sushmana are the most important. All three nadis are within the spinal cord. Ida and Pingala are on the left and right side respectively of the Sushmana. Breath-energy generally flows through each for about two hours alternately. When it flows through the Sushmana (the central nadi), the mind becomes steady. This steadiness is the highest state of Raja Yoga, for in this state there is wonderful meditation.

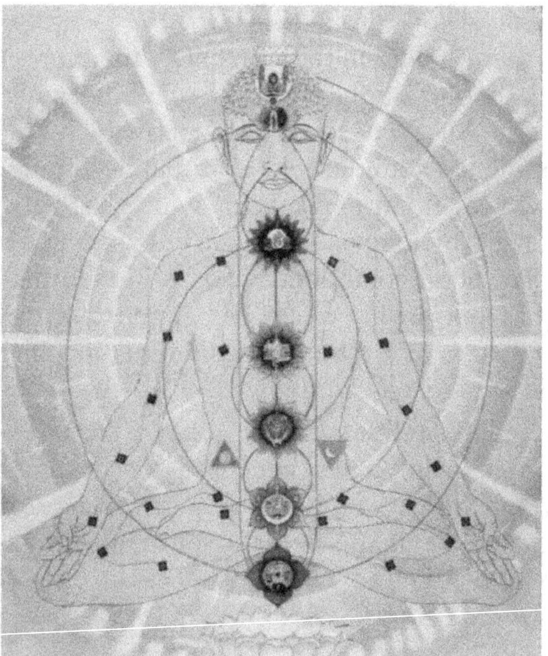

Gross prana travels in the nerves of the physical body, but the subtle prana moves in the astral tubes (nadis). The breath is an outcome of the manifestation of the gross prana. There is a very close and intimate connection between the gross and the subtle prana. If the mind and the prana cease to vibrate, no thought-waves will arise.

The cerebrospinal system is the mainstay of the physical body. The spinal column in yogic terminology is called 'Brahm Danda'. According to the Shiva Samhita, there are in the human system as many as 350,000 nadis, and out of these the following ten play key roles:

1. *Ida:* Starting from the lowest plexus (guda chakra), on the right side of the spinal column, it extends spirally around the Sushmana and goes as far as the left nostril. The ida is associated with the female elements of nature.

2. *Pingala:* Starting from the same chakra on the left side of the spinal column, it extends spirally as far as the right nostril. The pingala is associated with the male principle in nature.

3. *Sushmana:* The central nadi running the length of the spinal column from the base (guda) chakra to the third eye center (Brahmarendra), behind and between the two eyebrows.

4. *Gandhari:* Originates from the front of the Sushmana nadi running to the left eye.

5. *Hastijivha:* Originates from the rear of the Sushmana nadi running to the right eye.

6. *Pushpa:* Originates from the Sushmana nadi running to the right ear.

7. *Yashvini:* Originates from the Sushmana nadi running to the left ear.

8. *Alambhush:* Originates from the Sushmana nadi running to the shoulder plexus.

9. *Kuhu or Shubha:* Originates from the Sushmana nadi running to the tip of the generative organ.

10. *Shankhni:* Originates from the Sushmana nadi running to the rectum.

The central nadi (Sushmana) passes through the spinal column and runs through six major plexuses or chakras as follows:

1. *Muladhara:* Also known as the base or guda chakra, and is positioned at the rectum, characterized by a four-petal lotus.
2. *Svadhishtana:* Also known as the hypo gastric plexus, and is positioned at the generative organ and characterized with a six-petaled lotus.
3. *Manipuraka:* Also known as the solar plexus, and is positioned in the central abdomen or navel and characterized by an eight-petaled lotus.
4. *Anahata:* Also known as the heart plexus, and is characterized by a twelve-petaled lotus, the lotus of the un-struck sound.
5. *Vishuddha:* Also known as the pharyngeal plexus or throat plexus and is characterized by a sixteen petaled lotus and great purity.
6. *Aggya:* Also known as the ajna chakra or single eye, between and behind the two eyebrows, is the center of command and is characterized by a two-petaled lotus.

THE ELEMENTS OF ASHTANGA YOGA

The yogic art is long, tortuous and arduous. The reality of the self lies buried under the debris of the mind. In order to prevail over the mind, Patanjali gives a comprehensive account of his Ashtanga system of yoga and prescribes an eight-fold method consisting of: (1) Yama, (2) Niyama, (3) Asana, (4) Pranayama, (5) Pratyahara, (6) Dharana, (7) Dhyana, (8) Samadhi.

(1) Yamas and
(2) Niyamas

Yama: The term 'yama' literally means to expel, to eject, to throw out or to eliminate. It denotes abstention from vices and from entertaining any evil thoughts, or accepting any negative impressions which may tend to weaken the mind and the will.

Niyama: The term 'niyama' on the contrary, signifies acceptance, cultivation, observance and development of positive virtues, harboring good feelings, and absorbing these virtues into one's system.

Thus, these two words connote the simultaneous rejection of evil, and the assiduous cultivation and acceptance of good, respectively. The practice of both yamas and niyamas – restraints and observances – make up 'sadachar' or right conduct, which constitutes the bedrock of all the world's religions.

(3) Asana

The term 'asana' denotes the seat and the pose, position or posture, in the performance of yogic discipline. It is another external aid in yogic practice. The asana should be steady, firm, pleasant and comfortable, so as to keep the body quiescent but alert during the yogic discipline. The term 'asana' literally means easy and comfortable. Patanjali enjoined a posture both simple and pleasant. That posture is the best which may enable a student of yoga to remain motionless for a long time – two to three hours at a stretch – with an effortless ease, the object being to eliminate bodily reactions and to dissolve the mind into contemplation. By continual shifting of posture, one cannot successfully engage in the yogic practice, for with every change of posture the vritis are set in motion and the mind never grows steady and still. Hence the need for a firm and steady pose, but one characterized by ease and comfort, so that the practitioner may not feel fatigued and tired during the time he practices.

(4) Pranayama or Yogic Breathing

Prana is the sum total of all energy that is manifest in the Universe, the sum total of all the forces in nature. All forces, all powers and even the pranas themselves spring from one and the same source – the fountainhead of atman. The motor power behind the mind-stuff (chit) is that of prana and hence the regulation and control of prana is of prime importance and far above other psycho-physical disciplines. In the 'Gorakh Samhita' it is said that he who knows the secret of prana knows the secret of yoga, for in the rhythmic regulation of prana, lies the practical aspect of yoga par excellence.

Pranas are classified into five important categories according to the nature of their functions:

1. *Prana* is concerned with the respiratory system. It is the breath of life and gives vitality to the human system. Its seat is said to be in the region lying between the two eyebrows.
2. *Apana* helps the excretory system, as it has a tendency to flow downwards. It operates in the region below the navel.
3. *Samana* aids the digestive organs. Its seat is in the navel and it spreads on all sides, nourishing the body as a whole.
4. *Udana* is connected with swallowing. It has the quality of ascending, drawing or guiding breath, and its direction of movement is upwards. Its seat is in the neck and is active between the navel and the head.
5. *Vyana* helps in maintaining the circulatory system throughout the body.

The importance of pranayama as an integral part of Hatha Yoga and Raja Yoga is so great, that some have come to regard it as an independent form of yoga in itself and have given it the name Prana Yoga. However, it was never Patanjali's intention that any single feature of his eight-fold system would become a school of yoga in and of itself. He saw steady, rhythmic breathing as being vital in order to allow the body to benefit from effulgent prana and to avoid descending into shallow breathing. He was also, himself, a practitioner of pranayama. But in the Yoga Sutras, he doesn't state that the concentration of the attention (dharana) should be focused on the breathing itself. Yogic schools which isolate or emphasize a single feature of the Ashtanga system represent a subsequent adaptation to classical yoga.

Pranayama, or yogic breathing, can be practiced successfully under the guidance of a guru or an adept in the method. The great achievement of pranayama is to awaken and bring in to full play the coiled serpentine energy of Kundalini, lying in a dormant state at the spinal root-center.

(5) Pratyahara or Sense Withdrawal

This feature of classical yoga addresses the process of the control over the senses and sensory current withdrawal. The mind is rendered pure and limpid by the practice of yamas, niyamas, and pranayama, while pratyahara gives supreme mastery over the senses. The control of the senses is a key factor in the yogic science. The senses have to be withdrawn from the sensory plane and detached from outer impressions and influences. To shutter the mind resolutely against the onslaughts of the senses, it is necessary for the student of yoga to retire for some time every day into the 'monastic cell' of solitude, for it is a matter of common experience that muddy water becomes clear of itself if it is allowed to stand still for some time.

(6) Dharana or Absorbed Concentration

Having controlled the pranas through pranayama, and the senses through pratyahara, the student has now to fix his mind on something. It may be fixed on something without, such as an altar, a picture, or some type of icon. Within, it can be fixed on any area of the body, on one of the subtle centers of the astral body, or on an idea. Dharana consists, therefore, in fixing the mind's attention on a particular place, object, idea, or center. Any type of dharana helps in making the mind steady and is beneficial in and of itself.

The fixing of one's attention is the essential primary element in the practice of any yoga sadhana, and its importance cannot be overrated. It is because of this pivotal role that dharana is regarded by some as a form of yoga by itself, and is called mental yoga (mansik), the yoga of self-absorption. Pratyahara and dharana go together; for on the one hand the mind is to be weaned away from the attractions of the world and given something with which to occupy itself, which ultimately becomes more attractive than what it finds outside.

(7) Dhyana or Meditation

As a natural outcome of dharana (concentrated attention) there flows a continuous stream of perception. This flow of cognitive awareness is termed dhyana, or meditation. In the highest form of dhyana, the attention is fixed on the single eye, or tisra til, the still point of the body behind and between the two eyebrows. This is the intersection of time and the timeless, where the un-manifest becomes manifest. After some practice at this most vital center, the dark field of the inner vision becomes illuminated and gradually, with prolonged practice in deep concentration, the light assumes various forms, culminating with the radiant form of the master. This form is one's true spirit guide, competent to lead the soul into higher spiritual planes.

> *"When in meditation, the Master appears within, and one sees the secrets of Eternity like an open book."*

Rumi

The advantages of meditation are innumerable. Through contemplation of the attributes of God one can develop these very attributes within one's own self and be a witness of and a testifier to Heaven's glory.

(8) Samadhi

The term 'samadhi' is derived from two Sanskrit roots; 'sam' with its English equivalent 'syn' means 'together with', and 'adhi' means 'Lord' (primal being). Taken together, sam plus adhi denote a conscious state in which the soul, combined with mind (jiva), is completely absorbed in God. It is a state in which the individual, with his perception of individuality dissolved, experiences the great truth – 'I am Thou'.

Samadhi is the final and culminating stage in the long-drawn-out process of practical yoga, and may therefore be said to be the efflorescence of the yogic system. Meditation (dhyana) itself gradually develops into Samadhi when the practitioner loses all thought of himself, and the mind becomes the very form of its thought. In this state the adept is not conscious of any external object save the consciousness itself, a state of perfect bliss.

Those who achieve Samadhi do so by destroying the very nature of the mind-stuff which runs after material attractions by channeling the focused attention inwardly. In dhyana or meditation, one retains the distinction between the contemplator and the contemplated, but in the highest state of Samadhi, even these disappear as one identifies with the totality, his individuality now a figment from the past. In this state, known as 'nirvikalpa', one obtains deep insights into the subtle and the abstract aspects of existence. The more common state of Samadhi does accompany the consciousness of one's individuality and is called 'savikalpa'. Those who know or have known Samadhi, live and move in the world as liberated souls, appearing like any other human beings, but are permanently embedded in the consciousness of the divine.

The Evolution of the Yogic Systems

This concludes the summation of the Ashtanga yogic system as expounded by Patanjali and his mentor, Nandinath, the great Indian philosophers and thinkers, which is to this day, a primary component to the foundation of Indian philosophy. Nandinath, speaking of the herculean task ahead for any new aspirant, said, 'to pursue it was like attempting to empty the sea drop by drop with the aid of a blade of grass'. Today, conditions are no better suited for ease of practice and success.

Over the centuries, the original Ashtanga yogic system has changed and evolved from Patanjali's framework into new forms and a broader overall system of philosophy and practice. However, regardless of alterations in theme and emphasis, all subsequent schools of yoga are rooted, by and large, in Ashtanga Yoga.

NEWER FORMS OF YOGA
Mantra Yoga or the Yoga of Utterance

Mantra Yoga is the yoga of rhythmic repetition of sound formulae, usually considered sacred and secret, which were originally formulated by ancients who were adept in phonetics and the power of sounds, for the purpose of attracting certain deities and forces of nature.

Mantras represent vibrations. The most sacred of the Vedic mantras is that of the Gayatri, pronounced as the sacred syllable 'Aum'. It symbolizes the creative life principle itself, and hence is either the basis for or a component of many mantras. The Advaitists, who see the all-pervading power of God as imminent in all forms chant, 'Ah-aum Braham Asmi' (I am Braham) and 'Ay-aum Athma Braham' (I am Thou). These are often shortened to 'Ah-aum-sah' (I am He or He is I). Vedantists repeat 'Aum Tat Sat' (Aum is Truth), and Buddhists chant 'Aum Mani Padme Hum'. Mantras are often utilized in dhyana (meditation) where they help to discipline and focus the mind, and if given by a competent master, are charged with the life force of the teacher.

Hatha Yoga

Hatha Yoga essentially evolved as a form of Asana Yoga, with emphasis placed on performance of the various asana postures and on physical purification. The primary aim of Hatha Yoga is focused on the physical, not the spiritual, but proficiency in Hatha Yoga can provide a strong foundation for pursuing higher forms, such as Raja Yoga. Hatha means 'will-power'. Its first syllable, 'ha' represents the sun, and its second syllable, 'tha' represents the moon, and together form the conjunction of sun and moon. Hatha Yoga is taught by many teachers throughout the world, each with his own individual approach and emphasis. Some teachers incorporate much of the fundamental components of classical yoga, and many others focus primarily on the physical aspects.

Laya Yoga

Laya Yoga is the yoga of absorption or mergence. It is a fusion of Ashtanga's pratyahara, dharana, and dhyana. Laya literally means to lose oneself in some overpowering idea or ruling passion. By deep and continued absorption through concentration one is gradually led to a state of forgetfulness of everything else, including the body, and to having only one thought uppermost in one's mind, that being the objective before him for realization. The lowest form of Laya Yoga involves its usage in the quest of worldly gain, power and pelf, name and fame, and other mundane pursuits.

The highest form of Laya Yoga involves the absorption and contemplation of God, taking one above body-consciousness, leading to the divine ground of the higher inner regions. A devoted and prolonged single-mindedness is the key to success with this form. In contrast to other forms of yoga, rather than working to control the mind, it emphasizes controlling the latent Kundalini energy.

Raja Yoga

Raja Yoga is the path of self-analysis and discovery. It is well suited for persons having a scientific outlook and rational mind. It is based on the assumption that humans, in their current state of evolution, are far from their great potential. So, the yogin views his life and human form as an ongoing experiment, the goal of which is to find reintegration with Godhead. Outside authorities, like teachers and scriptural texts, are secondary to personal empirical evidence and awakening. The job of a Raja yogin is to unmask the reality within him by removing the numberless masks or false identifications, and thereby to separate the great Self from the enshrouding sheaths by which it is encumbered. Raja borrows much from Patanjali's Ashtanga system, with a new emphasis on awakening through discovery and experimentation.

Jana Yoga or Yoga of Knowledge

The path of Jnana is for those who are gifted with strong intellect and a keen insight, capable of penetrating into the why and wherefore of things, so as to reach the core of truth. It means right discrimination and knowledge, the very first component of Lord Buddha's eight-fold path of righteousness. Right understanding is essential for staying centered on the path to self-awakening. The aim of this yoga is to chase away the darkness of ignorance with the torch of knowledge. It is a highly analytical path and to find success through its practice, one has to adhere diligently to three things:

1. *'Shravan'* or hearing: By hearing the scriptures, great philosophical discourses, and the teachings of living spiritual mentors who are proficient in self-knowledge and God knowledge.

2. *'Manan'* or thinking: After hearing the truth, one engages in intense and thoughtful contemplation and looks for means to put intellectual truth into practice by replacing false ideas, methods, and institutions with versions that are based on truth.

3. *'Nidhyasan'* or practice: The yogin works to shift his awareness away from the personal self, and applies knowledge and truth to the quest for the higher Self, or Soul.

Bhakti Yoga or Yoga of Devotion

"He who with unwavering devotion (Bhakti Yoga), does God service, has crossed beyond the strands, and is fit for salvation."

Bhagavad Gita

Bhakti is a path of the heart, a yoga of worship with a loving faith, absolute and steadfast in one's reverent adoration. It is a very popular path and well suited for those who are endowed with an emotional nature and a tender heart. Selfless devotion is the key to success on this path. A devotee delights in rapturous strains, and is ever engaged in singing hymns in praise of his Lord and never gets weary of them. Bhakti begins on a principal of dualism, seeing God as a separate and superior being. The secret to union with God in Bhakti is that one becomes that which he adores. The principle of Bhakti is often successfully integrated in with other forms of yoga.

Karma Yoga or Yoga of Action

Karma is the essential law of man and his world. Our actions, whether physical or mental, all have consequences. The highest action is the selfless service of humanity and the natural world, for the benefit of God's creation. Service before self should be the guiding principle in one's life. Since creation springs from God, the fountain of all life, our thoughts, words, and deeds should be a perpetual dedication to Him. Through living for others, a yogin loses self-identity, and gains association and identification with God. Selfless devotion to duty is the key to success on the path of action. Karma Yoga is rooted in Patanjali's first two principles of Ashtanga Yoga: Yamas and Niyamas. Both the action rightly performed and the action rightly renounced lead to the same goal, for it is the right understanding of the nature of action that brings the yogic state.

*"He who does the task, dictated by duty, caring
nothing for the fruit of the action, he is a yogi."*
Bhagavad Gita

These three personal forms, Jnana, Bhakti, and Karma each contain elements of the others, so it is not possible to clearly isolate one from another. All three find their first clear exposition in the Bhagavad Gita, credited to Lord Krishna. The Gita is a compendium of the yoga systems prevailing at the time of its writing, mentioning as many as eighteen distinct forms. While Lord Krishna speaks of the various yogas which can be applied to accommodate the many variations of people and approaches to the divine, the practical esoteric principles underlying them are the same.

CHAPTER 5

SHABD YOGA
DHARANA NADA YOGA

"The greatest gift God can give is his own experience. Every object, every creature, every man, woman and child has a soul, and it is the destiny of all, to see as God sees, to know as God knows, and feel as God feels, to be as God is."

Meister Eckhart

"Those that received him, to them he gave the power to become the sons of God"

John 1:12

The practice of yoga has become popular and widespread throughout the world in recent years, taking on even more forms and adaptations. Most of the yoga taught today is aimed at benefiting and uplifting body and mind. Shabd Yoga, aimed at benefiting and uplifting the spirit, is the method of yoga practiced by all great saints and masters, both contemporary and historic. It is the simplest and most direct path to self and God realization. And like all forms of yoga, it incorporates much of Patanjali's Ashtanga system.

If you study the original texts of the Yoga Sutras you will find that in describing some features of his system, Patanjali was very specific in his exposition, but in other features, he wrote in a more general way, leaving the door open to the subsequent, inevitable evolution of yoga. For example, with respect to dharana, or absorbed concentration, he states that the attention must be focused somewhere, but he doesn't say where. If he had preferred some specific physical place, like an icon, a rendering of a god or goddess, or a mandala or chakra, or if there was a particular thought, perhaps of love, or a sacred place, or one's guru, he could have easily made his preference clear, but didn't.

Over the millennia, thousands of schools of yoga have formed which are based on pranayama, or yogic breathing sadhanas. In pranayama, the focus of the attention, in fact the focus of the entire practice, is the breathing. Many who practice pranayama claim that their method best represents Patanjali's originally intended mode of practice.

Patanjali was a great spiritual master who did practice pranayama. He also practiced Shabd Yoga, as evidenced by mystical references made in his writings. In his Yoga Sutra, he makes it clear that steady, rhythmic breathing is an essential component to yoga. However, he never states that the dharana, i.e., attention, should be focused on the breathing itself. Since both aspects, dharana and pranayama, are two of the eight limbs of his Ashtanga system, it would seem logical that if he intended that the attention be focused on the breathing, he would have stated so. But he did not. He did want the body-mind to be charged with prana, and steady, rhythmic breathing would ensure that. He also wanted to avoid having a practitioner slip into shallow breathing, which is a potential risk, especially when one sits in a posture (asana) for an extended period of time. He left the question of *where* to focus the attention open.

Patanjali practiced at least two forms of yoga. He was adept in pranayama. He was also a practitioner of Shabd Yoga. Some of his later writings make references to his inner communion with the light and sound. He knew that each practice required a different object of concentration. In pranayama, the attention needs to be focused on the breathing. In dharana nada meditation, the breathing is quiet and the attention is focused on the ajna chakra (third eye).

In our modern fast-paced world, human beings are engaged in the many facets of their physical lives, tending to jobs and families, illness and health, money and property. Our attention is fully invested in the necessities and attractions of this world and it is rare to find someone who is determined to unravel the mysteries of life, who truly wants to know and experience God.

> *"When the man of highest capacities hears of Tao (the way), he does his best to put it into practice."*
>
> Lao Tzu, Tao Te Ching

Human beings are the most highly evolved life forms. We are conscious; awake. Our intellectual capabilities are vast. Human potential is seemingly unlimited with respect to our ability to reason, imagine, and create. We are also the only life form with the capacity to know and realize God.

God is playing a game of hide-and-go-seek with us. Over the millennia, people have sought Him in every conceivable place: in books, in rites and rituals, in holy places, in temples, shrines, and mosques, in idols, superstitions, myths, and belief systems. But he's hiding in a place we'd never think to look; he's hiding inside of us. He is there, available, inside of everyone; young and old, rich and poor, saints and sinners, believers and non-believers, at all times, patiently waiting for us to find him.

> *"Knock, and it shall be opened unto you: For every one that asketh receiveth; and he that seeketh findeth; and to him that knocketh, it shall be opened."*
>
> Mathew 7:7-8

God and the heavens are hiding behind a doorway and this doorway is inside of us. It is located in the approximate location of the pineal gland, between and behind the two eyebrows. But this is not a physical door. It is a doorway within the spirit body that leads to the spiritual realms. Over the course of human history, many mystics have discovered this door and have passed through it to explore the mysteries of the beyond. Some have discovered it accidently or spontaneously while others have had a teacher who pointed out its existence and instructed them on how to traverse through it. It has been referred to by various names and terms: 'inner eye', 'third eye', 'single eye', 'divine eye', 'tisra til', 'shiv netra', 'the strait gate', 'ajna chakra', 'divya chakshu', 'Brahm-rendra', 'triambka', 'trilochana', 'nukta-i-sweda', 'koh-i-toor', 'mount of transfiguration'. Concentrating the attention at this door, and gazing within, is how we knock.

> *"Enter ye in at the strait gate...Because strait is the gate, and narrow is the way, which leadeth unto life, and few there be that find it."*
>
> Mathew 7:13-14

> *"Abandoning the two eyes I reached the third; And perceived the resplendence of the pure Lord".*
>
> Swami Ji

> *"In the focus of thine eye is a mole, wherein is hidden the entire mystery. Peep within and behold thou what lies beyond this dark curtain."*
>
> Tulsi Sahib

> *"The Lord will make, O Nama, the center of thine eye, His abode; And thine eye shall expand and contain the whole universe."*
>
> Namdev

> *"The sensuous eyes need sunlight to see. Use another eye. Vision is luminous. Sight is inflamed, while the sun-fired light darkens."*
>
> Rumi

*"Lanterns hang from the night sky so that your
eye might draw one more image of love upon
your silk canvas before sleep."*

Hafiz

*"The seat of the soul is between and behind the
eyebrows...It is at this point that the aspirant,
having closed his eyes, must focus his
attention..."*

Kirpal Singh

*"When you sit in meditation and close your
external eyes, please try to peep into the
darkness with the internal eye. By and by, you
will begin to perceive light."*

Sawan Singh

*"The light of the body is the eye: if therefore
thine eye be single, thy whole body shall be full
of light".*

Mathew 6:22

When asked about the cause of creation, Kirpal Singh
answered in very simple terms, saying "God was one and
wished to be many. There was vibration and vibration resulted
in two things: light and sound". This elemental vibration,
referred to by various mystics as the 'Word', is the basis of
everything in existence. Kirpal had his own term for it: 'the
God-into-expression-power'.

When Jesus was asked, "Where is God?", he replied,
"Behold the lord". Like so many of Jesus' statements, his
words were layered in meaning. He was himself, a perfect
master, the living manifestation of the Word. But he was also
declaring, "Look around you. Whatever it is that you see, that
is of God".

The Word, or Nada, being itself a wave structure, has its
dual nature, length and frequency. So, the power of God
which has manifested itself as creation, is itself, the archetype
of duality.

"No man hath seen God at any time".

John 1:18

In this passage, John is referring to absolute God, not the God-into-expression-power, or Word. Whatever existed before creation, whatever that singular power is, we as human beings cannot understand or know of it. Our mind, like everything else in creation, is vibrational. Through it, we can only experience and truly understand a thing or idea which has a dual structure.

So, are there two Gods, the 'pre-creation' singular one and the God-into-expression-power with its duality-based wave structure? No, because God had to put his power into a dual form in order for creation to be feasible. They are of the same essence, one created, and the other uncreated; one existing in being and the other existing in non-being. Is it possible, through concentration and absorption, to travel back to the source of this God-into-expression-power and experience it as One? Some mystics have said yes. Kabir and others write about a non-dual state of pure bliss. Certain passages in the Vedas concur.

Lao Tzu reflected on dualism long ago.

> *"It is because every one under Heaven recognizes beauty as beauty,*
> *That ugliness exists.*
> *And equally if every one recognized virtue as virtue,*
> *This would merely create fresh conceptions of wickedness.*
> *For truly, 'Being and Non-being' grow out of one another;*
> *Difficult and easy complete one another.*
> *Long and short test one another.*
> *High and low determine one another.*
> *Pitch and mode give harmony to one another.*

Actionless activity was Lao Tzu's respite from duality. It was his method. It was his way, or Tao. The combination of actionless activity, with the repetition of the mantra, provided by a Shabd Yoga teacher, will eventually result in a withdrawal of the sensory currents (pratyahara). This withdrawal begins in the lower extremities, the feet and legs, and continues up the trunk of the body to the neck. This experience of withdrawal is not the same kind of sensation one might experience when one's leg 'goes to sleep'. It happens gently, simply removing all physical sensation from the body, an important prelude to Samadhi.

So, the practice of the Shabd Yoga begins with wu wei, or actionless activity; being physically still. This skill must be fostered to a degree where it becomes habit. With sufficient practice, learning to become physically still for an hour or two or three at a time can be achieved. But Lao Tzu wasn't simply referring to physical stillness. What is more important, and much more difficult to cultivate, is mental quiescence, or in Patanjali's terms, 'elimination of the vritis in the mind-stuff'.

The God-into-expression-power, or Word, manifests within the human body primarily in two forms: light and sound. The practice of Shabd Nada Yoga involves the development of one's spiritual senses in order to meditate on these two manifestations of this power. By focusing one's attention in the forehead at the third eye, and holding it there in the eye center, one merges his attention with the visible light within. Through proper training, one learns to keep the attention pinpointed, fixed within the middle of the gaze. What a person sees, how much light, or how bright it is, or what form it is taking, if any, is not as important as learning to keep the gaze fixed and centered. At the time of initiation by a competent teacher, an aspirant is given a practical demonstration of this light and practical instructions on how to develop it further.

While focusing the gaze within, one may perceive a multitude of colors, lights, and forms. Some forms may be recognizable or describable. Others will be more difficult to describe. What an aspirant is hoping to find within is the 'guru dev', or radiant form of the master. This radiant inner master has also been referred to by Swami Ji, Jaimal Singh and other Shabd Yoga masters as 'Guru Swarup'.

In Rai Saligram's 1896 publication, 'Radha Soami Mat Prakash', the master goes into great length describing the relationship formed between disciple and this radiant, inner master.

> *"It must clearly be understood that the Guru Swarup, which manifests internally, is not of flesh and bones, but is spirituality personified, because the Omniscient Being, for the sake of His lovers and devotees assumes the form of Guru in spiritual regions.*
>
> *"This Chaitanya (endowed with cosmic intelligence) and spiritualized Form will guide and help the Abhyasi (disciple) all along. As the Abhyasi performs Dhyana (meditation) at a higher centre (third eye), this Form appears purer, subtler, finer and more refulgent.*
>
> *"Even in early stages of discipleship, Guru's form will keep the company of the Abhyasi up to Sat Lok (true home), continuously helping in the concentration and elevation of mind and spirit. No obstacles of mind and Maya can stand in the way of the Abhyasi so long as the Guru Swarup is with him.*
>
> *"Nay, as long as the Abhyasi's mind and spirit are engaged in the contemplation and*

meditation of this Form, no other thoughts of any kind can arise in his mind."

The guru dev appears out of golden and pale or purplish light and manifests first as a round disk which turns into the master's eye. Little by little, more of the face is revealed until ultimately the aspirant is face-to-face with his inner guide. The form may be a familiar form, perhaps one's own living teacher, or an ascended master from the past, such as the aspirant's teacher's teacher. In due course, with accurate and diligent practice, the inner master will communicate with the aspirant in the same way one would speak on the outside. It is the duty of this inner master to guide the soul through the lower planes and on up into the higher spiritual realms.

It should be clarified here that the light seen in meditation is not physical light. It is the radiance of the power of God or Word. It is self-existent, self-effulgent, shadow-less, and source-less. Even in bright sunlight, or in a brightly lit room, the inner light can be clearly witnessed.

In the same way we use our spiritual eye to perceive the radiant light of the Word, we use our spiritual sense of hearing to listen to the resonance of the Nada. The light and sound are integrated, emanating from the same source, but the contemplation of these two manifestations is done separately. A period of time is devoted each day to seeing, and another period to hearing. Later on, when one becomes more adept in the practices, the light and sound are contemplated simultaneously, but in the beginning, it is easier to separate the two practices. At the time of initiation, a competent teacher will provide a demonstration of the sound and instructions regarding daily practice and further development.

The spiritual senses of seeing and hearing are a part of the conscious make-up of everyone. So why doesn't everyone experience them naturally? If they are already there, why aren't we aware of them? The answer lies in where we focus our attention. Attention is the outward expression of the soul, and is the single most powerful component of our consciousness. It affords the mind its strength of concentration. It is also critical to the formation of memory. The more attentive we are to a particular moment in our life, the more likely we are to store that experience as memory. Attention gives life to memory. Attention determines where our life energy is. So where is our attention? It is in the physical world, in the experiences of the senses, the mind and the body. Therefore, we are not aware of our spiritual senses because we have done little to use them or develop them. Through the practice of Shabd Yoga, a person begins to utilize and develop them, and with regular practice they become a familiar component to one's consciousness.

Some people do, in fact, experience these spiritual senses, people who aren't practicing any discipline designed to awaken and develop them. These senses are, after all, a component to everyone's consciousness. There are people, for example, who experience their spiritual vision while conscious, even with open physical eyes. Some see the radiation of the astral body, or 'aura', around people. Others, even with no training, can sit in a posture of repose and see inwardly. Why some have these abilities while most do not, is a mystery.

It is even more common for people to experience their spiritual hearing. Tinnitus, or 'ringing in the ears', is an experience of the spiritual ear. This is not commonly understood by health professionals who have classified this ringing as a malady. What people with this so-called malady are experiencing are the overtones which are radiating off of the Nada. Some teachers have referred to this sound as the 'weak sound'. This sound is actually radiating around everyone but for some reason, certain people have their spiritual hearing attuned enough so that they hear it. Since it is not commonly understood what this ringing is, or where it comes from, it can understandably be a nuisance to those who experience it.

A practitioner of Shabd Yoga, while engaged in sound meditation, listens intently to the clearest of these inner sounds, hoping to catch the stronger, harmonic sounds of the higher planes. On the astral plane, the sound manifests as bells. In the beginning, it can sound like small, tinkling bells, but later, it will toll like a church bell.

Further up on one's spiritual journey in the causal realms, one hears the strong sound of trumpet, drum or thunder. Prophecy emanates from the causal planes and many historic accounts of prophetic visions describe them being accompanied by the sound of thunder. Native American mystics experienced this phenomenon and ascribed the term 'Thunderbird" when referring to the spirit of prophecy.

Further up, in a realm known as the 'super-causal' plane, sounds of strings like violin, sarod, sitar and harp are experienced. Still further up, in the spiritual realms, sounds resembling flute, pipes, oboe and shehnai are found. At the highest spiritual levels, masters tell us that all vibration dissipates and dissolves into pure bliss.

> *"So long as the sounds continue, there is the idea of âkâśa. When they disappear, then it is called Para Brahma, Paramâtmana."*
>
> Hatha Yoga Pradipika

> *"Blessed the ears attentive in receiving the flow of the Divine whisper, that do not let themselves be distracted by that of the world. Yes, blessed the ears that remain dead to the resounding voices outside, but listen to the truth that teaches inwardly."*
>
> The Imitation of Christ

Another form of spiritual hearing that may develop at some point within a seasoned practitioner is the hearing of voice. This phenomenon is an outcome of one's inner development, or 'receptivity'. Ideally, this voice will emanate from the guru dev, or spirit guide, and will provide positive, supportive communication. If so, this is a rare blessing. The voice may even sound exactly like one's own teacher's voice. In Buddhism's Lotus Sutra, we learn that a select group of advanced disciples were known as 'voice-hearers'.

> *"His voice-hearer disciples will be countless, boundless, beyond the scope of calculation...This Buddha will constantly dwell in midair, preaching the Law for the assembly and saving numberless multitudes of bodhisattvas and voice-hearers."*

While the voice an aspirant hears within will most likely come from his inner spirit guide, this may not always be the case. The inner realms are populated with psychic entities, some of which are not concerned for our welfare and benefit. You could rightly say that these entities are components of our own mental make-up, since it is through our own negative tendencies of thought and action that we have given life to them.

One important benefit to the meditation on light and sound is the cleansing and purification which takes place on the mental planes. But if the spirit voice begins to manifest at all, it will most likely come prior to the soul becoming completely pure. Deciphering these inner communications and trying to determine which are emanating from a positive source and which are not, illustrates that the spiritual path is fraught with risks and potential pitfalls. If one mistakes a voice as being his spirit guide, when in fact it is not, he can be deceived or led astray.

From Dara Shukoh's Compass of Truth, we are given a reference to the spirit voice.

> *"O friend! When thou shall begin to hear this voice, thou must attend to it very carefully and try to keep it with all thy might, so thou mayest be expert in hearing it; and may hear it, not only in the solitude of the desert and the*

In the field of psychiatry, the hearing of a voice or voices is considered to be a serious mental illness. It is a very real phenomenon, experienced by a good many people. But here we're not talking about ringing in the ears; we're talking about hearing voices. It appears that the cases which ultimately involve psychiatric doctors are, in fact, examples of the more malevolent type of psychic entities at work, and this, of course, is a very serious problem. Psychiatrists treat this condition with a class of pharmaceutical drugs.

As God is love and bliss, the inevitable outcome of someone who practices Shabd Yoga faithfully is that they will begin to manifest love within themselves. Love will be reflected in their behavior and relations with others. Some teachers have pointed out that it is not the actual experiences in meditation, i.e., what a soul sees or hears, which is the most accurate gauge of an aspirant's degree of spiritual advancement on the path. The best gauge of a person's spiritual development is the degree to which love has manifested within him or her.

Most of the mystics who practiced and taught Shabd Yoga through the ages had a mentor who had mastered the process themselves and who provided instructions and guidance. However, in some cases the process was simply discovered spontaneously. Lord Buddha, for instance, was in a state of repose when his inner vision opened and he witnessed the reality within. His spiritual development was such that he needed no mentor to guide him or instruct him. It appears that Mohammed, too, had his inner vision and inner hearing awakened spontaneously. Certain Christian mystics have also apparently discovered the light and sound without any teacher guiding or instructing them. But these souls represent the exception to the rule. Most of the great masters who appeared throughout history had a teacher or guru. Even great masters, like Swami Ji, Kabir, and Kirpal Singh, all of whom apparently had a very high level of development from birth, had a teacher who got them properly informed and trained.

Living in the world as we do, there is a myriad of obstacles and challenges which present themselves, making the successful practice of this ancient science more difficult. But by far, the most daunting challenge is our own mind.

> *"With all humility I submit to you, O Master,*
> *The wiles of mind are beyond limit and measure.*
> *Whoever claims he has conquered his mind,*
> *Never for a moment shall I believe this.*
> *No one was ever able to make his mind still,*
> *Except when the soul gets attached to the Divine Melody."*
>
> Tulsi Sahib

Thinking, the ongoing process of thought, is a mighty freight train, with the mind hurling images into our consciousness, one after the other, a perpetual onslaught of impressions, ideas, reactions, observations, memories, and on and on. Very few people have ever made a serious attempt to stop the process of thought. It is essentially impossible. It is like trying to hold back a mighty river. Even if you give the mind something to do, like engaging in the repetition of a phrase or an idea or image to focus on, thoughts will barge in anyway. You may have success for a few seconds, perhaps even a minute or more, but the mind will ultimately win. To counter this overwhelming force, a Shabd Yoga teacher will provide a mantra, a series of words or sounds which can be repeated slowly with the tongue of thought while the aspirant holds the attention in the eye center. Repetition of this mantra is called 'simran'.

Even with this task for the mind to engage itself in, the spontaneous, overpowering process of thought will impose its will and take command of the attention. When this happens, the aspirant must catch it, then initiate the process anew by refocusing the attention and beginning simran again. This process is repeated over and over, thousands of times, as the aspirant treads the spiritual path. In time, mind becomes more passive and begins to accept its role as a partner in the meditation process. Eventually, when one is able to catch the strong, harmonic sounds within, the mind finally surrenders and no longer interferes.

> *"Just as a dancer, though engaged with the musical instruments and beat of the music, maintains her attention on the pot balanced upon the top of her head;*
>
> *So the yogin, though engaged with the distracting host of objects and activities around him, never leaves off the mind contemplating on the repetition of simran."*
>
> Varaha Upanishad of Krishna-Yajurveda

One of the most informative books written on the practice of simran, "The Way of a Pilgrim", was written anonymously by a nineteenth-century Russian Christian (the book does not use the term, 'simran'). The book narrates the experience of the writer who learned that by reciting the 'Jesus Prayer' over and over, thousands of times per day, that it caused his mind to become inwardly centered, and induced strong feelings of inner peace and blissfulness. A Shabd Yoga practitioner uses the same process of repetition to help concentrate his attention, so that it can be more effectively absorbed within.

CHAPTER 6

THE GOD EXPERIENCE

"His devotees...never attain full knowledge of the infinite. Like streams tumbling into the ocean, they know not the depths therein...O great is the power of the Word, but few there be that know it."

Guru Nanak, Jap Ji

The word 'samadhi' is one which is used commonly in spiritual parlance. Patanjali devoted an entire book to the topic in his "Yoga Sutra", entitled "Samadhi Pada", a collection of fifty-one sutras. Many students of spiritual literature have some pre-conceived definition or notion as to what samadhi is. But these notions are typically based on the study of books, rather than on direct experience.

The term 'samadhi' is sometimes used by spiritual aspirants and writers to characterize their experiences. It is not uncommon for someone practicing meditation to experience blissfulness, flashes of light and intellectual revelations. Anyone who practices a form of meditation or contemplation which involves stilling the physical body can have these kinds of experiences. By referring to their experiences as samadhi, they feel a sense of achievement. As a result, the term samadhi has become diluted through misuse.

People who take up a religious or spiritual path often envision God as an abstract theory or concept, or they think of him as some kind of being living in a far distant place. But in fact, God is none of these things. For human beings, God is an experience.

The highest objective of Shabd Yoga is God realization. Few aspirants who take up its practice reach the goal. The reasons for this are the same reasons why people fail to reach any personal, religious or spiritual goal. They become distracted.   Their personal or professional responsibilities demand more and more of their attention. They lose interest. They find that they cannot adhere to some of the necessary disciplines or some destructive behavior creates a roadblock. Or perhaps they aren't making enough inner progress and they lose faith that they are on the right path.

Even if one doesn't attain his/her lofty spiritual goals, the practice of Shabd Yoga has many benefits. Learning to focus the attention in the third eye center during the practice of simran will reap rewards in one's personal life with enhanced powers of concentration and increased capacities of mental acuity and discernment. Disciplining the body to sit still will support every physiological system, especially keeping one's heart healthy. Tapping into our internal blissfulness can be a welcome respite from the ups and downs of daily life.

But for some who take up this arduous path, God realization is the goal and the yardstick. The 'God experience' is not a single, all-of-a-sudden eureka moment or event. It is not, actually, a single experience at all, but a class of experiences of infinite variety and possibility.   There is, however, a point where a soul can rightly say that he has experienced God, that he has experienced samadhi.

Samadhi is described in the fifteenth century yogic text, Hatha Yoga Pradipika.

> *"Now I will describe a regular method of attaining to Samâdhi, which destroys death, is the means for obtaining happiness, and gives the Brahmânanda (God knowledge).*
>
> *"The Yogî, engaged in Samâdhi, feels neither smell, taste, color, touch, sound, nor is conscious of his own self.*
>
> *"As salt being dissolved in water becomes one with it, so when Âtmâ and mind become one, it is called Samâdhi.*

"When the Prâṇa becomes effortless, and the mind becomes absorbed, then their becoming equal is called Samâdhi.

"This equality and oneness of the self and the higher self, when all thoughts cease to exist, is called Samâdhi.

"Indifference to worldly enjoyments is very difficult to obtain, and equally difficult is the knowledge of the higher Realities to obtain. It is very difficult to get the condition of Samâdhi, without the favor of a true guru.

"Those who have attained to Samâdhi, I salute thee! Even death itself, into whose mouth the whole of this movable and immovable world has fallen, has been conquered by thee."

Samadhi, as defined by Patanjali, begins when we lose all sense of self. Our name, age and gender, where we are in time and space – all awareness of self is gone. In samadhi, true samadhi, our individual consciousness has merged with the greater collective consciousness. The stream has emptied into the sea. We are awake, we are conscious, we are super-conscious…at least in most forms of samadhi. There is, actually, a type of samadhi that can be experienced in states of deep, dreamless slumber when we are not super-conscious. The way a person knows that he has experienced this type of samadhi is upon awakening, he is in a state of blissful intoxication and is disoriented. He has to think for a moment to remind himself who he is, his name, where he is, and the day and time.

But most forms of samadhi are experienced in a super-conscious state. The surest means, the surest path to samadhi is the sound current. Initially, we listen to the 'weak sound' in meditation; the variety of characteristics radiating off of the Nada's resonance. In time, with regular practice, one learns to catch the strong sound. Jaimal Singh, Baba Sawan Singh's guru, had a term for it; 'Shabd Dhun'.

When the Shabd Dhun comes in, it can come with power. It can take ahold of the soul and pull it up; drag it out of the body and into higher spiritual planes, into a state of samadhi. Catching the Shabd Dhun is like catching a bus. You have to be in meditation (the bus stop), but not just be there, you have to be paying attention. Otherwise, the bus will pass you by and you'll miss it. So, by paying attention, focusing on whatever sound is audible, loud and clear, this is how we catch the Shabd Dhun through the practice of Shabd Yoga.

The sound can also come in gently, quietly from above. When mystics speak of having an experience which comes from above, they are referring to an experience involving the crown chakra. The crown chakra is situated at the top of the head. It is a bridge to the higher realms. Even if someone is lying down, when the crown opens the experience still seems like it is coming from above.

During meditation, the aspirant should not put his attention at the crown. The attention should always remain either on the sound itself, or at the sixth, or ajna chakra, between and behind the two eyebrows. Keeping the attention fixed in the forehead acts like a trigger to open the crown.

When the sound comes from above, it comes quietly at first. It will manifest as beautiful, sweet harmonics. The sound itself has a mass to it, a discernable substance, and its harmonics produce color. The sound comes out of an inner sky that seems to spread out into infinity. The sound unites the crown with the sky with a column of sound.

An adept fortunate enough to catch the Shabd Dhun will find his consciousness merged with the sound. He will no longer be his lower self, listening to it. He will *be* the sound itself. Yet, even in this transcendent state, he will be able to alternate roles, back and forth; first as listener (audience), then as leader (conductor), and then as creator (composer).

The Shabd Dhun, like our musical art form, can manifest in an infinite number of ways. It can be a single-timbre strain, like a single instrument, or it can manifest as an orchestra of a thousand instruments. It can sing like a single voice or as a chorus of a hundred thousand. The sounds may be familiar; describable in terms of eastern or western classical instruments, or they may have a quality which is unfamiliar. A fortunate pilgrim will enjoy the concert with his guru dev (radiant inner guide).

With strong sound comes strong light and the sights of the inner planes. On the super-causal plane, the adept will bathe in Mansarovar, the 'Sea of Immortality', where the soul will become pure, and he will meet many glorious beings on the shoreline. But the guru dev is wary of the trappings of these intermediate planes, so he may protect the soul during some phases of the spiritual trek by placing the veil over the eye, so that just the sound is audible. He wants us to keep up the pace and not tarry while taking in the sights of the lower planes. During these periods the pilgrim may see the inner guide or he may see bright light or perhaps nothing. In time, the blinders come off and the soul is witness to the brilliant splendor of the higher spiritual realms.

Reaching to the state of samadhi is not the highest level of attainment. There is, in fact, no highest level of attainment. But beginning on the causal plane, samadhi can be experienced as the soul progresses within. Great masters and seasoned spiritual adepts are able to leave the body at will. It is not uncommon for an adept to experience regret when he finds himself leaving the higher realms and reentering the body.

Another characteristic of the god experience, which may develop around the time a soul begins to experience samadhi, is the manifestation, or secretion of 'Amrit' and spiritual fragrance. Amrit does not always manifest in someone who has begun to experience samadhi, but in some cases it does. Amrit is a sweet nectar which forms in the throat and drains down into the body. When it begins to develop, an aspirant will experience a piercing pain in the throat which may cause him to cough. But by enduring the pain, in due course the process will become established in the body.

Amrit causes a blissful intoxication. When present, it can cause the body to radiate divine fragrance. These fragrances can be detected by other people, especially spiritually attuned people. To experience a divine fragrance, one need not breathe in. The aroma will manifest directly in one's forehead. The phenomena of Amrit and fragrance are touched upon by some of the mystic poets, particularly Kabir, Hafiz, and Rumi. They are also referenced by the Gnostic leader, Valentinus, in his "Dialogue of the Savior".

> *"...the father loves his fragrance and manifests it everywhere. And when it mingles with matter it imparts his fragrance to the light, and by his silence he makes it superior in every way to every sound. For it is not the senses that smell the fragrance, rather it is the spirit that possesses the faculty of smell and draws the fragrance toward itself, for itself, and sinks down into the father's fragrance; thus, it nourishes the spirit and takes it to where it emanated from."*

PART II

Echoes from The Past

CHAPTER 7

BABEL AND BABBLE

Spiritual, religious and mystical writings abound with references to souls communing with the celestial light and sound. These references provide historic evidence of the practice of Shabd Yoga. But before exploring the world's sacred writings to discover some of these passages, it may be prudent to first detour into a discussion of some of the problems we face when attempting to use these ancient texts as authoritative sources, which include translation, manuscript corruption, misinterpretation, and limitations inherent with the use of language itself.

> *"And the lord said... 'Come, let us go down, and there confuse their language, that they may not understand one another's speech.' So the lord scattered them abroad from there over the face of all the earth, and they left off building the city. Therefore, its name was called Babel, because there the lord confused the language of all the earth;"*

Genesis 11:6

The word 'babble' no doubt derives from this Old Testament myth. Using language to convey our ideas presents a paradox. On the one hand, it is an imperfect and problematic medium, yet it plays an essential role in human communication. We cannot do without it. But the conveyance of meaning from communicator to listener or reader is plagued with unavoidable misunderstanding and misinterpretation.

Language itself is in a perpetual state of evolution with each new generation initiating its own expressions and idioms, complete with redefinitions and entirely new words. Studying word selections and their contextual relationships is one of the ways scholars date ancient manuscripts by placing word choices into time references. Even in a contemporary dictionary we often find many meanings for the same word, and this has been true throughout history. When you factor in the challenge of trying to convey religious and spiritual ideas, which are difficult to interpret to begin with due to their subjective nature, you compound the problem. Add to this the divisive nature of the milieu of religion itself and the problem compounds further.

For example, the word 'mystical' can mean *of, relating to, or resulting from an individual's direct communion with God or ultimate reality'.* The dictionary offers another meaning; *'of or relating to mysteries, esoteric rites, or the occult.'* Since the word 'occult' carries a negative connotation in some religious circles, the use of the words mystic and mystical carries the risk of misinterpretation, whether deliberate or otherwise. Even the use of the word 'meditation' carries the risk of uncertain meaning, since meditation is used to describe a wide variety of contemplative activities and techniques.

Extracting meaning from ancient texts raises these challenges to an even higher level. Many original religious manuscripts were written in languages which don't even exist today, or exist in forms which have evolved radically from their original forms. Then there are the challenges involved with translation. Many language pairs do not translate easily back and forth like European languages and East Asian languages. European languages use phonetic symbols that create the sound of the word, whereas Chinese, for instance, uses pictographs or ideograms that depicts a word, part of a compound word, a short phrase, or an idea. Modern Chinese has about 50,000 characters.

Language translation is a subjective business. It is an art, not a science. Even with compatible language pairs, every translation involves interpretation. When the translator has some personal interest in the meaning derived from the text, the problem compounds.

The process of copying ancient manuscripts is another source of inaccuracy that we tend to overlook or underrate because of our modern technologies. Today we can write, copy, store and print documents with almost no chance of them being corrupted or destroyed. In the ancient world, the exact opposite was true. The process of copying documents was a painstaking, tedious, and time-consuming task which produced mental fatigue and sloppy work. Every time a scribe copied a manuscript it was different from his original in almost every case. Scribes would leave out a word or copy a line twice or miss a line altogether. Spelling mistakes and poor penmanship were also a problem. When the original was torn or incomplete for some reason, the scribe would improvise and insert what he thought was originally there or what he felt should be there. Even the most innocent of mistakes can have a lasting impact on what we believe about our religious heroes.

> *"And in those days came John the Baptist, preaching in the wilderness...And the same John had his raiment of camel's hair, and a leathern girdle about his loins; and his meat was locusts and wild honey."*

Mathew 3:1

The book of Mathew was originally written in Hebrew, but our oldest surviving manuscripts are in Greek. The Greek word for locust is 'akris'. The Greek word for flatbread or cake is 'egkris'. Using the Greek alphabet, one word can be changed into the other by transposing only one Greek letter. Many scholars have concluded that the word 'egkris' was misspelled as 'akris' at some point.[3] If true, John's principal diet was most likely wild honey and flatbread, not locusts. Dining on insects does seem a bit radical, even for an ascetic like John.

---

[3] Dr. Edgar Goodspeed, History of Early Christianity, University Press

Sometimes changes made during the copying process were intentional, done to modify the text to mean what the scribe thought it actually meant or what it should mean. Often these kinds of alterations were made to accommodate the views of a particular group or sect. There are a number of places in the Christian Bible where these kinds of alterations are referenced in the footnotes.

Once a change or mistake was made to a manuscript, whether intentional or unintentional, if that copy was used as a source document at any time in the future, which was often the case, that mistake perpetuated itself into the future, along with all of the previous mistakes. Today, we have no original literary texts of any kind dating from antiquity. We have copies of copies of copies, of copies, many centuries removed from their originals.

Scholars have identified about 5400 versions of the New Testament, including both complete and partial manuscripts which date from the early 2nd century to the 16th century. The oldest complete copy we have of the New Testament dates to around 375 C.E. Except for the smallest fragments, no two are exactly alike. After analyzing and comparing all 5400 versions, and entering the data into computers, scholars estimate that the total number of differences in these documents exceeds two hundred thousand.[4]

Issues related to manuscript copying and translating are by no means limited to the Bible. The same problems plague all ancient religious texts in one way or another. In the case of Taoism, the issue of translation is critical, both the translation from the archaic Chinese to modern Chinese, and the subsequent translation to modern European-based languages. Archaic Chinese was a much simpler version of the language with fewer characters. With fewer character

---

4 Dr. Bart D. Ehrman, The Orthodox Corruption of Scripture, 1993, Oxford University Press

choices, the understanding of a passage was more open, less defined. Both modern and archaic Chinese have no 1st, 2nd, or 3rd person, no verb tense, no case, no singular or plural, no active or passive, and no mood. There is no punctuation, including periods, little if any use of connecting words, like pronouns and prepositions, and very often there is no subject to a sentence. In fact, a word can play nearly any role in a sentence's structure. For example, in Chapter 49 of the Tao Te Ching, Lao Tzu states, *'The hundred families all the time strain their eyes and ears, while the Sage all the time grandchilds them...'* Just how does a sage go about grandchilding? In another place he states, *'Good persons, I good them. Not good persons, I good them too.'* Archaic Chinese is vague. Even if it was your native tongue it is vague. It necessitates a higher degree of interpretation on the part of the reader than other languages. However, it appears to be the perfect language for Lao Tzu to have written in. He formulates his ideas within esoteric paradoxes allowing for numerous layers of meaning. He clearly intended for his writing to have no clear, objective meaning, but rather for it to convey personalized truths for each of his readers to discover.

Next to the Bible, the Tao Te Ching has been translated into English more times than any other book, over 100, since its first translation in 1868. Every translator has actually become an author of his own version due to the dramatic differences in these languages. But not only do we have Chinese to English translations, now we have English to English translations. English to English translations are also commonly used to create new versions of the Christian Bible. The purpose of same language translations is for the 'translator' to present his own theological interpretations. There are so many versions of the Christian Bible around that it is nearly impossible to track them all.

A line-by-line comparison of Chapter 1 of the Tao Te Ching by three translators helps to illustrate the sometimes-broad differences which can result. The first translator,

Dwight Goddard, used a Chinese document for his source in 1919. The second version, one commonly used by modern scholars, was translated in 1934 by Arthur Waley, who also used Chinese as a source document. The third, written by Wing-Tsit Chan in 1963, used Arthur Waley's English translation as his source document.

<u>Chapter 1: Line 1</u>

(Goddard) "The Tao that can be 'Tao-ed' can not be the infinite TAO (that is, the way that can be followed can not be the ultimate, pathless Way)."

(Waley) "The Way that can be told of is not an Unvarying Way;"

(Chan) "The Tao (Way) that can be told of is not the eternal Tao."

<u>Line 2</u>

(Goddard) "It is the same with the name of things: if things are explicable, the names we give them can not be the original Name."

(Waley) "The names that can be named are not unvarying names."

(Chan) "The name that can be named is not the eternal name."

<u>Line 3</u>

(Goddard) "(That is) The source of the universe is hidden in non-existence; existence is only the mother of its evolution."

(Waley) "It was from the Nameless that Heaven and Earth sprang."

(Chan) "The nameless is the origin of Heaven and Earth."

Line 4

(Goddard) "Since human beings are a small likeness of the great Universe, they can only realize their Taohood by making close imitations of it."

(Waley) "The named is but the mother that rears the ten thousand creatures, each after its kind."

(Chan) "The Named is the mother of all things."

Line 5

(Goddard) "One way to realize the wonderful mystery of TAO is to put away all thoughts and desires."

(Waley) "Truly, only he that rids himself forever of desire can see the Secret Essences;"

(Chan) "Therefore let there always be non-being so we may see their subtlety,"

Line 6

(Goddard) "The other way is to concentrate both true intention and sincere devotion."

(Waley) "He that has never rid himself of desire can see only the Outcomes."

(Chan) "And let there always be being so we may see their outcome."

Line 7

(Goddard) "These two ways of realization have different names but they both lead to a realization of the mystery that we call TAO."

(Waley) "These two things issued from the same mould, but nevertheless are different in name."

(Chan) "These two are the same, but after they are produced, they have different names."

Line 8

(Goddard) "Before one can attain the supreme perfection of Taohood,"
(Waley) "This same mould we can but call the Mystery,"
(Chan) "They both may be called deep and profound."

Line 9

(Goddard) "He must first realize its inmost mystery,"
(Waley) "Or rather the Darker than any Mystery,"
(Chan) "Deeper and more profound,"

Line 10

(Goddard) "That is, he must enter the door of this mystery of mysteries."
(Waley) "The Doorway whence issued all Secret Essences."
(Chan) "The door of all subtleties!"

If it was in fact Lao Tzu's conscious intent to produce a document which would spur a unique and personal interpretation for each reader, it appears from these three translations that he succeeded.

The early Christians argued over the question of Jesus' divinity. All of the most prominent groups, the Romans, the Marcionites, the Ebionites, and the Gnostics, all had their own view about this and they all produced either their own gospels or versions of the four main gospels which supported their view on this issue. This is but one example of disagreements over theological issues which have caused Christian documents to be altered and edited throughout the course of Christian history.

Another problem which has plagued the interpretation of religious texts is literary style. In the ancient world, the most common literary method for a teacher or philosopher to use to convey his message was through a fictional narrative. He would tell a story, or fable, and within the context of the narrative he would present his philosophical or theological message. This was the rule. This is how it was done and readers knew, expected that what they were reading was a narrative. Judaism, Hinduism, Buddhism, and a host of early Christian writings (which did not make their way into the New Testament), are all based in narratives.

Even as late as the seventeenth century, Galileo, a personage revered by all scientists and intellectuals, chose to present his theory of a sun-centered world within a fictional narrative, the same narrative that ultimately got him sentenced to house arrest. The four Christian gospels were actually a departure from this norm, as they were intended to be written as literal historic accounts. But still, even today in the twenty-first century, many religious figures want to apply a literal interpretation to these ancient fictional writings.

Using our modern-day versions of ancient manuscripts as source documents for any type of serious theological or mystical inquiry is problematic. They are not perfect. But collectively, the world's sacred writings represent some of humanities greatest treasures. The Tao Te Ching, the Koran, the Torah, the New Testament, the Adi Granth, the Vedas, the Buddhist Sutras, the mystical poetry of Rumi, Hafiz, and Kabir; what kind of world would this be without them? These great volumes, even in their imperfect states, have educated, awakened, and inspired billions of souls throughout the millennia.

CHAPTER 8

EVIDENCE FROM HISTORIC WRITINGS

Contained in this chapter are hundreds of excerpts from the writings of saints and sages which demonstrate their awareness of, and experiences with, the God-into-expression-power. Some of these sages were masters, teachers of Shabd Yoga. Others were mystics who communed with the light and sound and wrote about their experiences either in prose, or more commonly, in verse.

> *"O God, so many art thy names, that the poor tongue faileth to enumerate them."*

Guru Ram Das, Bhairon M.4

In the same way we have many names for God, such as, Ram, Allah, and Jehovah, many terms have been used to refer to the God-into-expression-power, such as; *Nada, Naam, Shabd, Word, Bani, Sound Current, Kalma, Sruti, Sraosha, Music of the Spheres, Music of all Harmonies, Nad, Udgit, et.al.* It is sadly ironic that the use of varying terms is one of the things which serve to help divide all of the world's schools of thought. One of these terms, 'Word', has been used by many sages including Hindus, Muslims, Christians, and Sikhs. In Christianity, it derives from the Greek term, 'logos' which means word, but it also means a thing's explanation or definition. Logos was also used by ancient Greek philosophers as meaning the 'explanation of everything'. Kalma means 'word' in Arabic and Nad and Udgit mean 'word' in Sanskrit. Another Sanskrit word appearing in the Vedas is 'Vak', meaning sacred word, and it is associated with the creation of the universe.

> *"In the beginning was the Creator (Prajapati). With Him was the Word (Vak), and the Word (Vak) was verily the Supreme Brahma."*

Rig Veda

Christians will recognize the parallel with the opening lines from the Gospel of John.

> *"In the beginning was the Word, and the Word was with God, and the Word was God. The same was in the beginning with God. All things were made by him; and without him was not any thing made that was made."*
>
> John 1:1-3

In these passages, Word refers to the utterance of the creator, the elemental, harmonic vibration of sound, out of which all of creation manifested; the vibratory disturbance of non-being, resulting in being.

> *"The unstruck Word is not the word which can be written or read; O Tulsi, the unlettered Word is indeed transcendent, known only through hints given by Saints."*
>
> Tulsi Sahib

The opening passage of John, and his use of the term 'Word', is interpreted by most Christian ministers as meaning the written and spoken words of the Bible. It has been used in this context by so many, for so long, that the original intent of its author, John, has been lost. This illustrates a good example of how a written passage, originally intended to impart an esoteric truth, becomes diluted by later generations who lack their own mystical experience and therefore lack right understanding.

> *"Some parrots have become so skilled with words, the blind turn over their gold and their very lives to caged feathers."*
>
> Hafiz

The following passages have been collected from the World's great wealth of spiritual literature. They provide examples of the awareness of the Nada, and the visual and audial experiences of mystics who established direct inner contact with it.

Commenting on how fortunate his disciples were to have been given God's gift of inner vision and hearing when less fortunate souls were not, Jesus stated;

> *"It is given unto you to know the mysteries of heaven, but to them it is not given…Therefore, I speak to them in parables: because they seeing, see not; and hearing, they hear not; neither do they understand…For verily I say unto you that many prophets and righteous men have desired to see those things which ye see, and have not seen them; and to hear those things which ye hear, and have not heard them."*

> Mathew 13:11-17; Luke 10:24

A version of this passage also appears in the fourth chapter of Mark, followed by Jesus' parable of sowing the Word, where he casts himself as the sower, saying, *"The sower soweth the Word…"* In this parable, Jesus makes the point that the power of God, or 'Word', can only take root and flourish in a person who leads a life of purity and Godliness. Jesus did not initiate the usage of the term 'Word', as it appears at various places throughout the Old Testament. The term had also been used by Greek mystics such as Plutarch, Socrates, and Pythagoras to mean essentially the same thing; the essence of the human soul. By the dawn of the Christian era, Greek philosophical ideas and terms had become well established throughout the former Greek Empire.

In the opening chapter of John, the apostle points out that even in a place of utter physical darkness, the self-effulgent light of the Word is visible to those whose inner eyes are open.

> *"And the Light shineth in the darkness, and the darkness comprehendeth it not…That was the true Light which lighteth every man that*

> *cometh into the world...And the Word was made flesh, and dwelt amongst us."*

John 1:5-14

Jesus explains his vital role as a living master, or Word made flesh, when he declares;

> *"I am the Light of the world. He that followeth me shall not walk in darkness, but shall have the Light of Life."*

John 8:12

Perhaps no canonical book has stirred the imagination of Christians more than the Book of Revelations. This last book of the New Testament falls into a literary category referred to by scholars as 'apocalyptic', meaning that the book explores unknown mysteries or hidden truths. The author identifies himself as John. It was originally written in Greek, although scholars have concluded that Greek was not the author's first language. Since it makes reference to the island of Patmos, and we know that the apostle John lived there, most Christian scholars have concluded that he was indeed the author.

Some scholars believe that the book represents a more or less literal account of the author's own mystical experiences. However, there are others who disagree, who feel that it is most likely a colorful narrative. Either way, it is highly probable that the author was a mystic adept, well-established in the causal plane, who had advanced inner development of seeing and hearing. It is also highly probable that, even if it does not represent a literal account of an inner vision, it is nonetheless based on the author's own mystical experiences. The sights and sounds he describes are fully consistent with those of other mystic writers. John testifies to seeing multiple ascended masters and the radiance coming off of their feet. He describes the sounds of running waters, thunder, trumpet, and roaring voice, all of which are sounds emanating from the causal plane, the source of prophetic vision. As examples;

"I was in the Spirit on the Lord's day, and heard behind me a great voice, as of a trumpet..."

"I saw...one like unto the Son of man...His head and his hairs were white like wool, as white as snow; and his eyes were as a flame of fire; And his feet like unto fine brass, as if they burned in a furnace; and his voice as the sound of many waters."

"The first voice which I heard was as it were a trumpet..."

"I saw four and twenty elders sitting, clothed in white raiment...And out of the throne proceeded lightenings and thundering and voices..."

"And I heard, as it were the noise of thunder..."

"Hurt not the earth, neither the sea, nor the trees, till we have sealed the servants of our God in their foreheads."

"And there were voices, and thundering, and lightening, and an earthquake."

"And I saw another mighty angel come down from heaven, clothed with a cloud: and a rainbow was upon his head, and his face was as it were the sun, and his feet as pillars of fire...and [he] cried with a loud voice, as when a lion roareth: and when he had cried, seven thunders uttered their voices."

"And I looked, and lo, a Lamb stood on the Mount Zion, and with him a hundred and forty-four thousand, having his Father's name written in their foreheads. And I heard a voice from heaven, as the voice of many waters, and as the voice of a great thunder: and I heard the

voice of harpers harping with their harps. And they sung as it were a new song before the throne...and no man could learn that song but the hundred and forty-four thousand which were redeemed..."

"And I heard as it were the voice of a great multitude, and as the voice of many waters, and as the voice of mighty thundering, saying, Alleluia..."

"His eyes were as a flame of fire...and his name is called The Word of God."

"And they shall see his face; and his name shall be in their foreheads. And there shall be no night there; and they need no candle, neither light of the sun; for the Lord God giveth them light..."

The Christian tradition is replete with great mystics and mystical accounts.

> *"The Word of God became man that you also may learn from a man, how a man becomes a God."*
>
> Clement of Alexandria

> *"Absolutely unutterable and indescribable are the lightning-like splendors of Divine Beauty; neither can speech express nor hearing apprehend. Shall we name the brilliance of the morning star, the brightness of the moon, the radiance of the sun – the glory of all these is unworthy of being compared with the true light, standing farther from it than does the gloomiest night and the most terrible darkness from midday brightness. This beauty, invisible to bodily eyes, comprehensible to soul and mind only; it illumines some of the saints and leaves in them an unbearable wound through their desire that this vision of Divine beauty should extend over an eternity of life."*
>
> St. Basil the Great

> *"I entered even into my inward self, you being my Guide…and I entered and I beheld with the eye of my soul (such as it was), above the same eye of my soul and above my mind, the Light Unchangeable. Not this ordinary light which all flesh may look upon, but as the brightness of this should be manifold brighter, and with its greatness, take up all space. It was not a common light but different; yes, far different from all others…Whoever knows the truth, knows what that Light is, and whoever knows that Light, knows Eternity."*
>
> St. Augustine, Confessions 7:10

"Those in whom the eternal Word speaks are delivered from uncertainty. From one Word proceed all things and all things tell of Him."

The Imitation of Christ

"For all whatsoever has life, liveth in the Speaking Word; the Angels in the Eternal Speaking and the temporal spirits in the re-expression or echoing forth of the formings of time, out of the sound or breath of Time, and the angels out of the Sound of Eternity; viz., out of the Voice of the Manifested Word of God."

Jacob Boehme, 'Mysterium Magnum'

"If you should in this world bring many thousand sorts of musical instruments together, and all should be tuned in the best manner most artificially, and the most skillful masters of music should play on them in concert together, all would be no more than the howlings and barkings of dogs in comparison of the Divine Music, which rises through the Divine Sound and tunes from Eternity to Eternity."

Jacob Boehme, 'The Aurora'

"The highest Divine illumination, incomparable Light, is the source of all the gifts and all the virtues…In this light, the Spirit merges in relief of a beatitude that cannot be measured, or sounded, but can only be known by experience."

John Ruysbroeck, The Spiritual Espousals 2: LXX

"A particular phenomenon occurs when the brain is overcharged by Astral Light; sight is turned inward instead of outward; night falls on the external and material world, while fantastic brilliance shines on the world of spirit; even the physical eyes experience a

slight quivering and turn up inside the lids...Pythagoras defined God as a living and Absolute Truth clothed in light; he defined the Word as number manifested by form...He said also that God is supreme music; the nature of which is harmony."

Father Eliphas Levi

"I asked for the most intimate experience with the Christ. No one would believe what happened in a vision, more true than this world; the Sacred Chord pulsated Light throughout the universe, and I nursed my own Lord at my breast."

St. Francis of Assisi

"Who must God have made love to in order to have given birth to all this sound, to this sacred spectrum of color, scents, and music...I am a swimming galaxy tonight. Angels surround me hoping I will share a piece of this light."

Meister Eckhart

"When my sight became clearer, I could see auras around different foods. And I know now – should I say this? – that everything can sing. The songs of fruits and grains will calm. Why not put them into yourself? A new language you will learn. More generous eyes we need. The songs of light will help you."

St. Catherine of Sienna

"What percentage of God is unseen? What percentage of the truth of Him do we know? He led me to a place where only Light existed...This Light which never sets, which nothing can obscure because it is eternal, is suddenly placed in front of us by God."

"There is a divine world of Light with many suns in the sky. I slept with my Lord one night. Now, all is luminous; I know we conceived."

"If only I could give the slightest idea of what I saw? But thinking about it I find it is impossible, because the very Light of that region which is all Light is so different from ours, that the brightness of the sun seems, in comparison, rather pale and gray."

St. Teresa of Avila

"This voice, or loud sound of water, fills the soul with such copious benefits and gives it such a great strength that it seems to hear not only a sound of rivers but also a crash of thunder."

St. John of the Cross

Thomas Aquinas, like Augustine, embraced both faith and reason in his quest for knowledge. One day, three months prior to his death, he was overtaken by a divine revelation while conducting mass and was unable to continue. Later he reflected on the experience, saying;

"I can no longer write, for God has given me such glorious knowledge that all contained in my written works are as straw – barely fit to absorb the droppings that fall in a stable."

The gospel of Mary Magdalene was not included in the canon, and is little known to most Christians, largely due to its now fragmentary condition. In one passage, Mary, speaking to Jesus, describes seeing the radiant form of the Master within during meditation.

"I saw the Lord in a vision and I said to him, 'Lord I saw you today in a vision.' He said to me, 'congratulations to you for not wavering at seeing me, for where the attention is, there is the treasure'."

GNOSTICISM

Christian Gnosticism thrived in the early centuries, especially in areas distant from the watchful eyes of the Roman officials who were responsible for monitoring new, potentially subversive religious movements. While Gnosticism was highly diverse, with many sects with radically differing views, the principal theme which ran throughout was that knowledge, particularly spiritual knowledge, was something to be acquired through the direct, mystical experience of each person. The following sources are all considered to be components of the Gnostic library of writings.

"Jesus said, 'If they say to you, where are you from? Say to them; It is from the light that we have come – from the place where light, of its own accord alone, came into existence'."

"When you see one who has not been born of woman [radiant form of the master], fall upon your face and prostrate yourselves before that one: it is that one who is your father."

"There is light existing within a person of light. And it enlightens the whole world."

Gospel of Thomas

"Soul and Spirit are constituted of water and fire...I do not mean worldly fire, which has no form, but another kind of fire, whose appearance is white, which is beautifully luminous, and which bestows beauty."

"The demons do not see those who have put on the perfect light, and cannot seize them. One will put on the light in a mystery, through the act of union...In other words, no one can obtain this grace without putting on the perfect light and becoming, as well, perfect light."

The Gospel According to Philip

"Then Jesus said to his disciples, 'did I not tell you that just like a visible flash of thunder and lightning, so will the good be taken up to the light?'"

Dialogue of the Savior

"The Word of the father goes forth in the entirety, being the fruition of his heart and an outward manifestation of his will."

"His wisdom meditates upon the Word."

"The Word that is in the heart of those that declare it, has come forward. It is not just a sound, but it became a man."

"Speak from the knowledge of the superior day, in which there is no night; and from the star that does not set, since it is perfect. Speak, therefore, from the heart, for it is you who are the day that is perfect, and it is within you that there dwells the star that does not set."

"Their hope, toward which they strive, is striving toward them: it is their image, the light in which there is no shadow."

Valentinus, The Gospel of Truth

"I am the Word who dwells in the ineffable Silence. I dwell in undefiled Light. A Thought emerged from the Great Sound...I am the Thought of the Father, the perfect Glory, and the immeasurable Invisible One who is hidden. The Sound exists from the beginning in the foundations of the All. But there is a Light which dwells hidden in Silence and it was the first to come forth...I alone am the Word, ineffable, incorruptible, immeasurable, inconceivable. The Word is a hidden Light; unreproducible, the source of All...It is the foundation that supports every movement of the Aeons that belong to the mighty glory. It is the founding of every foundation. And it is a Word by virtue of the Sound ... I, the Word, became a foundation for the All."

The Trimorphic Protennoia

THE ESSENES

"I have reached the inner vision, and through Thy spirit in me, I have heard Thy wondrous secret. Through Thy mystic insight, Thou has caused a spring of knowledge to well up within me, a fountain of power, pouring forth living waters, a flood of love and all-embracing wisdom, like the splendor of eternal Light."

The Book of Hymns

JUDAISM

"For with thee is the fountain of life: in thy light shall we see light."

Psalms 36:9

"The grass withereth, the flower fadeth, but the Word of our God shall stand forever."

Isaiah 40:8

"By the Word of the Lord were the heavens made...For He spake and it was done."

Psalms 33:6-9

"Forever, o Lord, thy Word is settled in heaven...Thy Word is a lamp unto my feet, and a light unto my path."

Psalms 119:89-105

BUDDHISM

The Surangama Sutra, one of Buddhism's most revered texts, was written anonymously in Sanskrit by a master (Buddha) around the 1st century, C.E. Literally translated, Surangama Sutra means 'The Buddha's Great Crown Sutra'. Approximately one third of the sutra is devoted to a dialogue that the Buddha and Manjusri have with their twenty-five most advanced disciples; Bodhisattvas and Arhats. The Buddha asks each of them to testify as to how they attained to Samadhi and achieved perfect emancipation from the eighteen spheres of mentation; i.e., the six organs of sense, the six sense perceptions, and their corresponding objects of perception. (Buddhism recognizes six sense perceptions, adding *cognition* to the five common ones.)

As the disciples begin to testify, they describe a variety of methods and practices, including;

1. development of transcendental sight
2. meditation upon the originality of phenomena

3. the realization of the non-existence of all phenomena

4. the acquisition of perfect health and perfect intelligence

5. the development of perfect clarity of consciousness

Two disciples describe their method as being 'concentration of mind upon in and out breathing (pranayama). In the Buddha's summation, he explains the shortcomings of this method, and why it is not prescribed for novice disciples.

> *"Breathing is a spontaneous activity of the organism but it is conditioned by moods and emotions. The novice has not attained to a refined state of in and out breathing because the mind and the breathing are not yet united into an evenly balanced state of tranquility, which is difficult to attain, so it will be difficult for him to attain the essential nature of perfect accommodation by merely concentrating his mind on his in and out breathing."*

Several disciples testify that their method for achieving perfect accommodation was through the practice of 'intrinsic', or transcendental hearing.

> Kaundinya – *"It was while I was concentrating my mind in my practice of dhyana on the contemplation of the transcendental sound of the Dharma, that I attained my first experience of Samadhi and became an Arhat."*

> Samantabhadra – *"The transcendental and intrinsic hearing of my Essential mind became very pure and transparent, so that I could use it to discriminate the understanding and ideas of all sentient beings…I would say that in my case it was through the intrinsic hearing of my Essential Mind."*

Purna Metaluniputra – *"Since these ancient days, since the Lord has been among us, I have offered my services in turning the Dharma Wheel, and have lately attained to the degree of Arhat by means of the development of my hearing, by reason of which I am conscious of the transcendental sound of the Dharma, reverberating like the roar of a lion...I would answer that my first thorough accommodation of mentation was the subjugation of my internal attachments...by means of the intrinsic sound of the Mysterious Dharma."*

The testimony of the Buddha's most advanced disciple, Avalokitesvara, who had taken the name of his Buddha from a previous incarnation, is saved for last. The author devotes a disproportionate amount of text to a description of Avalokitesvara's method, Transcendental Hearing, and the nature of his subsequent spiritual development.

Avalokitesvara – *"I recall that ages ago, there was present in the world a Buddha called Avalokitesvara, by whose instruction I was encouraged to begin seeking Enlightenment. I was taught to begin practicing by concentrating my mind on the true nature of Transcendental Hearing, and by that practice, I attained Samadhi. "As soon as I had advanced to the stage of Entering the Stream, I determined to discard all thoughts of discrimination as to where I was or had been. Later I discarded the conception of advancing altogether, and the thoughts of activity or quietness in this connection did not again arise in my mind. Continuing my practice, I gradually advanced until all discrimination of the hearing nature of my self-hood, and of the intrinsic Transcendental Hearing, was discarded.   As soon as all arbitrary conceptions of rising and disappearing of thoughts were completely discarded, the state of Nirvana was clearly realized.*

"Then all of a sudden, my mind became transcendental to both celestial and terrestrial worlds and there was nothing in all the ten quarters but empty space, and in that state, I acquired two wonderful Transcendencies. The first was a Transcendental Consciousness that my mind was in perfect conformity with the Essential, Mysterious Enlightening Mind of all the Buddhas in all the ten quarters, and was also in perfect conformity with the Great Heart of Compassion of all the Buddhas. The second transcendency was that my mind was in perfect conformity with the minds of all sentient beings of the Six Realms, and felt with them the same earnestness and longing for deliverance.

"Blessed Lord! Because of my adoration for Buddha Avalokitesvara, he taught me how to attain the Diamond Samadhi by the single method of concentrating my mind upon Transcendental Hearing. And moreover, he helped me to attain the same compassionate capacity that all the Buddhas had, by reason of which I attained the thirty-two kinds of transformations that are instantaneously available in response to the prayers for deliverance from any part of the world, at any time. These transformations have all been attained and exercised with perfect freedom and spontaneity in the mysterious Diamond Samadhi which I had attained by concentrating my mind in the practice of Dhyana on Transcendental Hearing...

"But in addition to the acquirement of perfect accommodation by means of my attainment of Supreme Enlightenment, I have also acquired another Four Kinds of Inconceivable, Wonderful Transcendencies of Spontaneity. The first developed because when I first attained to my Transcendental Hearing, my mind became abstracted into its essential nature, and all the natural powers of hearing, seeing, smelling, tasting, touching, and understanding attained to a state of pure, glorious Enlightenment of perfect mutuality and accommodation in one perfect unity of Awareness. Because of this, I have acquired this great Transcendental Freedom, so that when I give deliverance to sentient beings, I can transform myself into wonderful appearances. The second inconceivable, wonderful Transcendency of Spontaneity developed because of my emancipation from the contaminations of the six sense-objects. It is as if sound were passing through walls without any hindrance. Thus, I can skillfully transform into different kinds of appearances, and can transform these appearances to give the Transcendental Power of Fearlessness to sentient beings. The third inconceivable, wonderful Transcendency of Spontaneity developed because of my practice upon the pure, original Essence of perfect accommodation, so that wherever I go, I inspire sentient beings to sacrifice their lives and possessions in order to pray for compassion and mercy. The fourth inconceivable, wonderful Transcendency of Spontaneity developed because of my

acquirement of the Buddha's Intrinsic mind, so that I can give all different kinds of offerings to all of the Buddhas of all the ten quarters of the universes.

"As my Lord has enquired of us as what was our means of perfect accommodation...I answer that my first perfect reflection of Samadhi was by means of my Intrinsic Hearing and Transcendental Mental Freedom from objective contaminations, so that my mind became abstracted and absorbed into the Divine Stream and thus I acquired the Diamond Samadhi and attained Enlightenment. Blessed Lord! In those far-off days, my Lord and Buddha Avalokitesvara, praised me for my skillful acquirement of the all-accommodating Door of dharma. As such my Transcendental Hearing reaches to the ten quarters of all the universes."

The Buddha and Manjusri conclude with their summations, by declaring that the method of 'Entering the Stream' by way of 'Transcendental Hearing of the mysterious Dharma' was in fact the means employed by them. Manjusri further explains that the reason some had found success through other methods, was due to two factors: 1) they were monks and were able to devote a full-time effort to their quest for enlightenment, and 2) their efforts were supported by the transcendental powers of the Buddha.

"Then the Lord Tathagata addressed Manjusri, Prince of the Dharma, saying: - Manjusri! As sentient beings wish to return to their origin where their nature will be in perfect unity there are many different ways that may be used as expedient means for attaining it. But there is one way, no matter what the conditions for practicing it may be – difficult or

not difficult – that is available to all, that is accommodating to all, that, though the period of practicing may vary with different disciples, is sure to bring them to the goal.

"Then Manjusri addressed the Lord Buddha, saying: - Blessed Lord! Since my Lord has descended from the Deva Realms to this Saha World, he has helped us most by his wonderful enlightening Teaching. At first, we receive this Teaching through our sense of hearing, but when we are fully able to realize it, it becomes ours through a Transcendental and Intuitive Hearing. This makes the awakening and perfecting of a Transcendental Faculty of Hearing of very great importance to every novice. As the wish to attain Samadhi deepens in the mind of any disciple, he can most surely attain it by means of his Transcendental Organ of Hearing.

"For many a kalpa – as numerous as the particles of sand in the river Ganges – Avalokitesvara Buddha, the hearer and answerer of prayer, has visited all the Buddha-lands of the ten quarters of the universe and has acquired Transcendental Powers of boundless Freedom and Fearlessness and has vowed to emancipate all sentient beings from their bondage and suffering. How sweetly mysterious is the Transcendental Sound of Avalokitesvara! It is the pure Brahman Sound. It is the subdued murmur of the sea-tide setting inward. Its mysterious Sound brings liberation and peace to all sentient beings who, in their distress, are calling for aid; it brings a sense of permanency to those who are truly seeking the attainment of Nirvana's Peace...

"All the Brothers in this Great Assembly, and you too, Ananda, should reverse your outward perception of hearing and listen inwardly for the perfectly unified and intrinsic sound of your own Mind-Essence, for as soon as you have attained perfect accommodation, you will have attained to Supreme Enlightenment.

"This is the only way to Nirvana, and it has been followed by all the Tathagatas of the past. Moreover, it is for all the Bodhisattva-Mahasattvas of the present and for all in the future if they are to hope for Perfect enlightenment. Not only did Avalokitesvara attain Perfect Enlightenment in long ages past by this Golden Way, but in the present, I also, am one of them.

"My Lord enquired of us as to what expedient means each one of us had employed to follow this Noble Path to Nirvana. I bear testimony that the means employed by Avalokitesvara is the most expedient means for all, since all other means must be supported and guided by the Lord Buddha's Transcendental Powers. Though one forsake all his worldly engagements, yet he cannot always be practicing by these other various means; they are special means suitable for junior and senior disciples, but for laymen, this common method of concentrating the mind on its sense of hearing, turning it inward by this Door of Dharma to hear the Transcendental Sound of his Essential mind, is most feasible and wise."

The Lotus Sutra, another of Buddhism's revered texts, was also written anonymously. Its origins are unknown, but its first translation into Chinese was done in 255 C.E.

The text is written in a narrative format, and it addresses its topics in both a literal and lyrical style. It makes reference to various Buddhas and describes visions of light, sound, and divine fragrance associated with them.

> *"Manjusri, why from the white tuft between the eyebrows of our leader and teacher does this great light shine all around? Why do mandarava and manjushaka flowers rain down and breezes scented with sandalwood delight the hearts of the assembly?"*

> *"Beneath these jeweled trees are lion seats, and the Buddhas seat themselves on them, adorning them with their brilliance like a huge torch burning in the darkness of the night. A wonderful incense exudes from their bodies, pervading the lands in the ten directions. Living beings are wrapped in the aroma, unable to restrain their joy."*

> *"Again, he will see Buddhas, their bodies marked by a golden hue, emitting immeasurable rays that light up all things, employing Brahma sounds to expound the doctrines."*

> *"The Buddha emitted a light from between his eyebrows, manifesting signs that are rarely seen."*

The Buddha promises to manifest himself in his radiant form (guru dev).

> *"If those who expound the Law are alone in an empty and silent place, and in that stillness where no human voice sounds, they read and recite this sutra, at that time I will manifest my pure and radiant body for them."*

The sutra goes on to describe other various mystical experiences involving light, sound, and fragrance.

"When these Bodhisattvas saw this beam of light that illumined the Buddha lands everywhere, they gained what they had never had before. They wished to know the causes and conditions that had occasioned this light."

"Sandalwood and aloes in a jumble of fine powder rain down; like birds flying down from the sky they scatter as an offering over the Buddhas. In the midst of the air heavenly drums of their own accord emit wonderful sounds."

"In the Brahma heaven and above, the light Sound heaven, the All Pure heaven, and up to the Summit of Being heaven, the sounds of the voices speaking there – the teacher of the Law, dwelling here, can hear them all."

"One who upholds this sutra will also be able to detect the odors of the various heavens in the sky above. The scent of sandalwood, aloes, various kinds of powdered incense, and incense made of an assortment of flowers – of heavenly scents such as these, there are none that he cannot detect and identify. He will also be able to detect the scent of the bodies of heavenly beings…Thus extending his awareness upward to the Brahma heaven, by detecting their scent, he knows all those who enter meditation or emerge from meditation. In the Light Sound and All Pure heavens and up to the Summit of Being, those born for the first time, those who have departed – detecting their scent, he knows them all."

"The lands that he passed through on his way quaked and trembled in six different ways, and in all of them seven jeweled lotus flowers

rained down and the instruments of hundreds and thousands of heavenly musicians sounded of themselves without having been struck."

The Buddha describes his advanced disciples as 'voice-hearers'.

"Great hero and stalwart, World-Honored One, Dharma king of the Shakyas, because you have pity on us, favor us with the Buddha Voice!"

"When the voice-hearers and bodhisattvas hear this Law that I preach, as soon as they have heard one verse, they will all without doubt be certain of attaining Buddhahood...You, Shariputra, and the voice-hearers and bodhisattvas, you should understand that this wonderful Law is the secret crux of the Buddhas."

TIBETAN BOOK OF THE DEAD

"O nobly-born, five colored radiances - vibrating and dazzling like colored threads, flashing, radiant, and transparent, glorious and awe-inspiring, will...strike against thy heart, so bright that the eye cannot bear to look upon them...be not afraid of that brilliant radiance of five colors, nor terrified; but know that Wisdom to be thine own. Within those radiances, the natural sound of the Truth will reverberate like a thousand thunders. The sound will come with a rolling reverberation...Fear not. Flee not. Be not terrified. Know these sounds to emanate from thine own inner light."

TAOISM

The Tao Te Ching is foundational to all Chinese philosophy and is so revered by Buddhists that many consider it to be an auxiliary Buddhist text. It was written anonymously sometime prior to 250 B.C. by a spiritual master who wrote under the pen name, 'Lao Tzu'. Lao Tzu was a skillful communicator whose couplets were layered with multiple meanings and purposes. He used his criticism of the ruling classes of his time as a literary vehicle for teaching his esoteric wisdom by presenting an argument, then jumping to a completely different train of thought to conclude each passage. His objective was to get the reader to think about the two seemingly unrelated things and how they might be somehow connected. His chapters are not intended to have a single, objective meaning, but are rather a kind of muse for his readers to discover some truth, personal to them.

> *"My words are very easy to understand and very easy to put into practice. Yet, no one under heaven understands them…but it is upon this very fact that my value depends."*

Chapter 70

Lao Tzu writes of many aspects of mysticism and the spiritual life, including spiritual seeing and hearing, the importance of stillness and contemplation, cause and effect, duality, the role of the master, and returning to the source of all life.

"The great Form is without shape.
For Tao is hidden and nameless."

Chapter 41

"Because the eye gazes but can catch no glimpse of it,
It is called elusive.
Because the ear listens but cannot hear it,
It is called rarefied...
Endless the series of things without name
On the way back to where there is nothing...
For to know what was once there, in the beginning,
This is called the essence of the Way."

Chapter 14

"Push far enough towards the Void,
Hold fast enough toward the Quietness...
This return to the root is called Quietness;
To know the always-so is to be illumined."

Chapter 16

"Being substance-less,
Tao can enter even where there is no space;
That is how I know the value of action that is actionless,
And teaching without words.
The value of action that is actionless,
Few indeed can understand."

Chapter 43

"Block the passages, shut the doors...
Good sight means seeing what is very small...

He who having used the outer light,
To return to the Inner Light,
Is thereby preserved from all harm.
This is called resorting to the always-so."

Chapter 52

"Tao is called the mysterious power.
This mysterious power is so deep-penetrating,
So far reaching,
That it follows things back –
All the way back to the Great Concordance."

Chapter 65

"The practice of Tao consists of subtracting,
day by day;
Subtracting and then subtracting,
Til one has reached inactivity.
But by this inactivity,
Can everything be achieved."

Chapter 48

"If one looks for Tao, there is nothing solid,
If one listens for it, it is faint to the ear,
Yet if one uses it, it is inexhaustible."

Chapter 35

HINDUISM

The ancient, highly diverse Hindu culture is rooted in the Vedas, perhaps humanity's oldest collection of written wisdom. Within the various sutras are found references to the God-into-expression-power with terms including Nada (the primordial essence of creation), Vak (sacred Word), and Akash Bani (voice coming down from the heavens).

"Let yogi sit on Sidh Asana, and while practicing the Vaisnavi Mudra, should hear the sound through his right ear. By communion

with the Nada, he will become deaf to the external sounds, and will attain the Turya Pad, or a state of equipoise within a fortnight. First, the murmuring sounds resembling those of the waves of the ocean, the fall of rain, and the running rivulets and the Bheri will be heard intermingled with the sounds of bell and conch."

Nada Bind Upanishad

"The door of the True One is covered with a golden disk. Open that, O Pushan, that we may see the nature of the True One."

Isha Upanishad

"Uttering the sacred syllable 'Aum', rise above the three regions, and turn thy attention to the All-Absorbing Sun within. Accepting its influence, be thou absorbed in the Sun, and it shall in its own likeness make thee All-Luminous. He who transcends the effulgence, is this Aum."

Rig Veda

"Salutation to the Gurû, the dispenser of happiness to all, appearing as Nâda…one who is devoted to Him, obtains the highest bliss."

Hatha Yoga Pradipika

JAINISM

"Hearing the Sound resembling that of the conch and witnessing the Lotus Light like that of a newly blossomed flower between the two eyebrows, one faces the Sat Guru [radiant form of the Master]."

"When the mind finds an anchorage in Knowledge, there flashes forth the Light."

"The aspirant is enjoined to sit in solitude and meditate with a single-pointed attention, on the Maha Mantra of Panch parmesti and to perceive the Light."

Suttagame, Part II

ZOROASTRIANISM

From the 'Gatha Ushtavaiti', thought to have been written by the original Zoroaster, also known as Zarathustra, we have an invocation to the Mazda Ahura, praying for the gift of Sraosha, literally translated as 'resounding fire', or Word.

"Thus, I reveal the Word, which the Most Unfolded One has taught me, the Word which is the best for mortals to listen to. Whosoever shall render obedience and steadfast attention unto Me, will obtain for his own self the All-embracing Whole Being and Immortality; and through the service of the Holy Divine Spirit will realize Mazda Ahura (Godhead)."

"Divine Guidance of the Eternal Master, accomplishing long life in the Right Paths leading to the Absolute Kingdom of the Divine Mind, wherein the Omniscient, Self-existent Life-Giver dwells by His all-pervading Reality, I invoke that divine Sraosha, which is the greatest of all divine gifts for spiritual succor."

BAHAISM

"O Essence of Negligence! Myriads of mystic tongues find utterance in one speech, and myriads of mysteries are revealed in a single melody; yet alas, there is no ear to hear, nor heart to understand."

Bahaullah, Hidden Words

ISLAM

"God is Light on Light, and He guides whomever he wants to his Light."

Koran 24:35

In Dara Shukoh's pamphlet, "Compass of Truth", he discusses the Prophet's communion with celestial light and sound and his inner vision of the Guru Dev.

"Once they asked our Prophet; 'In what manner did the inspiration for the Koran come to you?' He replied, 'I hear a sound sometimes like the sound of a boiling cauldron, and sometimes like the sound made by bees, and sometimes I see an angel in the form of a man, who talks with me, and sometimes I hear a sound like silvery bells or the beating of a drum.'

In Chapter 2 of "Compass of Truth", Dara Shukoh further describes contact with the Guru Dev and other celestial beings.

"O friend! Thou shalt practice with diligence and perseverance, the methods of meditation to be described herein, and the mirror of thy soul will become bright, and thou shalt see reflected in it the forms of prophets, saints, and angels.

There thou shalt meet also with the form of thy Master, who will lead thee to the holy Prophet, and to the mighty companions of the Prophet, and to powerful saints and friends of God. And whatever difficulties you might have, you can ask for their solutions from these forms mentally and you will get reply from them...Thou shouldst meditate on these appearances carefully and observe them minutely; so that the truth regarding the subtle world, which is actually the real world, may become fully revealed to thee. Then thou shalt be able to see whatever thou desirest to see in that world."

SUFISM

Hazrat Inayat Khan (1882-1927) left a large collection of writings which originated from his discourses. The following excerpt is to be found within the volume entitled, 'The Mysticism of Sound'.

"All space is filled with the Abstract Sound. The vibrations of this Sound are too fine to be either audible or visible to the material ears or eyes. This Sound is the source of all revelation to the Masters to whom it is revealed from within and, therefore, they know and teach the one and the same Truth.

This Sound goes on continually within, around, and about man. It develops through and into ten different aspects, because of its manifestation through the different tubes of the subtle body (nadis), and sounds like thunder, the roaring of the sea, the jingling of bells, the buzzing of bees, the twittering of sparrows, the vina, the flute, and the sound of the conch.

The knower of the mystery of sound knows the mystery of the whole universe."

Jalaluddin Rumi (1207-1273) is remembered as being one of humanity's greatest mystic poets. He was born in the eastern provinces of the Persian Empire to a father who was a religious scholar. At a very young age he met and was mentored by Persia's most renowned poet, Attar, who immediately recognized Rumi's spiritual eminence. Rumi inherited his father's position as head of a madrassa, but in 1244, Rumi journeyed to Damascus where he met his spiritual master, Shamz Tabriz. Shamz claimed that he had been wandering throughout the empire in search of a true disciple, a successor to carry forth his spiritual mission. Rumi became known for his continual state of God-intoxication, which took tangible form as a perpetual outpouring of poetry, a disguise for his mystical testament.

"Don't worry about saving these songs!
And if our instruments break,
It doesn't matter.
We have fallen into the place
Where everything is music.
The strumming and the flute's notes
Rise into the atmosphere,
And even if the whole world's harp should burn up,
There will still be hidden instruments playing."
"There is a seed grain of light inside.
Fill it with yourself, or it will die."
Don't go to sleep one night.
What you most want will come to you then.
Warmed by a sun inside, you'll see wonders."

"We rarely hear the inward music,
But we dance to it nevertheless,
The pure joy of the light,
Our music master."

"The sound of drums rises on the air,
Throbbing, it is God's heart.
A voice inside the beat says,
'I know you're tired, but come on,
This is the Way'."

"Take the cotton out of your ears,
The cotton of regret and consolation,
So you can hear the sphere-music...
A Gnostic says little, but inside is full of
mysteries,
And crowded with voices."
"The universe of the Creation-Word,
Where the divine commands, 'To Be',
That universe of qualities is beyond reckoning;
More intelligent than mind,
And more spiritual than spirit.
No being is unconnected to that reality,
Of which no mortal can speak."

Hafiz of Shiraz (1320-1392) began writing poetry to a beautiful girl after falling in love with her, but after having a vision of an angel, he began dedicating his poetry to God. Soon afterward, he met his spiritual master, Mahmud. Hafiz managed to secure the position of court poet to the Shah, gaining fame and notoriety. But since he was writing from his own experience, many clerics considered him a heretic. Hafiz left an extensive and rich body of work addressing virtually every aspect of spirituality.

> *"I can see angels sitting on your ears,*
> *Polishing trumpets, replacing lute strings,*
> *Stretching skins on the drums,*
> *And gathering wood for the evening's fire.*
> *These angels made sweet music last night.*
> *Did you hear them?"*
>
> *"You still listen to that old tavern song,*
> *That brings your body pain.*
> *Now, chain your ears to his flute and pulsing drum.*
> *Inside the veins of the petals of a blooming redbud tree*
> *Are hidden worlds where sometimes Hafiz resides.*
> *I will spread a Persian carpet there,*
> *Woven in Light."*
>
> *"There are some who can visit that luminous sphere,*
> *Which sings, 'this world never was'.*
> *The truth of that experience,*
> *Is reserved for so very few."*
>
> *"I have made the journey into nothingness.*
> *I have become that flame which needs no fuel."*
>
> *"Let's all join hands, and drink of the sun,*

And sing sweet songs to God until He joins us
With a few sublime notes from His lute and
drum."
"It takes great courage to plunge into the
darkness,
Tracking God into the unknown, and not panic,
Or get lost in the startling new scents, sounds,
and sights."
"Noise is a cruel tyrant, who is always
imposing curfews
While repose and quiet break out the vintage
elixir,
And awaken the true music…
Now the sky drum plays all by itself in my head,
Singing all day long, the Lord's name."

Bulleh Shah (1680-1758) is considered by many to be the greatest mystic poet of Northwestern India, and is often compared to Rumi and Shamz Tabriz.

"The flute has suddenly burst forth into
melody!
On hearing it I have forgotten all other things.
I am shot with the wondrous shafts of Unstruck
Music;
And the world appears fake, false in its
pursuits.
O Master, I have come to bargain
For a glimpse of your face."
"We are powerless in our halls of learning.
He Himself brought us under His pen,
We are ignorant without the Word,
And without the Word, none can cross."

SANT TRADITION - TEACHINGS OF THE MASTERS

Most of the great spiritual adepts who have appeared in the world over the ages are probably unknown to us because no one wrote about them and they left no writings of their own. This section contains a small, but noteworthy sampling of masters who did.

Ravidas (1460 – 1540) was a contemporary of Kabir, about 20 years younger in age. Both were from Benares and since Ravidas refers to Kabir in his writings as 'master', we must assume that Kabir was his guru. The famous poet-saint Mirabai, a member of a royal family, names Ravidas as her guru, so we must also assume that Ravidas was Kabir's successor. Ravidas inherited his father's position as a low-caste cobbler, lived in utter poverty, and due to his lowly social status, higher caste people, like Brahmins, rarely sought him out for spiritual training. However, some members of the ruling class did, including Mirabai. One day Mirabai brought a diamond to give to Ravidas so that he could improve his living conditions. He refused to accept the generous gift but she wedged it into his thatched roofing so that he would have access to it, if and when he changed his mind. Some months later, she returned to his hut and found the diamond exactly where she had left it. Ravidas thanked her, then humbly explained that he already had all the inner wealth he would ever need.

> *"How canst thou maintain the distinction of high and low, when all have arisen from the same Divine Flame? How canst thou give discriminatory names to some, sayeth Ravidas, when the Audible Life Current in all remaineth the same?"*
>
> *"Perform your devotions in the inner sky, by merging yourself into the Sound Current.*

There the throne of the Thousand-Petaled Lotus is adorned, and the unstruck Divine Symphony is eternally played."

"Obtained is the Divine Nectar of God's Name, and I remain immersed in its taste; And I ever keep it on my tongue. Drinking that Nectar, I am steeped in Divine ambrosia, and I remain absorbed, day and night. By a single drop of that Nectar, the thirst of countless lives was quenched, fetters of birth and death were broken, and Ravidas was released forever."

Dadu (1544-1603), lived during the reign of the enlightened Mogul ruler, Akbar the Great. Dadu was once invited to one of Akbar's spiritual symposiums. After listening to his inner wisdom, the participants asked from whence such knowledge originated. Dadu replied that God belonged to the caste of love, that his body was comprised of love, that he was the color of love, and that his currency was the wealth of love.

"All are bound by the Word,
And the Word abides in all.
All arise from the Word,
And in the Word do all merge back, sayeth Dadu.
That, from which the wave of knowledge arises,
From which the spiritual sight emerges;
In the Word alone does that Source abide.
The realm where the unstruck Music is sounded,
Where the lustrous Form shines forth;
That realm, a true servant of the lord alone beholds.

There, he plays his instrument in perfect harmony,
Where melody is the essence of the body,
And through the self is the Melody expressed.
"The knowledge of the Sound Current,
Imparted by the Guru,
Merges one easily into Truth.
It carries me to the abode of my beloved,
Sayeth Dadu.
By enabling people to hear the sound,
The Master can awaken them at his will.
He may, at his pleasure, speak within them,
And fuse them into his own form.
The aspirant who fills his pot
With drops of Celestial Melody,
He alone survives.
How can he die, O Dadu?
He drinks the divine Nectar."

Namdev (1270-1350) met his master, Khechar, as a young boy outside of a Hindu shrine. He told the boy that he had been waiting there for him in order to deliver him from the illusion of mythology and superstition. Khechar gave Namdev initiation on the spot. In a poem to his young disciple, Khechar says;

"Serve thy master, who will impart to thee the secret of the path of true knowledge.
Then shalt thou see the Lord within and thy delusion will vanish.
Within thy body is the abode of the Lord,
Where shineth beauteous light and constantly, day and night, resounds the Word.
There thou shalt meet the Supreme Lord."

In his poetry, Namdev characterizes the process of sensory withdrawal from the body as 'dying while alive', a phrase also used by the Greek master, Plutarch.

> *"The thundering resonance of the Word,*
> *Has liberated me while living;*
> *Through the Word of my guru*
> *I have realized my true self;*
> *And while still living, I have learnt to die;*
> *I have now no fear of death.*
> *Visoba Khechar says: 'Death we transcend,*
> *O Nama, when we experience it while living."*
>
> *"Whenever I see Him, I sing His praises,*
> *And then I, His servant, attain peace and bliss.*
> *On meeting my master, I merge in Divine Melody.*
> *Where the effulgent light is seen,*
> *There rings the boundless Word.*
> *I became fused in Divine Light;*
> *At this union arranged by my Master*
> *In the lotus chamber within*
> *There are gems of brilliant hue;*
> *They sparkle with dazzling sheen*
> *Like flashes of lightning.*
> *He is near, He is not far;*
> *My soul is replete with Him.*
> *Where the Unstruck Melody is luminous,*
> *Nama has realized the Truth,*
> *Through the grace of his Master,*
> *And has attained the blissful state of Union."*

Kabir (1440-1518) is remembered both for his spiritual legacy and his many volumes of mystical verse, which will endure for all time in the library of humanity's greatest literary works. His popularity in India today has never been greater; ironic considering he was despised and persecuted by so many in his own time.

Kabir was an iconoclast, a reformer, and his field of action was the holy city of Benares where he battled Brahmins and Mullas alike. His weapon was the pen and his tactics were sarcasm, humor, and mockery. With a Socratic wit he decried ascetics and holy men, questioning; "If saffron-colored robes could give salvation, what about saffron colored dogs? Are they liberated? If shaven heads could, what about sheep who are shorn twice a year? If tree-sitting sadhus found salvation, what about the birds? If river bathing led to salvation, what about the fish?"

He compared Qazis who delivered memorized discourses with prattling parrots, and book-learned Vedantic scholars with donkeys, carrying loads of carrots too large to consume. He challenged established convention with piercing wit, denouncing the authority of the gods and goddesses, idol worship, superstitions, rites and rituals, and the entire apparatus of Muslim and Hindu piety.

Kabir describes the God experience, disguising it as poetry.

> *"The moon shines within me,*
> *But these blind eyes cannot see it;*
> *The sun and the moon, both are within,*
> *But my deaf ears cannot hear it."*
>
> *"O how do I describe that secret Word?*
> *How can I say He is like this, or He is like that?*
> *If I say He is within me, the universe is ashamed;*
> *If I say He is outside of me, it is a lie.*
> *He makes the inner and outer worlds indivisible;*
> *The conscious and the unconscious are His footstools.*
> *He is neither manifest nor hidden;*
> *Neither revealed nor unrevealed.*
> *There are no words to convey that which he is."*
>
> *"Where Spring, the lord of the seasons reigneth,*
> *There the Unstruck Music sounds of itself,*
> *There the streams of light flow in all directions;*
> *Few are the men who can cross to that shore!*
> *There is my Lord self-revealed;*
> *And the scent of sandalwood and flowers,*
> *Dwells in the depths."*

"The middle region of the sky, home to the Soul,
Is radiant with the music of light;
There, where the pure and white music blossoms,
My Lord takes His delight.
In the wondrous brilliance of each hair of his beard,
The light of millions of suns is lost.
On the shore of that region is a city,
Where the rain of nectar incessantly pours.
Kabir says; come pilgrim,
Behold my great Lord's reception."
"The light of suns and moons illumines the way,
And the melody of love swells forth,
As the rhythm of detachment, beats time.
Day and night, the sky chorus fills the heavens,
And Kabir says;
'My Beloved One radiates lightning.'
Time and the universe sing hymns of worship,
While invisible bells ring in adoration.
Kabir says; 'While the Lord watches from his throne,
Creation bows in exaltation.'
Held by cords of love, Joy sways to and fro,
And the sky chorus breaks forth in song.
A lotus of wonder, spinning creation's hub,
Pure souls know its true delight.
Radiant music surrounds it,
And the heart bathes in the Sea of Infinity.
Kabir says, 'Dive into that sweet ocean,

And let the regrets of life and death wash away'."

In his own lyrical way, Kabir declares as Christ did; "I and my Father are One".

"I have taken my seat on the Self-poised One,
I have drunk from the cup of the Ineffable,
I have found the key to the Mystery, and
I have reached the Root of Union.
Traveling without feet,
I have entered the Land without sorrow,
Welcomed by the Lord's great mercy.
They sing of Him as invisible and unattainable,
Yet in my meditations,
I have seen Him and know Him."

SIKHISM AND THE SIKH GURUS

The Sikh sacred scripture, the Adi Granth, is a collection of hymns, most of which were penned by one of the ten gurus who appeared in their lineage, which spanned 200 years.

"One merged in the Word lives in the light of God.
The Word makes manifest the inner light,
And leads the soul Godward.
One escapes all bondages and lives in Truth,
The Word is a rare gift in this age,
And a true disciple gets it.
He who practices the Word,
Not only is he saved,
But many more are saved with him."

Guru Amar Das

"By hearing the Sound Current,
One reaches the Source and finds comfort.

By hearing the Sound Current,
One knows the Truth, and escapes the angel of death.
By hearing the Sound Current,
One becomes self-luminous, and darkness departs.
O Nanak! By hearing the Sound Current,
One glows with Divine Light.
The Word becomes fully manifested
And one becomes the Word Personified."

Guru Ram Das

"Word is the sovereign remedy for all ills;
It is a Comforter and a Bestower of bliss.
We wish for nothing else but the light of Thy Word,
O Master! The light that permeates in all hearts."

Guru Arjan

"Those who are fulfilled in Thy Word
Are completely saturated with it,
O Nanak! There is but one Amrit
And none beside it.
Those who are dependent on Thy Word
Are completely dyed in Thy color,
O Nanak! There is only one exhilarating vintage
And no other."

Guru Angad

"One gets the merit of all religions
By listening to the Divine Melody."

Guru Teg Bahadur

Sikh theology regarding the nature of and practice of the Word is best articulated by the founding master of the Sikh lineage, Guru Nanak.

PART III

The Radha Soami Lineage

The 'Radha Soami' lineage of teachers officially began in 1861 with the public mission of Swami Ji, at least in name. However, according to Swami Ji, the modern lineage of teachers actually began nearly 400 years earlier with Kabir and Guru Nanak, the source of the stream.

CHAPTER 9

NANAK – THE SOURCE OF THE STREAM

In the year 1469, a divine meteorite struck northwestern India about 40 miles outside of Lahore (now a part of Pakistan). They named this heavenly flame, Nanak. The shock waves from Nanak's visit to this world resounded from the lofty heights of Tibet to the jungles of Sri Lanka, from the lowlands of Burma across and beyond the Hindu Kush to Mecca, Baghdad and Jerusalem. Even today, the aftershock of Nanak's earthly mission still resounds in every corner of this planet. Few outside of India today realize the impact that he had on humanity, and is still having, and will continue to have for centuries to come.

Guru Nanak was born to fulfill a unique and noble purpose; to bridge the divide between people of different faiths and to inspire common people to seek God-realization. The life of Guru Nanak is recorded in a narrative called Puratan Janamsakhi, which historians consider to be the most reliable source of biographical information. While the account is somewhat brief, leaving out large segments of his life while he was engaged in his famous travels, it does provide a revealing picture of the man-teacher-saint.

At the time of his birth, and throughout his life, the Moguls were securing power throughout Northern India and would eventually rule a vast empire which would endure for 330 years. Islamic kingdoms had been in place in Northern India for some time, but with the Moguls came an increasing dominance of Islam and seeds of conflict with people of other faiths, such as Buddhists and Jains, but especially Hindus who were the majority. The official position on religion for most of the Mogul rulers was one of tolerance, but it was the Muslim clerics and administrators who used their positions of authority to make life difficult for Hindus. With the Moguls in power, Islam had the upper hand and the animosity between Hindus and Muslims deepened and widened. It was in the midst of these circumstances that Nanak appeared.

Nanak's father was the village accountant, an important position, appropriate to his merchant (Bedi) caste and social status. The village elder assured the young boy and his father that when it came time for his father to retire from active service, the job would go to Nanak. The tradition of a job or trade being passed on from father to son is a time-honored mainstay of Indian culture. Educational opportunities were scarce in his rural village, but he was tutored in Persian and Hindi as a preparation for his career.

While his father groomed him to be a merchant, Nanak developed his own interests. From a very early age, he investigated the subject of religion with anyone he could find who seemed to have any insight into the subject or any theological literature. As he got older, he sought out ascetics, sages, and yogis and centers of religious learning and as a result, gained a sound footing in scriptural literature and theology. His family had him married as a teenager and arranged for various village jobs, such as herding buffalo, shop keeping, and trading in horses, trying to pave the way for their son's inevitable life as a householder. But Nanak preferred the company of his religious and ascetic friends and performed poorly at the jobs his father arranged for him.

Running out of favors in his local village, Nanak's father made arrangements for him to apprentice as a merchant in a nearby town, Chuharkhana. He bankrolled his son with enough money to secure living accommodations and to set himself up in business. But along the route, Nanak met some ascetics and holy men and gave all of his money to them. Upon return, his family was bewildered. Nanak, they concluded, had gone mad. His father even called in a physician to examine him. Nanak tried to explain that he was smitten with pangs of love for the Lord and suffered simply from God-intoxication.

Maru, M.1

Eventually his brother-in-law, Jai Ram, intervened and offered to take Nanak with him to Sultanpur, where he set him up with a merchant's position. Nanak carried out his duties during the day to the best of his abilities but when night came, he engaged in meditation.

It was at Sultanpur that Nanak's fate would forever change. One morning, while bathing in the Kali Bein, a stream near town, he wandered off into the forest. His family and friends wondered what had happened to him. Did he drown? Three days later he emerged from the forest with a blissful radiance about him muttering, "There is no Hindu, there is no Muslim". Everywhere he went, Nanak chanted the phrase. People really did begin to believe that he had gone mad.

Nanak's equating Hindus with Muslims offended many people. On one occasion, a formal complaint was filed against him and he was brought before the governor, where a local Qazi (priest) presented the complaint. The governor could see that Nanak was God-intoxicated and offered him a seat next to his. He explained to the Qazi that Nanak was a faqir and that his words were easily misunderstood. The hearing recessed for afternoon prayers and Nanak accompanied the Qazi, who conducted the prayer. Nanak did not kneel, as is customary, but instead remained standing.

Upon return to the hearing, the Qazi used Nanak's behavior at prayers as further evidence against him. When the governor asked Nanak to explain, he replied that the Qazi had also not prayed. Yes, he kneeled down, but at no time did he

have his mind on God. Instead, the Qazi was thinking the
entire time about his new foal that was loose back home,
worried that the foal might fall into a nearby well. The Qazi
was ashamed. He apologized to Nanak and to the governor
and withdrew the complaint.

    Sometime around 1497, Guru Nanak left Sultanpur and
began his journeys. This period would occupy the next
twenty-five years of his life. He began with a small troupe,
including his good friends Mardana, a Muslim, and Bhai Bala,

a Hindu, but the numbers would soon swell. He took four main journeys and one minor one. His longest one, which may have spanned as long as twelve years, took him as far as Egypt and the Middle East, all the way to Jerusalem and Turkey. To the north, Nanak crossed the snow-capped Himalayas where he met the Tibetans and Chinese, and gave light to the Naths, the Siddhas, and the Lamas. To the east, he crossed the North Indian plains as far as Bengal. And to the south, he traversed the subcontinent as far as Sri Lanka. He traveled not for the purpose of reaching a particular place, but rather in search of the hearts of sincere seekers wherever he might find them.

Nanak was a reformer, always challenging the old ways and methods. He saw that people everywhere were just going through the motions of their religious observances. He sought to inspire them to really want to know God, while always careful to seek a point of equilibrium with them and their traditional faiths. Underlying his efforts was a vision for people adopting a completely new and practical means of seeking and realizing God through the practice of the Word.

When Nanak visited Hardwar, he observed the pilgrims at the river throwing water toward the east, which is a customary way of relieving the burdens of the departed ancestors. Nanak waded in and began throwing water toward the west. When the people asked him why he was throwing water to the west, he replied that he was watering his fields in Lahore. They asked how such a thing was possible, to which he replied that if these waters could reach the heavens, then surely they could reach Lahore which was much closer by comparison. He was at all times focused on his mission of weaning people away from their archaic, ritualistic observances.

Given the political turmoil of the time, anyone sincerely seeking spirituality usually became an ascetic and left the towns and villages behind to live a life of self-abnegation and rigid disciplines in the mountains, forests, and jungles. Nanak was concerned to see these sincere souls driven away from mainstream society. He wanted the quest for spiritual awakening to be integrated in to the fabric of everyday life for all people, regardless of their style of living or stature in society.

When visiting Gorakhmata, Nanak met with a group of yogis who immediately took to him and asked him to join their order. Nanak answered with the following hymn;

> *"Yoga lies not in the yogi's patched garments,*
> *Not in his ash smeared body, nor walking staff.*
> *Yoga lies not in large earrings, shaved heads,*
> *Nor in the blowing of the conch.*
> *One who lives in the world, uncontaminated,*
> *Has found the secret of yoga.*
> *Religion lies not in empty words.*
> *One who takes all men as his equal is religious.*
> *Religion lies not in pilgrimages,*
> *Not in postures of contemplation,*
> *Religion lies not in places of bathing*
> *Nor roaming about begging.*
> *One who lives in the world, uncontaminated*
> *Has found the secret of Religion."*

Nanak was a masterful teacher. From the very beginning, he had a clear vision of his goals and the means by which he would realize them, which were well-planned and calculated. When he prepared his visit to a city or village, he would intentionally visit places of religious study, sites of pilgrimage, shrines and holy places and religious festivals. Nanak and his evangelical troupe amounted to a traveling minstrel show. They would find a strategic spot and begin singing and playing their instruments and people would gather around. Then he would stop in the middle of a verse and expound on the deeper, esoteric meaning. He was also a prolific writer. The collection of Nanak's hymns that have been preserved and which are contained within the Adi Granth numbers 974.

Nanak had a flair for the dramatic. He often carried a staff in one hand and a collection of hymns in the other. He wore costumes which were carefully designed for each journey to convey the precise image that he wanted people to see. Sometimes his dress would incorporate elements of Hindu and Muslim attire. At other times, his attire would be carefully planned without any possible inference to either. In general, he dressed the way he thought best for each situation in order to facilitate his communication and integration with the local people.

When he visited Multan, the land of faqirs and holy men, he was greeted at a village gate with a bowl brimming over with milk, meaning that the place was already awash with saintly men and there was no room for another. Nanak placed a jasmine flower on top of the milk and had the bowl returned. His reply meant that he would float above the fray giving sweet fragrance to all.

The love of God and service to man was at the core of Nanak's message. He bore witness to the glory of one God, one brotherhood, and the principles of human fellowship and universal love. He came to reconcile all religions and all faiths, with a reverence for all past saints and masters. He proclaimed the harmony inherent in all the scriptures of the world by announcing a singular truth within all the great traditions; that the same flame of love shone in all of the churches, temples, shrines, and sacraments of man. Nanak was the manifested heart of religion.

When the Mogul ruler Babar met Nanak, the king asked him if there was some favor he could grant. Nanak politely, yet firmly declined, telling Babar that to beg from a king would be foolhardy since God is the only true benevolent giver. He added, "I hunger for God alone, and ask for naught". Later, Babar learned that Nanak had been imprisoned and ordered his immediate release. He sent for Nanak and this time he asked the master for the favor of his advice. Nanak counseled the King in spiritual matters, using Islamic references and terminology out of respect, and concluded by saying, "Have love of God uppermost in thy heart and hurt not the feelings of His creatures".

One evening in Mecca, Nanak entered a mosque to meditate and fell asleep. He was awakened later by a man who complained that he was in a 'sinful posture', as his feet were pointed toward the crown of the mosque, the direction toward which people prayed. Nanak answered, "Kindly tell me in which direction God is not, so that I may point my feet accordingly". When questioned in Mecca as to whether he was a Hindu or a Muslim he explained he was neither because he saw the same spirit of God inherent in both. Speaking to the Muslims, he told them to make Allah the rosary as he interpreted the wisdom of the prophet. In Mecca some cried out, "God is speaking to us through Nanak". When Sheik Farid greeted Nanak he stated, "Thou art Allah". The master replied, "Allah is the only aim of my life and is the essence of my being".

Nanak addressed his followers lovingly as 'Bhai', or brother. To him, all were brothers, a part of the brethren of God. He viewed all as equals, whether they be rich or poor, high caste or low. He formed a new social consciousness everywhere he went by creating groups of 'Bhais' who helped spread his message.

In 1520, Nanak retired from his travels and returned to Kartarpur and his humble roots to work the soil with his family and devotees. For 25 years, Nanak had journeyed far and wide in search of true seekers. Now it was time for them to travel to him. And travel they did. For the remainder of his life, his disciples journeyed from far and wide to the Punjab to bask in the glory of his light. Nanak had gained considerable renown by this time, and many of his visitors had never previously met him; only heard of his spiritual eminence. They poured in from the Middle East, Central Asia, Afghanistan, and the subcontinent, including Brahmins and Sufis, the Siddhas and Naths; people of all colors and castes.

Prior to his death, the master appointed his devoted disciple, Lehna of Khadur, to succeed him in his spiritual mission and renamed him 'Angad'. He instructed Angad to move across the river to found a new community, as it would be needed in the future to further the work. After Angad had gotten settled in, Nanak found that he continued to spend long hours in meditation, as was his custom. Nanak counseled his dear disciple saying that his meditations had been successful, and now a suffering humanity would need him soon, so it was time to begin to lead a more active life in the world in preparation for Nanak's departure. Nanak left his mortal frame on September 7, 1539.

The tradition of successorship begun by Nanak spanned 200 years with nine subsequent spiritual masters, culminating in the mission of Guru Gobind Singh. The fifth guru, Arjan, collected Nanak's writings, along with the writings of his predecessors to create the 'Adi Granth', a canon of sacred scripture for the Sikh Society. In addition to Nanak's 974 hymns, Arjan included 541 hymns from Kabir's repertoire, and in keeping with the Sikh view of respect and recognition for past saints and masters, Arjan also added another 300 hymns from 25 saints outside of the Sikh tradition, including works by Ravidas, Namdev and Dadu.

Arjan chose to open the Adi Granth with a special collection of Nanak's hymns known as Jap Ji, which represent the core of Nanak's mystical teachings. 'Jap' means 'meditation upon', or 'mergence with', and 'Ji' means 'new life'. Taken together, Jap Ji means 'solving the mystery of life through meditation'. Nanak implores us to seek the source of life through communion with the Word. In his hymns, Nanak uses a mixture of Hindu and Islamic references and symbolism to drive home his points. The objective of the spiritual path, according to Nanak, was to become so immersed in God that any distinction between ourselves and God becomes lost. Nanak was qualified to teach the process by which one could attain this objective because he had mastered it himself.

The prologue of Nanak's Jap Ji is somewhat reminiscent of the opening of John's gospel. The term 'Naam' means Word, or Living, Conscious spirit.

> *"There is one reality, the Unmanifest-manifested;*
> *Ever-existent, He is Naam.*
> *The Creator; pervading all;*
> *Without fear; without enmity;*
> *The Timeless; the Unborn and the Self-existent;*
> *Complete within Itself...*
> *He was when there was nothing;*
> *He was before all ages began;*
> *He existeth now, O Nanak,*
> *And shall exist forevermore."*

In the first stanza, Nanak laments the futility of seeking God through ineffective means. Like Lao Tzu, he proclaims that there is a 'way' after all.

> *"How may one know the Truth and break through the cloud of falsehood?*
> *There is a way, O Nanak, to make His Will our own..."*

In his fourth stanza, Nanak reveals that 'communion with the Word' is the way.

> *"True is the Lord, True His Holy Word;*
> *His love has been described as infinite.*
> *Men pray to him for gifts, which He grants untiringly.*
> *When all is his:*
> *What can we offer at His feet?*
> *What can we say to win his love?*
> *At the ambrosial hour of the early dawn,*
> *Be you in communion with the Divine Word*

And meditate on His Glory.
Our birth is the fruit of our actions;
But salvation comes only from His grace.
O Nanak, know the True One as immanent in all."

In the next stanza we can appreciate Nanak, the 'minstrel-teacher', encouraging us to sing God's praises in the spirit of Bhakti.

"Let us sing of Him and hold communion with the Word,
With hearts full of loving devotion;
For then shall all sorrows end and we be led joyously Homeward".

In stanza six, Nanak implores us to follow the instructions of our master, as Jesus did when he said, 'If ye love me, keep my commandments'.

"If I may only please Him, tis pilgrimage enough;
If not, nothing – no rites or toils avails;
Whichever way I look, I find that in His creation,
None has won salvation without His Grace – regardless of karmas.
You can discover untold spiritual riches within yourself;
If you abide by the teachings of your Master.
My Master has taught me one lesson:
He is the Lord of everything, may I never forget Him."

In stanzas eight through fifteen, Nanak describes the ultimate fate of one who devotes himself to the practice of the Word.

"By communion with the Word, we can escape unscathed through the portals of death...

By communion with the Word, one can have yogic insight with the mysteries of life and self all revealed...

By communion with the Word, one becomes the abode of truth, contentment, and true knowledge...

By communion with the Word, the spiritually blind find their way to Realization...

O Nanak, His devotees live in perpetual ecstasy, for the Word washes away all sin and sorrow.

By practice of the Word, one rises into universal consciousness and develops right understanding...

By practice of the Word, one is freed from sorrow and suffering...

By practice of the Word, one speeds on to the Higher Spiritual planes unhindered...

By practice of the Word, one saves not only himself, but when he becomes an adept, many others whom he guides...

O, great is the power of the Word,

But few there be that know it."

In stanza twenty-one, Nanak explains that once a soul reaches the 'Sea of Immortality' on the causal plane, our actions here on the earth plane, whether righteous or not, no longer determine our spiritual destiny.

"Pilgrimages, austerities, mercy, charity, and alms giving, cease to be of any consequence, when one gets an ingress into the Inner Eye;

Communion with the practice of the Holy Word, with heart full of devotion,

*Procures admittance into the Inner Spiritual
Realms,
Washing away the dirt of sins at the Sacred
Fount within. "*

In the next stanza Nanak acknowledges that God's
creation is beyond comprehension, and then in stanza twenty-
three, he puts it into perspective.

*"His devotees praise Him, yet never attain full
knowledge of the Infinite;
Like streams tumbling into the ocean, they
know not the depths therein.
Even kings and emperors with heaps of wealth
and vast dominion,
Compare not with an ant filled with the love of
God. "*

In stanzas twenty-eight and twenty-nine, Nanak lends
encouragement to the aspirant.

*"Let contentment be your earrings...
Let preparedness for death be your cloak...
Let your master's teachings be your supporting
staff...
Let the Divine Music vibrating in all be your
trumpet. "*

In stanza thirty-eight, he encourages us further.

*"Make purity your furnace, patience your
smithy,
The Master's word your anvil, and true
knowledge your hammer.
Make awe of God your bellows and with it
kindle the fire of austerity,
And in the crucible of love, melt the nectar
Divine.
Only in such a mint can man be cast into the
Word. "*

In his finale, Nanak sums up our ultimate fate.

> *"Air is the Master, Water the father, and the Earth the mother,*
>
> *Day and Night are the two nurses in whose lap the whole world is at play.*
>
> *Our actions: good and evil, will be brought before his court,*
>
> *And by our own deeds, shall we move higher or be cast into the depths.*
>
> *Those who have communed with the Word, their toils shall end,*
>
> *And their faces shall flame with glory.*
>
> *Not only shall they have salvation,*
>
> *O Nanak, but many more shall find freedom with them."*

Guru Nanak paved the way for a lineage of Masters to follow him by naming Guru Angad as his successor. One poignant question which has come up with respect to Nanak, and which has been debated for centuries is; 'did he have a living master'? We know that as a young man he had many teachers who instructed him in theology and various spiritual methods, but none of them trained him in the science of the Word. The official position of the Sikh brotherhood is that he did not. Having a highly evolved master soul appear in the world spontaneously who is ready to embark on a great spiritual mission is certainly not without precedent. Lord Buddha, for example, appears to have had no living mentor. Nanak was once asked, "Who is your master?" He replied, "Shabd is my master, and my attention is its disciple". However, in his writings, he suggests that perhaps he did have a living master.

> *"I attached myself to the Word, given by my Master."*

Ramkali, Sidh Gosht, M.1

"I have made sure by asking it of my Master;"

Sri Rag, M.1

"I am a sacrifice to my Master."

Asa-di-Var, M.1 and Ramkali Onkar, M.1

"My Master has taught me one lesson."

Jap Ji 6

When Guru Nanak reappeared out of the forest in Sultanpur, after having spent three days apparently lost to the physical world, along with repeating the phrase, "There is no Hindu, there is no Muslim", he also reported that while in the forest he had met the Lord. He went on to say that he had been given certain esoteric instructions regarding meditation and his spiritual mission. So, did he meet his master in the forest that day physically, or perhaps in his radiant form? According to Kirpal Singh, incidents like this are not without precedent. "There are instances, though rare, when the sincere aspirants have seen, and received Initiation from the Master even without meeting him physically".[5]

If in fact Nanak did have a guru, it could only have been one person: Kabir. While we do not have any specific written accounts of what took place during Nanak's travels, we do have general information. We know that he deliberately sought out any and all spiritual luminaries who were alive at the time. During Nanak's eastern journey, he certainly visited Benares, a city known as a spiritual hub. Kabir, by this time, was famous in Benares, or in the eyes of some, infamous. It is difficult to imagine the two men not meeting personally. Kabir was about thirty years older, an ideal age difference for a guru-disciple relationship. But the most compelling case for the Kabir-Nanak relationship is their teachings. If you were to walk into the middle of a lecture on one or the other's teachings, you wouldn't know if the subject of the lecture was

---

[5] Kirpal Singh, Spiritual Elixir, Sant Bani Press, 1970

Nanak or Kabir. They're that close. They were as one soul in two bodies. They were both musical and both prolific writers. They were both reformers, condemning archaic religious practices. They even used similar imagery and terminology in their hymns. For example, Kabir attacks the yogic lifestyle in a way strikingly similar to Nanak.

> *"The Yogi dyes his garments, instead of dyeing his mind in the colors of love;*
>
> *He sits within the temple of the Lord, leaving Brahma to worship a stone.*
>
> *He pierces holes in his ears; he has a great beard and matted locks, and looks like a goat;*
>
> *He goes forth into the wilderness, killing all his desires, and turns himself into a eunuch;*
>
> *He shaves his head; he reads the Gita and becomes a mighty talker.*
>
> *Kabir says; 'You are going to the doors of death, bound hand and foot'."*

In another hymn, Kabir attacks religious observances using the term, 'True Name', a term adopted by Nanak (Sat Naam).

> *"O brother! When I was forgetful, my true Master showed me the way.*
>
> *Then I left off all rites and ceremonies, I bathed no more in the holy water;*
>
> *From that time forth I knew no more how to roll in the dust in obeisance;*
>
> *I do not ring the temple bell;*
>
> *I do not set the idol on its throne;*
>
> *I do not worship the image with flowers;*
>
> *It is not austerities that mortify the flesh which are pleasing to the Lord.*
>
> *When you leave off your clothes and kill your senses, you do not please the Lord.*

The man who is kind and who practices righteousness,
Who remains passive amidst the affairs of the world,
Who considers all creatures on earth as his own self,
He attains the Immortal Being, and the true God is ever with him.
Kabir says; 'He attains the True Name whose words are pure, and who is free from pride and conceit'."

In this hymn, Kabir equates Allah with Ram, in a spirit akin to Nanak.

"Hari is in the East; Allah is in the West.
Look within your heart, for there you will find both Karim and Ram.
All the men and women of the world are His living forms.
Kabir is the child of Allah and of Ram.
He is my Guru, He is my Pir."

Kabir, like Nanak, uses the term 'Word' to mean the elemental essence of creation.

"Receive that Word from which the Universe springeth!
That Word is the Guru; I have heard it, and become its disciple.
How many are there who know the meaning of that Word?
O Sadhu! Practice that Word!
The Vedas and the Puranas proclaim it,
The world is established in it,
The Rishis and devotees speak of it;
But none knows the mystery of the Word.

> *From that Word the world-form has sprung.*
> *That Word reveals all.*
> *Kabir says; 'But who knows from whence the*
> *Word cometh'!"*

If there was no direct tie-in between the two, either physical or mystical, the equivalency of their teachings is extraordinary. Nanak created a great flood of spirituality which was damned up in Amritsar and throughout the Punjab, benefitting ten generations of Indians. But spirituality, like water, finds its own course to run, and run it did, around and over the dam, across all of India, and ultimately, throughout the rest of the world.

CHAPTER 10

TULSI TO SAWAN – THE RAPIDS

"O God! Thy Saints have at all times been in the world. O God! Throughout the ages the line of gurus has been in existence. The succession of Satgurus continues throughout, and they have ever preached the lesson of the Word."

The Adi Granth

Shabd Yoga Masters have always been present in the world because they have an essential role to perform. Humanity is in a continual state of spiritual evolution, and there are at all times new souls who are ready to embark upon the spiritual path and others ready to complete their development toward God realization. There is food for the hungry and water for the thirsty, as per the law of supply and demand. Humanity is ever in need of spiritual succor.

Historically, there are cases where a spiritual master has appeared at a time and place to fulfill this need but then left no competent successor to carry on the spiritual work. There are other cases where the teacher did leave a successor, and in some cases, established a rich spiritual tradition which endured for generations. The Sikhs gurus, the Sufi masters, and the Buddhas are all examples of lengthy traditions. But eventually these lines dry up, for one reason or another, and a spiritual master appears in another culture somewhere else.

The Sikh line of living masters ended with the tenth guru, Guru Gobind Singh. He is famously known as the 'warrior guru', due to his role in organizing an army of peasants which ultimately drove the Moguls out of northwestern India once and for all. Since his death in 1708, the Sikhs have considered their holy scripture, The Adi Granth, to be their guru, even though the Adi Granth itself states that the world is never without a living master.

Tensions between the Moguls and the people of northwestern India reached a boiling point during Gobind Singh's life. His father, Guru Teg Bahadur, the ninth Sikh Guru, had been murdered by the Moguls and the Mogul authorities feared that Gobind Singh might be out for revenge. As a result, Gobind Singh himself became a target.

He stayed on the move for much of his life, traveling throughout the subcontinent establishing friends and allies, while initiating sincere souls into the practice of the Word wherever he could find them. While traveling in southwestern India, he met the Peshwa of Poona in Maharashtra, India, southeast of Mumbai. A Peshwa served as a governor or viceroy over a particular region for the emperor, but in fact had complete authority and functioned like a king. Gobind stayed with the Peshwa for a period of time and initiated the entire royal family and much of the royal court into the practice of the Word.

> *"The Rani (Queen) of Ratan Rao Peshwa,*
> *accompanied by Bhai Nand, came to the feet of*
> *Guru Gobind Singh for spiritual instruction."*[6]

Because of the decentralized nature of his spiritual mission, Gobind Singh established the 'Khalsas' or 'pure ones'. These were disciples who had achieved a certain level of spiritual attainment and who Gobind entrusted with carrying on the task of initiation on his behalf during his absence. One member of the Peshwa's royal family, Ratnagar Rao, was not only a Khalsa but became a spiritual adept in his own right. During Gobind Singh's life, he initiated souls on Gobind Singh's behalf, but after his death, he carried on with his own mission and a rich spiritual tradition was established in Poona which would endure for many generations.

---

[6] Shri Des Raj, 'Hindu Sikh Ithras'

In 1720, twelve years after Gobind's death, Baji Rao I succeeded to the throne. Two generations later his grandson, Amrit Rao, as first born, was due to succeed as Peshwa. However, just prior to his coronation the young man disappeared. His family attempted desperately to locate him but to no avail. As a result, his younger brother took the throne and came to be known as Baji Rao II.

It is impossible to know precisely why the young man renounced his privileged destiny and disappeared, but historians who have researched the incident have concluded that Amrit Rao, who had been initiated into the spiritual science at a young age, made rapid inner progress in his youth, spending long hours in solitude out in the jungles. When it came time for him to assume his inherited role as peshwa, he decided that life at court was not for him, electing instead for the life of a contemplative and ascetic.

These conclusions are based on the research of a prominent local historian, Shri Vitthal R. Thakar, which was completed and published in 1980. Shri Thakar has also concluded that Tulsi Sahib, the great saint of Hathras, author of the 'Ghat Ramayana' and 'Ratan Sagar', is none other than the same Amrit Rao of Poona.[7]

Amrit Rao changed his name to Sham Rao immediately upon leaving Poona. He clearly did not want to be found or identified. He wandered throughout India for many years, eventually settling in Hathras, 30 miles north of Agra in 1808. By that time, he had become known as Tulsi Sahib. He was also popularly known as 'Dakhani Baba' which means 'sage from the South'.

Some have speculated that Ratnagar Rao was Tulsi Sahib's master. This is unlikely due to the fact that Ratnagar Rao would have been beyond 100 years of age in Tulsi's

---

[7] J.R. Puri and V.K. Sethi, 'Tulsi Sahib, Saint of Hathras', 1978

youth. Amrit Rao was probably initiated by one of Ratnagar Rao's surviving disciples, perhaps a family member.

Tulsi Sahib (1763-1843) is said to have adopted the name 'Tulsi' because he believed that part of his mission was to clarify the epic work, 'Ramayana', written by the great poet saint Tulsidas (1532-1623). The 'Ghat Ramayana' is aimed at clarifying the earlier work, especially pointing out the subtle spiritual truths underlying its allegorical literary format. Like so many other ancient religious texts, the Ramayana had been widely misunderstood for centuries because people had come to interpret it literally, thereby missing its spiritual undertones.

While many choose to discount a possible connection between Tulsi Sahib and the Sikh lineage, if one compares his writing to that of the Sikhs, it would appear that they were all in fact a part of the same spiritual tradition.

> *"Listen, O friend, to the thunderous roar of the Word,*
>
> *Which reverberates throughout the firmament.*
>
> *The invisible world is contained within the human eye,*
>
> *Behold Brahmand within, through your astral eye;*
>
> *When that eye is opened, everything stands revealed.*
>
> *The soul in Sunn (third plane) will hear resounding peals of Sound.*
>
> *She will uncover and know the essence of the Word."*

Shabdavali Pt. II

> *"Lightning flashed in my eye, O friend,*
>
> *While basking in the light of the moon.*
>
> *I got a glimpse of the Invisible within,*
>
> *And thirst and longing for the Lord were aroused.*

My ears received the boon of Unstruck Music,
And knowledge came in an explosion of light,
O friend.
Dark clouds began to scatter
And the sight of the Divine Mansion
Was revealed to me.
Beyond the sun, the moon, and the tunnel,
Tulsi beheld the abode of the Lord Almighty."

Shabdavali Pt. II

"The Universe is contained within the human
frame,
Tulsi has himself seen what to others is beyond
reach.
Not only the macrocosm within the microcosm
did I behold,
But, piercing the veil,
I also perceived the One pervading all.
Within my own body,
I have discovered the universe;
One who has tasted the Divine Nectar within,
Will alone know the effulgence of the Supreme
Lord."

Ghat Ramayan Pt. I

"Word, Word, sayeth everyone,
But that Word is found beyond Sunn;
That alone is called the True Word.
True Word is transcendent, it is unstruck
melody.
The unstruck Word is not the Word
Which can be written or read;
O Tulsi, the unlettered Word is indeed
transcendent,

Known only through hints given by Saints."

Shabdavali Pt. I

As Tulsi's reputation grew, he was often visited in his small hut on the outskirts of Hathras by Brahmins and Pundits looking to engage in debate with the master. He was always hospitable and patient, giving them the opportunity to speak their minds. But before they left, he would offer a simple explanation of the teachings of the saints, or 'Sant Mat' as he called it. Sometimes his visitors, upon hearing of the spiritual science, would request initiation before returning home. On one occasion, a monk named Priyelal Gosain, after realizing that what Tulsi was describing was what he had sought his entire life, discarded his saffron gown, his beads, and sacred threads and asked for knowledge of the Word. Tulsi replaced the beads and robe around the monk's shoulders and explained that our outer modes of attire have no relevancy either way.

Tulsi frequently visited the towns and villages in the area, including Agra. Among his Agra disciples was a Sikh family, including the young Sikh couple, Seth Dilwali Singh and Mahamaya. On his trips to Agra, Tulsi Sahib would usually stay in their home. On one of his visits, Tulsi informed the couple that they had been chosen to bring a great saint into the world. One year later, on August 25, 1818, the couple gave birth to a son, Shiv Dayal Singh, who would later become known as Swami Ji Maharaj.

Swami Ji is an example of one of the rarest types of saints who is born realized. On the last day of his life, he told his closest disciples that he had been practicing the inner Sound Current since the age of six. He further stated that his Sant Mat path was a continuation of the path of Sat Nam begun by Guru Nanak and his successors, and that his own master, Tulsi Sahib, had been a subsequent exponent of the same tradition.

Spiritual enthusiasts and scholars enjoy friendly, and at times, not-so-friendly debates over successorship of their guru, their guru's guru, or somebody else's guru. The question of whether or not Swami Ji had a spiritual master is a popular case in point. Some argue that Tulsi Sahib was his spiritual master, while others argue that he had no master, that he didn't need any master.

Advocates to both sides often have personal interests at stake. Saligram, for example, seemed to initially accept that Tulsi was Swami Ji's mentor. But it appears that later on, he backtracked from that position, apparently because it didn't fit neatly into the intricate Radha Soami theology which he was instrumental in formulating following Swami Ji's death. Tulsi Sahib's followers have always insisted that Tulsi was his guru.

Regarding this particular question, some simple logic may be all that is required. Swami Ji's parents had been initiated by Tulsi, who they had a personal relationship with. They understood that their son had a unique, spiritually-related destiny which lay ahead of him. Prompted by this knowledge, Shiv Dayal Singh probably received all the meditation instructions he needed from his parents. It's really fairly simple. "Plug you ears and listen, and then fix your gaze here." A highly evolved soul like Swami Ji really wouldn't need much more.

Swami Ji learned as a child that he would one day inherit Tulsi Sahib's spiritual work. There are also stories of Swami Ji, who as a young man, would trek the 25 miles up to Hathras to enjoy Tulsi's darshan. Tulsi's legs had begun to fail him as he aged, partly the result of sitting in Samadhi for long periods with too little exercise. Swami Ji used to throw the old man onto his back and haul him around for nearby visits and errands. Swami Ji later adopted the term 'Sant Mat', a term which Tulsi Sahib had coined.

After Tulsi left his mortal frame in 1843, Swami Ji spent the better part of the next 17 years in a small room at the back of the family home in continual samadhi. Then, in 1861, largely at the behest of his beloved disciple, Rai Saligram, he began his public mission.

Swami Ji's communication style was simple and straightforward, and at times, even terse. He produced two written works; the Sar Bachan in prose, and the Sar Bachan in verse. The prose work is essentially a collection of his sayings written down by disciples during and after his public discourses.

"Three things alone will lead to salvation in this age of Kali Yuga (iron age);
1. Implicit obedience to the teacher;
2. The company of a Saint;
3. Simran (light meditation) and Bhajan (sound meditation)

Everything else leads to worry and confusion. Time spent in anything else besides these three things is time wasted."

Sar Bachan 41

"They are greatly mistaken who try to verify the teachings of the Saints by reference to the Vedas. Even the author of the Vedas did not realize the exalted status of the Saints. How then can the Vedas know of them? Saints are not chained to anything. They promulgate whatever path they consider proper and suitable for their time. Those who accept will stand to gain. Those who do not, will remain unfortunate."

Sar Bachan 149

"Only he who has suffered in the world and is afraid of it will come into the Satsang (gathering) of the Saints. It is not possible for others to stay before Them. When the soul is thus convinced of the authenticity of the Saints, he will not fall into the snares of the priests and false masters."

Sar Bachan 151

"It is difficult for a person to come to the Satsang of a Sat Guru. Even if somehow he does come, he finds it difficult to stay. For when the Saints refute the Vedas, the Puranas, and the Quran, and describe their own teachings as being valid and true, it will not be possible for him to bear hearing it. Only a true seeker, or one afflicted with the pangs of Divine longing will be able to stay."

Sar Bachan 146

"One should first get on the right road; then he can reach the goal. The right road cannot be

found until one contacts a Sat Guru. But instead of seeking a Sat Guru, people busy themselves in pilgrimages, fasts, idol worship, Namaz (Muslim prayer), and book learning. Such acts lead only to egotism and confer no spiritual benefit."

Sar Bachan 141

"The Lord loves humility first of all. It behooves you, therefore, to do that which will induce humility. The society of the Saints is the best place to develop it. Keeping the company of priests and pundits who care for nothing else but wealth and good food will not develop humility, nor will the Lord be pleased. Until one comes across a merciful Saint, he should not accept anyone as his guru."

Sar Bachan 111

"Leaving everything else aside, one must implicitly obey the Sat Guru of his own time, and faithfully follow his instructions. This will lead him to success. This is the long and the short of everything."

Sar Bachan 116

Swami Ji could be a harsh critic of organized, institutionalized religion and religious claims. In one of his writings, "Hidayatnama", he describes the soul's journey through the lower spiritual region.

"When your eye turns inwards in the brain and you see the firmament within, and your spirit leaves the body and rises upwards, you will see the Akash in which is located Sahas-dal-kanwal, the thousand petals, which performs the various functions pertaining to the three worlds. Its effulgence will exhilarate your spirit. You will, at that stage, witness Niranjan,

the lord of the three worlds. Several religions which attained this stage, and took the deity thereof to be the lord of all, were duped. Seeing the light and refulgence of this region, they felt satiated. Their upward progress was stopped. They did not find the guide to higher regions. Hence, they could not proceed further."

Swami Ji continues to remark on the journey through the intermediate spiritual regions.

"At the apex of this Akash (in Sahas-dal-kanwal), there is a passage which is very small like the eye of a needle. Your focused attention should penetrate this eye. "Further on, there is Bank nal, the crooked path, which goes straight and then downwards and again upwards. Beyond this passage comes the second stage.

"Trikuti (having three prominences) is situated here. It is one lakh yojan in length and one lakh yojan in width (an expression describing vast dimensions).

"There are numerous varieties of glories and spectacles at that plane which are difficult to describe. Thousands of suns and moons look pale in comparison to the light there. All the time, melodious sounds of Ong Ong and Hoo Hoo, and sounds resembling thunder clouds reverberate there. On obtaining this region, the soul becomes very happy, and purified and subtle. It is from here onwards that the soul becomes cognizant of the higher spiritual regions."

Swami Ji then speaks of the lower regions of pure spirit.

"The refulgence of this region (Daswan Dwar) is twelve times that of Trikuti. Pure pools of ambrosia, called "Mansarovar," abound here.

There are innumerable flowers and gardens. Spirits, like beauties, dance at various places. Everywhere, fountains of nectar are overflowing and the streams of nectar are gushing out.

"How may one describe the splendor and decoration of this region? There are platforms of diamonds, beds of emeralds and plants of jewels, all studded with rubies and precious stones.

"Bejeweled fish, swimming in pools there, display their beauty and ornamentation, with their glitter and sheen, attract attention.

"Beyond this, there are innumerable palaces of crystals and mirrors, in which spirit entities reside at their respective places, as allocated by the Lord. The denizens there are spiritual and free from physical taints. Full particulars of these regions are known only to Sants. It is not feasible to describe them in greater detail."

Swami Ji continues, attempting to do justice, in mortal words, to the purely spiritual realms.

"The soul, thereafter, ascends to Hootal Hoot, which in Hindi, has been described as Bhanwar-gupha. There is a rotating swing here which is all the time in subtle motion, and the spirits ever swing on it. All round, there are innumerable spiritual islands from which the sounds of "Sohang Sohang" and "Anahoo Anahoo" rise continually. Spirit entities playfully and rapturously enjoy these sounds. Whiffs of scents of various kinds and sweet fragrance of sandalwood are enjoyed by the spirit there, and the melodies of flutes are heard, while the soul proceeds onwards."

Finally, Swami Ji speaks of Sach Khand, the true home of the soul.

"On crossing into this place (Sach Khand), the spirit entity reached the outpost of Sat Lok, where melodious sounds of "Sat Sat" and "Haq Haq" were heard as though being sung by a vina. On hearing this, the soul penetrated further on, rapturously. There rose to view, silver and golden streams full of nectar, and vast gardens, each tree thereof is one crore yojans in height (50 million miles), and crores (vast numbers) of suns and moons hang from them as flowers and fruits. Innumerable spirits and Hansas sing, chatter, and play on those trees like birds. The wondrous beauty of this region is ineffable.

"While enjoying it, the spirit entered Sat Lok and came into the presence of Sat Purush. Now as regards the glory of the person of Sat Purush, each hair of His is so brilliant that crores of suns and moons look pale in comparison. How may one describe His eyes, nose, ears, face, hands, and feet? They are all nothing but refulgence. Even to describe them as oceans of light does not convey the remotest idea adequately.

"After witnessing the glory of this region, the spirit proceeded on to Alakh Lok and got darshan of Alakh Purush. Thereafter, the soul continued and attained Agam Lok. The spirit entity sojourned there a long time, and as it proceeded further, it experienced the darshan of Radhasoami; that is, Anami Purush, and merged in Him. Radhasoami Dham is boundless, infinite, endless and immeasurable. It is the Nij Sthan, the special resting place of

Swami Ji, Hidayatnama

Swami Ji implores us to faithfully follow the instructions of the Master of our own time. One of his own instructions was to keep the company of a living Sat Guru. Swami Ji lived in Agra and most of his disciples were either from that area of India, or traveled to Agra to have the benefit of his personal attention. During that period, in the mid nineteenth century, there was no way to conduct a spiritual mission on a global scale due to the limitations of transportation and communication.

Today, in the twenty-first century, the world community has become smaller and more intimate and spiritual and educational missions can, and are scaled globally. However, with people spread all over the planet, it is not feasible for most disciples of a teacher to have the kind of physical access that Swami Ji's disciples had to him. This fact illustrates a good example of how the circumstances of each generation, such as technology and the ongoing evolution of culture, help determine how a teacher will go about reaching out and conducting his mission.

Swami Ji's leading disciple was Rai Saligram (1829-1898). He is also referred to by some under the honorific, 'Huzur Maharaj'. A few years after Swami Ji's death, Saligram inaugurated his own spiritual mission and is widely recognized as being Swami Ji's principal successor. He is named in Swami Ji's will as such. It is also generally recognized that Swami Ji had multiple successors.

Many of Swami Ji's associates had already suspected that Saligram would continue Swami Ji's work. Swami Ji had stated that sometimes he was Saligram's teacher, but that other times, Saligram was his teacher.

Rai Saligram is credited for cataloging and codifying Swami Ji's teachings. He founded the Radha Soami movement, as a tangible, organized entity. He was Swami Ji's Paul, his evangelist. Not on the scale of Paul, but equal in spirit. Saligram authored and published over a dozen books on the spiritual path.

You can feel Saligram's evangelical spirit in the opening preface of one of his most important written works, "Radha Soami Mat Prakash".

Saligram had a distinguished career in the Indian Postal Service, rising to the high position of Postmaster General for the North Western provinces. He was the first Indian to hold the post, having been previously held by English administrators. He is remembered for significant achievements in modernization and innovation.

Rai Saligram learned about Swami Ji from a co-worker, who happened to be Swami Ji's brother. He met Swami Ji and became his disciple. As a young man, Saligram had studied religion, philosophy, and yoga, so in an academic sense he was an ideal disciple for Swami Ji. Saligram understood the spiritual science theoretically, in terms of religion. After two years of discipleship, Saligram proposed that he retire from his position in the postal service. Swami Ji declined, saying that his career would not interfere with his spiritual progress. Saligram and Swami Ji developed a close relationship with

Saligram taking responsibility for many aspects of his master's welfare.

As a teacher, Saligram was a hard worker, often conducting satsang five times a day. After his death in 1898, the question of successorship, and various issues pertaining to the direction which this fledgling organization should take moving forward, were left a bit murky. This murkiness, over time, resulted in the Radha Soami Agra group being splintered into three principal factions; Soami Bagh, Dayal Bagh, and Peepal Mandi. A fourth faction would ultimately be spawned in the Punjab by another of Swami Ji's beloved disciples, Jaimal Singh.

Saligram's writings contain some of his own insights on various aspects of spirituality, including how love plays a role in binding souls together. He writes about the effects of experiencing one's own inner bliss. He also writes about certain stages of inner development, such as the development of the connection with the radiant form of the master in meditation.

> *"The Supreme Being is a boundless ocean of spirit, or love, and the human being a drop or current of spirit or love from this ocean; and love being the very essence and means of existence of the whole creation, it follows that no effort in any direction, temporal or spiritual, unless actuated by love or affectionate regard, can be crowned with success, and the work or labor rendered easy, sweet and harmonious.*
>
> *"Every wave of love rising in a lover's heart brings tidings of goodness and joy from the beloved, and every thought springing up in such a heart is a harbinger of good works and good services for the sake of the beloved.*
>
> *"Knowledge, without love for the Supreme Being, is futile and tends towards untruth or*

darkness or materialism. Pure, spiritual love turns everything to good use and leads to enlightenment and truth. Even worldly love, such as filial and conjugal, is accompanied with goodness, happiness and comfort for all concerned. How much more goodness would then ensue for mankind, in general, if this same love were to become spiritual, and be directed towards the Supreme Being, the Merciful Parent of the whole creation.

"The noble passion of love is most powerful and strong. Where pure love dwells, there sheds the light of Grace, as it forms a link with the spirit or love current from its source, the Supreme Being. Love, or the power of attraction, is the basis of the entire creation and the cause of its sustenance and preservation.

"The sound heard internally is a current which has originally emanated from the Supreme Being and is the means not only of concentrating the attention, but also of raising the spirit to the source from which it emanates.

"Due to excessive bliss in Bhajan (sound meditation) or Dhyana (light meditation), an Abhyasi (practitioner) may experience great ecstasy and detachment. He may become somewhat averse to the pleasures and activities of the world. In this condition of ecstasy, the Abhyasi should never think that he is perfect and that his task is completed.

"Such an Abhyasi must not give up his family, avocation or anything else in a fit. He should not consider this state of ecstasy to be stable and lasting. If he takes any action in haste he

would repent. He should try his utmost to control his feelings and conceal them from people of the world."

Rai Saligram was a rational and scientifically-minded thinker, which is one of the reasons he became such an effective teacher. In 1896, nine years prior to Albert Einstein publishing his theory of relativity, Saligram wrote on the phenomenon of life (spirit) and its relationship to atomic structure.

> *"Scientists say that Matter and Motion are the principal factors in the creation. This is true so far as the lower material regions are concerned, but they do not, or cannot say how or whence this motion originated. Motion needs a motor, and this motor is the same spirit or word current issuing forth like rays from the sun, from various centers or spiritual-material suns and diffused over all the space comprised in the second and third grand divisions.*
>
> *"Every atom is in itself a ray or current issued from a center and is endowed with spirit power, which on the physical plane is called energy by the scientists. Unmanifested energy or spirit power is called latent or potential, and that which is brought into action or full play, kinetic. Both the above names apply to the impulse from the spirit force which is the origin and beginning of all.*
>
> *"The atoms playing their part in this world, for instance, issue forth from our physical sun or the internal Sun, of which the former is a star. They are manufactured in the above orbs before they issue forth as rays or currents and are thus fitted for the work of creation or for*

forming parts of the bodies they combine to form or give existence to.

"The spirit current latent in these atoms is much steeped in matter of the lower spheres and it requires the impulse from a higher current, appertaining to and descending from the higher sphere, to awaken its energy, or actuate it into action.

"It will thus be seen that spirit power or force is all in all, or it is the principal force or actor in the whole creation; or in other words, it is the life and soul of everything."

One of Swami Ji's most ardent disciples was a young Sikh boy named Jaimal Singh (1838-1903). Jaimal was born in the Punjabi village of Ghuman into a family of pious Sikh farmers who had prayed for a saintly son. His village had been home to the famous Namdev a few centuries earlier and had become a place of pilgrimage for sadhus and holy men.

Jaimal's early years can be closely compared to Nanak's. He had a keen interest in religion and at the age of five, was put in the charge of a Vedantist scholar who lived nearby. By the age of nine he had memorized large sections of the Adi Granth and had a sound training in Hindu literature as well. And like Nanak, he sought the company of the many Sadhus and holy men who were to be found locally in the hopes of finding the true path to enlightenment.

Jaimal had discovered that in the Adi Granth, there were repeated references to the five-sounded Word, or 'Panch Shabd', and that self-realization and God realization could only be achieved through communion with the Word. He realized that unlocking the mystery of these passages was the key to finding God, but no one in his village could give him a satisfactory explanation or demonstration.

Like Nanak, Jaimal showed little interest in mundane affairs, preferring to associate with the many holy men who frequented his village. His father sent him off to live with his sister, hoping that the new surroundings would help him break the habit of 'wasting all of his time' with sadhus. He was given some goats to look after but soon after his relocation, he met a yogi who instructed him in pranayama. When his father learned that the boy was spending all of his time practicing yoga, at the expense of his little herd of goats, he ordered him back home. A few months later his father died, leaving Jaimal Singh free to begin his spiritual quest in earnest.

At the tender age of thirteen he left home, determined to find a guru who could unlock the mystery of the Word. For a year he traversed northwestern India on foot, back and forth, in search of a true master. He met many teachers along the way who instructed him in their methods, but none could unlock the mystery of the Word. Eventually he returned home, exhausted and dejected.

He spent the next eight months applying himself to family duties and obligations but a passage out of the Vedas continually haunted him; "*Awake, arise, and stop not until the goal is reached!*" One day, the urge to solve the mystery of the elusive Word overcame him and at the age of fifteen, he set out again, hoping this time to complete his quest.

Not long into his journey, he found himself on the banks of the sacred Ganges in Hardwar, a community known for its many holy men. After meeting and talking to some of the locals, he learned of an old ascetic, over 100 years of age, who lived off in the jungle, and who was thought to have great spiritual powers. Jaimal managed to locate the old sadhu, finding him in his posture, suspended in a swing, hanging from a tree branch. Jaimal took a seat off to the side in hopes of eventually getting the sadhu's attention. Nightfall came and Jaimal stayed on.

The next day, the sadhu finally acknowledged him and asked what he wanted. The boy replied that he was in search of enlightenment and had heard of the sadhu's great powers. He sought instruction in his disciplines. The sadhu closed his eyes and went silent. Later he came out of his trance and explained that his disciplines were very difficult to practice and that they had not led to spiritual freedom. Then the sadhu climbed back into his swing, closed his eyes, and meditated there for the remainder of the day and the following night. Jaimal stayed on.

The next morning the sadhu arose, bathed and then joined Jaimal. He told the boy that in his meditation he had seen the master he was seeking, and that he lived in Agra where he gave public discourses on the Adi Granth in his home. Jaimal immediately began the long trek down to Agra, and after a week of searching, located Swami Ji.

Jaimal sat in on Swami Ji's discourse and afterward, questioned him privately. Jaimal was satisfied with what he heard, but was a bit surprised that Swami Ji didn't dress in the traditional Sikh attire. In fact, he blended in so much with the other men that he almost seemed too ordinary to be a great saint.

> *"Only a perfect one, who is always laughing at the word 'two', can make you know of love. His greatness is built on this foundation: the ability to appear, speak, and act as the most common of men."*

> Hafiz

Swami Ji took Jaimal to a private room, where he gave him meditation instructions and left the boy alone. Jaimal immediately went into Samadhi, where he remained for the next 48 hours. Eventually, one of Swami Ji's disciples asked about the young Sikh boy. They returned to the room where they had left him and found Jaimal, still out of his body in deep samadhi. They shook him a bit to help him regain his physical consciousness. Jaimal Singh could not speak but Swami Ji did, saying; "Well dear boy, do you still wonder whether or not your master is a true Sikh or not?" Swami Ji went on to explain that the path of the Saints is not concerned with outer forms and appearances, and that each must live by the best traditions of the community in which the Lord has chosen to place us.

Swami Ji was a teacher of teachers. On the last day of his life, he named no less than four of his disciples to continue on with the spiritual work. Rai Saligram founded the Radha Soami school in Agra. But it was Jaimal's destiny, a few years after Swami Ji's earthly departure, to re-establish Guru Nanak's spiritual mission in the Punjab by way of Swami Ji's Sant Mat panth. In Northwestern India, the presence of a living shabd yoga master had been absent since the time of Gobind Singh.

Jaimal Singh was not attracted to life as a householder. Instead, he joined a Sikh Regiment in the Indian/English army, where he served as a private in the infantry, eventually rising to the rank of sergeant. As a career military man, Jaimal developed self-discipline habits which would serve him well in his sadhanas. He would ultimately find success in his spiritual pursuits.

Jaimal Singh left a collection of his letters sent to his leading disciple, Sawan, which have been published under the title, "Spiritual Letters". While much of the letters deal with personal matters, others provide valuable insight into their master/disciple relationship and the spiritual guidance offered by Jaimal. As a re-clarification of terminology, Jaimal uses 'surat' to describe the attention, 'shabd' to describe the sound characteristic of the Word, and 'Dhun' to refer to the stronger and more harmonic aspect of the sound current. He also uses 'sarup' to refer to the radiant form of the master seen in meditation.

"Now, about the four means of controlling the mind:

1. Following the instructions of the Sat Guru
2. Shabd Dhun (strong sound)
3. Getting attached and devoted to the Dhun
4. Finding enjoyment and bliss in it.

"When you begin to gain control of the mind, then the form of the Sat Guru appears in the eye focus. Just as you see your face reflected clearly in the mirror, in the same way the sarup (radiant form) of the Sat Guru will be seen inside, within the eye focus. The mind, which works conjointly with the surat, and the vritis, will become pure by daily practice.

"When all worldly desires have been driven out of the mind, the mind won't wander off. It will be fixed in the form of the Master. As the merciful face of the Sat Guru falls upon the mind, all its material desires will disappear. The mind will then obey the surat. Then the Dhun will merge the surat with Itself, and thus give some amount of bliss. The Shabd Dhun will then pull the mind up and control it in the same way animals, like goats or cattle, are kept tied by means of a rope. Thusly does the Shabd Dhun pull the mind.

"After rising up gradually, and taking the mind along with it, the surat leaves the mind in Trikuti (second spiritual plane). When the surat comes back from Trikuti to the lower levels, then it brings the mind along with it. After that, the surat is no longer subject to the mind, which does not give rise to any trouble. That is the way to control the mind through practice of the Word.

"When you sit for sound practice, whatever sounds you hear in the beginning,

Spiritual Letters 28

Saints often leave the question of successorship open so that surviving disciples are unclear as to who is best-suited to carry on the spiritual mission. One day, while Jaimal Singh was visiting Sawan Singh, his closest disciple, he stated that the two of them had come for the good of mankind. Sawan didn't know what to think of his master's statement and replied that Jaimal had come for the good of mankind but that he was just an ordinary man. Jaimal repeated the statement and Sawan repeated his reply. Then Jaimal's eyes lit up and he repeated the statement a third time, firmly. Sawan sat silent and dumbfounded. Sometime later, Jaimal asked Sawan to join him on the Dais during the monthly gathering and announced openly that Sawan would inherit his job.

The two masters' styles could not have been more different. Jaimal was the humblest of beings, happy living a simple existence in his small hut by the river. Sawan, the prominent government engineering officer, immediately went to work with engineering and building plans for the future. Eventually, he would turn Baba Jaimal Singh's property by the river into a thriving community, capable of serving the needs of 100,000 people.

Sawan's teachings are preserved in the form of a collection of his public talks which were transcribed and published under the title, "Discourses on Sant Mat". There is also a collection of his letters to disciples published under the title, "Spiritual Gems". In one of his letters, Baba Sawan Singh explains that even though the way the teachings are presented may change to suit the times, the underlying spiritual principles do not change.

> *"Man, himself, is the perfect book, for all books have come out of him. Inside of him is the Creator, with all His creation. The study of books gives us second-hand information, while the study of ourselves gives first-hand information. So why not read ourselves and see what is there?*

> *"From books we are able to grasp the central idea upon which they are based. If you examine religious texts in that spirit, you will find that the central idea of religion, and of Sant Mat of course, is the practice of the Sound Current. Many different words and names have been used to express the theory. Christ, Buddha, and the Vedic Rishis practiced and preached the same. The fundamental core of all of their teachings is the Sound Current.*

> *"The way the teachings are presented depends upon the language of the people, their customs, and their intellectual development. And as these customs, manners, and so forth change with time, their books go out of date; hence, the necessity of giving out the same age-old principles of the Sound Current, afresh. The message must be kept modern, and so adapted to the times and people to whom it is presented.*

"This Current is present in man; all human beings. It is natural in man, not artificial. It can be neither altered nor modified; nor added to, nor subtracted from. All else in this world changes continually, but not this Current. It is an emanation from, or wave of, the Great Source of all – the Supreme Creator, by whatever name you wish to speak of Him. Each individual is a spark or a drop of that same Infinite Source.

> *"The Creator is at the top of this Current and the individual soul is at the other end, with the Current itself acting as the connecting link between the two. By this Current, the life – even the very existence of the individual is sustained. But the individual is unaware of it due to the thick veils of mind and matter which cover it at this end. But it sustains creation, and in man is found in the eye focus from where it permeates us within and outwardly, through the various sense organs. To catch it, the scattered and scattering attention must be controlled and held in the focus where connection is established with the astral, mental, and spiritual planes; finally merging in the Source at the other end.*
>
> *"The first essential thing, therefore, is to enter this laboratory within ourselves, by bringing our scattered attention inside of the eye focus. While this is a slow process, we should not be deterred. It is the most worthy of pursuits. It is our job to control the thoughts arising within us, and we must do it! And we must do it now, in this very lifetime, while in this human form."*

Spiritual Gems 157

After Swami Ji's departure in 1878, the proliferation of Radha Soami groups swelled, and along with multiple groups came multiple shabd yoga masters. Many of these masters are worthy of note. However, one of them, Baba Faqir Chand (1886 to 1981), stands out as being a refreshing voice for candor and critical thinking.

Faqir Chand is best-remembered as the 'honest guru'. He was refreshingly straightforward regarding certain aspects of the role of the guru and the guru's abilities. His assertions include:

Gurus should not take credit for their disciples' inner experiences and mystical revelations

Gurus should not take credit for otherwise inexplicable events in the lives of their devotees, events that could be characterized as 'the workings of God', or 'miracles'

Gurus should admit that they don't know everything

Gurus should admit that they suffer from the same human vulnerabilities as everyone else

Faqir Chand was born into a Brahmin family in the Punjab. His father was employed in a low-level position with the Indian Railway Police and the family lived a simple, working-class existence. As a young boy, Faqir Chand devoted himself to mastering various Hindu scriptures.

At the age of eighteen, he secured a humble position with the Indian Railway as a signaler for construction projects. In this job, he interacted with co-workers, most of whom were tough, earthy men who ate meat, smoked tobacco, drank alcohol and used coarse language. As a result of these influences, Faqir Chand became a meat eater, and developed some of their unseemly personal characteristics. But his family quickly intervened and guided him onto a more proper course. He adopted the vegetarian diet and other principals of Hindu Dharma appropriate for a young Brahmin. But he felt shame and regret over his moral weakness.

One night, while in prayer, lamenting over his lapses and transgressions, his inner vision suddenly opened and he witnessed the radiant form of a sadhu with a glowing white beard. The sadhu asked Faqir Chand what made him weep, and what did he want?

He answered that scriptures claimed that God appears on the earth as a human being and that he wanted to meet God in human form. The radiant sadhu replied; "For you, your God in the human form is already on this earth. You will come into His contact and all your sins will be pardoned." After saying these words, the radiant sadhu vanished.

He continued to yearn for a chance to meet the lord. One day, his longing became so great that he wept continually for 24 hours. Early that morning, he had a vision of a living Radha Soami master, Maharishi Shiv Brat Lal. In the vision, the master drew water from a nearby well and offered it to Faqir Chand. Then, the radiant master disclosed to Faqir Chand his address in Lahore.

Faqir Chand began writing letters to this address provided in the vision. Since he didn't know Shiv Brat Lal's name as yet, he simply addressed his letters to God. After a year of letter writing, he received a reply from Maharishi Shiv Brat Lal who invited him to Lahore. The letter said, in part; "I value your sentiments and your passion for the Lord. I myself have discovered Reality, Truth, and Peace at the feet of Rai

Saligram Ji of Radha Soami Mat. Provided you feel no reluctance in following this path, come and see me at Lahore."

Baba Faqir Chand traveled to Lahore, where he met master Shiv Brat Lal and received initiation instructions. He was also given one of Swami Ji's books; 'Sar Bachan'. He initially objected to Swami Ji's writings, since they were critical of established religious teachings, including Vedanta. Shiv Brat Lal suggested that he put the book aside and then revisit it after he had gained more inner experience and awakening. Faqir Chand applied himself to his spiritual practices and quickly made contact with the inner radiant master, or guru dev. He continued making inner progress with regular meditation (simran and bhajan).

Faqir Chand had his first encounter with guru politics when he met another Radha Soami devotee who had been initiated by a different teacher, Babu Kainta Prasad Sinha, who was at that time the spiritual head of the Radha Soami Satsang at Ghazipur in Uttar Pradesh. This other Radha Soami devotee belittled Faqir Chand, saying that since he had not been initiated by a true guru, he was therefore not a true Radha Soami follower. This incident became foundational for Faqir Chand's later views regarding sectarianism and organizational biases.

During World War I, Faqir was stationed in a post which allowed him the opportunity for long, uninterrupted meditation sessions. During these years, he made rapid inner progress. In 1918, he was granted leave, so he headed for Lahore to be with his guru. He posed the question to Shiv Brat Lal; "How does the goal of Radha Soami Mat differ from that of other religions?"

Shiv Brat Lal answered, saying; "Faqir, you are yourself a true Master of your generation. Begin delivering spiritual discourses to true seekers and initiate them into the path of Sant Mat. In due course of time, your own disciples will prove to be your 'True Guru', and through them all secrets of Sant Mat will be revealed".

In Faqir-like humility, he responded; "Your Holiness, I am myself ignorant of the Truth. How can I lead others on this sublime path?" His master replied; "Faqir, you may be suffering from ninety-nine shortcomings. But you possess one sure virtue; that of Truth. Truth resides within you in abundance and it will be everything you'll ever need to realize all of your life's goals".

His teacher advised him further, saying; "Your name is Faqir. Be true to your name. Have pity upon the helpless, ignorant and the weak. With your sincere love and affection, help them out of this sphere of illusion, and guide them to their true Home. Remove the barriers that divide mankind and lead them to the supreme state of Nirvana."

Thus, it was that at the young age of 32, Faqir Chand began his work as a spiritual teacher. He served eminently in this role for the next 63 years.

He initially wrote two books, and mailed copies to Baba Sawan Singh for review. Sawan Singh had been a close friend of Faqir's guru, Maharishi Shiv Brat Lal. Sawan Singh wrote back, saying; "You are a true Faqir. You are doing highly desirable service to the Radha Soami Mat."

Faqir remained in somewhat of a quandary about his feelings about gurus and the role that they play. He was worried that his ideas were too radical. He didn't want Sawan Singh, or any other Radha Soami teacher to think he was openly criticizing them, and he certainly didn't want to do anything that could undermine their work.

In 1942, Faqir visited Sawan at Beas and explained that he wanted to be open and honest with people about his avant-garde ideas. But he also expressed his reservations. He was so conflicted about it, he was actually contemplating retirement from his spiritual duties.

Sawan offered him a candid response. He stated that he could not disclose the truth about these issues in their totality for two reasons;

1. Satsangis, in general, are not prepared to fully understand these matters, and
2. He was bound by certain institutional requirements to uphold the status quo.

He further stated; "Please continue to fulfill your assigned duties fearlessly. You shall have my full support under all circumstances."

Sawan's reply to Faqir acknowledged an indelible feature of Hindu culture. Indians love to adore their teachers. This is a good thing because Bhakti helps to ensure that the bond of love created between teacher and student will endure, and that this bond will help the stronger carry the weaker into higher spiritual realms, both here on the earth plane and also beyond death. (It's usually the teacher who is more spiritually advanced, but not always.)

Now, if you're a spiritual pilgrim, and you're going to devote your heart and soul to your teacher, you certainly want your teacher to be special. You want him to have special abilities. It would be wonderful to love somebody unconditionally who is bigger than life, an answerer of prayers; a truly divine being. Over the centuries, Indians have elevated their spiritual heroes into mythical dimensions.

What Sawan communicated to Faqir Chand was essentially this; it is true that many disciples of spiritual teachers misunderstand the abilities and limitations of the living master. But nothing can be done about this because these beliefs are too ingrained within Indian thought.

That being said, a Shabd Yoga master is not an ordinary human being. He has a highly evolved consciousness with heightened perceptions and awarenesses. Masters do sometimes have special abilities, but the nature of these abilities are unique to each master. One thing common to all masters is that love guides their thoughts, words and deeds.

It's not inherently harmful for disciples to believe these things about their teachers. The truth is that spiritual masters, in a physical and emotional sense, are just like us. Their physical lives often defy the ideal of 'perfection' that we want them to measure up to. They experience emotions essentially the same way we do. But they have achieved remarkable inner spiritual revelations and attainments. As a result of these realizations, they have gained special esoteric knowledge and are now in a position to lead and guide others.

The warm relationship enjoyed between Baba Sawan Singh and Baba Faqir Chand serves to illustrate the futility of engaging in organizational politics. Both masters were co-workers in the divine plan, working to further the cause of human spiritual evolution.

Baba Sawan Singh had a good number of disciples from Europe, America, and other places outside of India. But it was his favored disciple, Kirpal Singh, who ultimately took Sant Mat to the far reaches of the globe.

Chapter 11

SANT KIRPAL SINGH – THE WATERFALL

"Let the law of Love prevail amongst you, which should be radiated to all nations and races. Give up hatred, eradicate egoism and anger. Eschew violence. Abandon war. Abandon lust for power. Pledge yourself to love, sincerity, humility, forgiveness, and non-violence. Transform your nature by living a life of goodness. Manifest truth, purity, love, selflessness, and righteousness in every aspect of your life. Make a true religion of the heart as the ruling factor in your lives. Love all, serve all, and have respect for all, as God is immanent in all forms. Preach the gospel of oneness and live the life of oneness. This is the way to peace on earth. This is the mission of my life, and I pray that it may be fulfilled."

Kirpal Singh

Kirpal Singh has been referred to as a 'perfect Master', an archetype guru. There are generally three benchmarks attributed to a perfect Master. One is their level of spiritual attainment; a fully liberated soul who has merged his individual soul with its source. We cannot know with any reasonable certainty what Kirpal's level of attainment was, any more than we can discern anyone else's attainment. The second benchmark is that they lived an ideal human life, and in that respect, we can say that he certainly led an extraordinary life, imbued with service and self-sacrifice. The third earmark of a perfect master is that even after he leaves the world physically, he continues to work in the physical world directly through his disciples.

The life of Kirpal Singh has been well documented in a book entitled, "Love, Light, and Life", by Devinder Narendra and Eileen Wigg. He was born in Sayyad Kasran in the Punjab, now a part of Pakistan. He was an ardent student as a young boy and as a college student in religious studies, would read the entire contents of his school's library in his search for knowledge. As a child, he had extraordinary abilities, often knowing of events in advance. One day in school, he requested to leave at once as his grandmother had just died. His headmaster dismissed the request as an attempt to cut class. A short while later, Kirpal's uncle arrived to take the boy out of school due to the sudden death of his Grandmother. After this he was nicknamed, 'little saint'.

Even from a young age, Kirpal was committed to service and self-sacrifice. One poignant incident from his youth took place when his older brother had been promised to wed the daughter of a good Sikh family. Normally, the bride and groom are perfect strangers until their actual wedding day, but Kirpal's brother snuck over to her home to catch a glimpse of his bride-to-be. When he announced to his family that she was not to his liking and that he refused to wed her, his parents were in shock. To deny marriage in these circumstances was a great insult to the girl's family and a source of shame to his own. But Kirpal jumped in and agreed to marry the girl, saving the day for both families.

Even without the direction of a competent master, Kirpal was able to leave the body at will and experience long states of samadhi. He counseled his wife about this and told her to be careful not to allow anyone into their home when he was in this state, and trained her to use pressure points to bring him back into physical consciousness. One day, some neighbors did find him in samadhi and cried out for a doctor, thinking that Kirpal had possibly died.

As a young man, Kirpal inquired into spiritual matters and received some training, but he longed for the day when he would meet a true spiritual master. He began seeing Sawan Singh in his meditations as early as 1917. Then in 1924, he met Sawan in person and immediately realized that this was the master who had been guiding him within during the previous seven years.

As a disciple, Kirpal embodied the highest type of Bhakti, when the soul merges with the object of its devotion. Once he was satisfied that Sawan was a true master, he surrendered himself to his master and his meditations. He would have been very happy to remain in his role as disciple for the entirety of his life, if only his master could have somehow lived so long.

During partition in 1947, when Pakistan was formed out of Northwestern India, millions of people died due to the horrendous violence which erupted between Muslims and Sikhs. Muslims were slaughtered by marauding bands of Sikhs and Hindus and Sikhs were slaughtered by marauding bands of Muslims. It was a sad time in the history of civilization. Kirpal put his own life at risk, inviting refugees from both sides, Muslim and Sikh alike, into Sawan's ashram, refusing to hand them over to the death squads. In one incident, he even left the ashram unarmed to plead with a group of armed, bloodthirsty Sikhs to allow the Muslims who were hiding in the ashram safe passage out of the area. To the amazement of many, the Sikh band did an about-face and escorted the Muslims to safety themselves. It is estimated that he saved the lives of thousands of innocent people during this period.

Later that year, Sawan called for Kirpal Singh and informed him that he would be leaving the world soon. He had a special assignment for him which included the responsibility of providing spiritual initiation. Six months later, in April 1948, Sawan called Kirpal to his bedside. Sawan gazed intently into Kirpal's eyes for several minutes, filling him with an overpowering, blissful intoxication. Then Sawan closed his eyes, not to open them again. Kirpal later explained that the mastership is passed through the eyes, and that this was the moment it was passed to him.

Kirpal retired to the Himalayas for six months of samadhi. While he didn't acknowledge this openly, he also needed time to mourn the loss of his close friend and teacher, Sawan Singh. Then Kirpal returned to Delhi, and with the help of some devoted associates, acquired some property and founded an ashram. His work took place in two arenas. As a spiritual master, he took on the task of providing spiritual initiation to thousands of souls during his twenty-five-year mission. But he was also a founder and initiator of projects and organizations.

Partly as a result of Kirpal's involvement with these ambitious projects, and partly as a result of his career as India's deputy military accounts officer, he was connected at the highest levels of Indian government and society, giving him a unique entrée onto the world stage. In the 1950's, Kirpal developed a close relationship with Jawaharlal Nehru, becoming his confidante and spiritual advisor. Later, he served in the same capacity with Indira Gandhi, who participated in of Kirpal's special events during the time she served as Prime Minister.

Kirpal's first large undertaking was the World Fellowship of Religions. The WFR actually came about as the result of a combination of circumstances and influences. Sawan had earlier shared with Kirpal a concept he had for a symposium where world religious leaders could come together to meet and discuss each other's faiths and explore ways to cooperate with each other to help mitigate religious divisions and strife. Kirpal kept the idea in the forefront of his thinking and planning, and would occasionally share the idea with others whenever the opportunity arose. When he discussed it with the prominent Jain leader, Muni Sushil Kumar Ji, he found an enthusiastic ally. Kumar Ji offered to host an international conference and from there, the WFR was born.

Coincidently, at that same time, India was experiencing some internal problems stirred up by fanatical religious entities. They were making certain demands, and some had organized belligerent gangs who were threatening to riot. The situation became so dire that the government had to send in the Indian Army to help maintain order.

Nehru called in Kirpal for help. He asked him to intervene with religious leaders, in the hopes of garnering their support in quelling the unrest. Kirpal spent the next two months crisscrossing the subcontinent, by car and by train, visiting with religious leaders. During these meetings, he promoted the upcoming WFR conference. Kirpal won them over. They pitched in to help settle the unrest, and later became delegates to Kirpal's WFR.

The first WFR conference was held at the Red Fort in Old Delhi in November, 1957, drawing an estimated 200,000 participants. Attending dignitaries included the Indian Prime Minister, Jawaharlal Nehru, plus the Indian President, Vice President, and Education Minister. Kirpal was elected unanimously as its first president, a position he occupied for the next 17 years. The first conference focused on a number of issues, including: 1) tolerance, 2) fellowship, 3) understanding, 4) parallels in teachings, 5) acknowledgement of one common Supreme Being. While the concept for the WFR drew many skeptics and opponents, it was a rousing success and laid the groundwork for a vital entity going forward, which would continue to convene and work together, even beyond Kirpal's passing.

The fourth WFR conference was held at the Ramlila Grounds in New Delhi in 1970. The conference adopted four resolutions and a Universal Charter of Religions, as follows:

Resolution No. 1

This conference of the WFR resolves to establish an International Institute for the unbiased and systematic study of comparative religions.

Resolution No. 2

The basic fundamentals underlying all religious faiths are essentially the same, those being; non-violence, justice, compassion and equality, eternal love, service, and truth.

Resolution No. 3

The WFR will establish a delegation to collaborate and cooperate with the United Nations and UNESCO, to help transmute the moral, spiritual, and religious vacuum which currently retards the spiritual evolution of humanity.

Resolution No. 4

The WFR will cooperate with scientists in finding ways to create a synthesis and common ground for sharing knowledge and information on matters related to the upliftment of humanity.

Universal Charter of Religions

We solemnly affirm and declare that:

1. It is our sacred duty to promote peace, human relations and understanding, through non-violent means on the basis of equality, friendship, compassion and love.
2. It is our sacred duty to assist all individuals in their attempts to develop themselves spiritually.
3. It is our sacred duty to strengthen the universal principles of religion and their application to human life.

4. It is our sacred duty to help facilitate the educational, economic, cultural and moral development of all human beings.
5. It is our sacred duty to enhance the dignity of man.
6. It is our sacred duty to render selfless service to all human beings regardless of their caste, creed, race and nationality.
7. It is our sacred duty to work to quell tensions and misunderstandings amongst various religious entities, social groups, and nations.
8. It is our sacred duty to promote religious pluralism in order to foster human unity and brotherhood.
9. It is our sacred duty to promote environmental purity and reverence for life, including clean air, water, land and food.
10. It is our sacred duty to promote a higher standard of living for all people
11. It is our sacred duty to help curb problems associated with overpopulation.
12. It is our sacred duty to help eliminate outdated religious practices, including superstitions and factional prejudices.
13. It is our sacred duty to strive to keep religion free from political influences.
14. It is our sacred duty to work to manifest the foregoing affirmations through all available means at our disposal.

In his remarks to the delegation, Kirpal said:

> *"We have with us here, friends, both from the East and the West, to whom we extend our welcome. We have great appreciation and love for you all, especially as you come for the cause of God. All of us should join the army of God...Truly speaking, religion is the expression of divinity already existing*

1974 was a busy year for Kirpal. He organized and convened the first world conference on the Unity of Man, attended by hundreds of thousands of delegates from across the globe.

He also continued construction work on the five 'Man Centers' scattered around India. These centers were self-sufficient communities, designed to provide services to the needy, including:

1. A place of universal worship, which would accommodate the requirements of all religious faiths.
2. Assistance and accommodations for the indigent in the elderly population.
3. Free medical care and a free kitchen for the indigent.
4. Agricultural husbandry, to supply vegetarian foods for the center.
5. Language education, aimed at fostering communication between varied social and religious groups.

That same year, Kirpal organized the 'National Unity Conference' in conjunction with the 'Kumba Mela'. The mission of the conference was to attempt to consolidate the efforts and resources of many of India's sadhus, holy men, and spiritual leaders toward improving the economic plight of the poor and needy and toward the elimination of religious strife. It was the first time that anyone had ever been able to bring this many holy men together at the same place and time for any reason.

On August 1, 1974, Kirpal was asked by Indira Gandhi to address the Indian Parliament to explain the concept of his 'Man Centers'. As an impoverished nation, India has few resources to devote toward social services and they hoped that some of the master's ideas could be applied in other areas of the country.

Kirpal's writings and recorded talks have been carefully preserved in electronic and published formats. He is the author of no less than fourteen books and numerous other writings. Digesting such a sizeable library of teachings is a large undertaking but they can be looked at within six general themes:

1. <u>Man-Making</u> – *"There are basically two stages to be gone through before the struggling disciple rises above body consciousness and begins to enjoy the spiritual disciplines and to firmly tread the Path of Spirituality. The first stage is where the disciple has little or no knowledge of self-introspection and is in a state of abysmal ignorance. The second stage is when the disciple begins to realize that he has innumerable faults and failings which must be corrected before he can hope to rise above body consciousness, at which state this Path really begins. This second stage, which is for most a long, drawn-out struggle with lower tendencies of the mind, is known as 'man-making'. Spirituality, or rising from the lower realms of existence to higher realms of untold bliss and harmony, is not difficult. It is the 'man-making' which is difficult."*

Morning Talks

2. <u>Finding a Competent Teacher</u> – *"As like attracts like, man must of necessity have a human teacher, for nothing else can teach him. The way to God, therefore, lies through man. When people see the Guru living like an ordinary human being, eating, drinking, etc., they become careless in thought and perception. You should always remember that a Master's life is two-in-one. He is the son of man, accepting all as brothers, having no ill thought for anyone, living like a true*

human being, sharing happiness and misery with others. He also suffers in the sadness of others, and sometimes sheds tears of sympathy too. But as his true Self, he leads the souls within and up. Those unfortunate people, who consider him merely a man, remain at the level of man and lose a golden opportunity."

Sat Sandesh, Sept. 1972

3. <u>The Path of the Masters; Surat Shabd Yoga</u>
"The references to Light and Sound, say the Masters of the Surat Shabd Yoga, are not figurative but literal, referring not to the outer illuminations or sounds of this world, but to inner transcendent ones. They teach that the transcendent Sound and Light are the primal manifestations of God when he projects Himself into creation. In His Nameless state He is neither light nor darkness, neither sound nor silence, but when He assumes shape and form, Light and Sound emerge as His primary attributes. The course of Surat Shabd Yoga, as described and taught by Guru Nanak, is the most natural one. Even a child can practice with ease. It is designed by God Himself and not by any human process, and therefore is complete in itself, not requiring addition, alteration, or modification."

Spiritual Elixir

4. <u>Meditation</u> – *"God is not found in books, as only statements about Him are given there. Nor can He be found in temples made of stone by the hand of man. In these*

we gather together only to pray to God or to thank Him for all that He has given. He resides within you. The body is the true temple of God. When you have understood this, then where do you go to find Him? First within your own self. Withdraw from outside, withdraw from the mind and outgoing faculties and come up to the seat of the soul at the back of the eyes. Once you are able to rise above body consciousness, you enter into an awareness of the higher order, which lies beyond the reach of all philosophies and psychologies, for then you are on your way to the Causeless Cause, the Mother of all causes, knowing which everything else becomes known of itself, like an open book. The whole of this life's purpose is to become still – to withdraw from outer environments, and to concentrate. You have great strength in you; you are the child of a Lion."

Morning Talks

5. <u>Detachment</u> – *"So all true Masters say that realizing God is a simple matter – what is there to realizing the Lord? Just uproot the attention from here and plant it there. It is simply a matter of withdrawing and gathering together the scattered attention, which is the outward expression of your soul. Wherever you keep it engaged or attached, those very thoughts will always be reverberating within you. If we can only attach our soul to something higher within us, we would be alright. But if our attention is diverted through the*

outgoing faculties, so much so that it becomes identified with the outer things, what is the result? You cannot withdraw your attention from them. It is a question of the attention or surat, whether you keep it engaged toward the outside things or invert and attach it to your Overself."

Morning Talks

6. <u>Initiation</u> – *"It is the 'Word' personified or the Master Power that gives initiation, and it does not matter where the Master is physically at the time of initiation. Regardless of whether the Master himself is near at hand, or far away overseas, the Master Power always works. In case of distance, the authorized representative conveys the Initiation instructions, generally in the morning hours. At the time of Initiation, the Master takes His seat at the Third Eye of the initiate and looks after him henceforth. The accepted aspirants, who are sincere and receptive during initiation, do have a perceptive first-hand inner spiritual experience at which time the spiritual eye is opened to see the Light of God and the inner ear is opened to hear the Voice of God – the Creative Sound of the Beyond which has a soothing and healing effect. The instructions in the esoteric teachings consist of the exposition of Bhajan (Sound Practice) and Simran (Light Practice), including the repetition of the words (mantra), which are charged with the power of the Master; concentration or meditation, by fixing the inner gaze at the*

*center of the two eyebrows; and then
linking the spirit with the saving lifeline
within, ever reverberating in the form of
the perennial Sound Current, the very life-
breath of the Universe, of which the
Master himself is the living embodiment.
As soon as a devotee is able to transcend
the physical body, the Radiant Form of the
Master (Guru Dev) appears in the subtle
realm, bringing him back to the True
Home of his Father."*

Naam or Word

During his life, Kirpal Singh conducted three world tours, introducing thousands of souls on five continents to the age-old spiritual science. Spirituality, once the prized, exclusive gem of Central Asia was now global. What began five hundred years earlier with Guru Nanak and his roaming band of minstrels, singing Nanak's hymns and providing esoteric instructions; this same teaching was now available to anyone, virtually anywhere in the world.

Kirpal left his earthly frame in August, 1974, and to the lament of some, did not publicly name any particular successor. He said that it was in God's hands and that He would provide. In the case of Kirpal's mission, the question of successorship makes for an interesting case study which will be further explored in Part IV.

PART IV

Instructions for Seekers After Truth

The following five chapters are dedicated to those souls who seek the highest degree of development, who take up the path toward God realization in earnest. While some of the information may have already been addressed in previous chapters, it is all consolidated together here in PART IV.

Chapter 12

FINDING A COMPETENT TEACHER

"The cook says to the Chickpea, 'I was once like you, fresh from the ground. Then I boiled in time, and then boiled the body; two fierce boiling. My animal soul grew powerful. I controlled it with practices, and boiled some more; and then boiled once more beyond that and became your teacher'."

Rumi

Regardless of what field of endeavor you choose to pursue, whether it be intellectual, spiritual or mundane, having a competent teacher to guide you, especially in the beginning phases, is essential to your future success. This is certainly true for anyone who embarks on the spiritual path. Even great masters like Swami Ji and Kirpal Singh had teachers who provided critical information and instructions to facilitate their early quests. But how does one go about identifying a competent teacher, especially a teacher of Shabd Yoga?

In the world today, existing side-by-side, are many thousands of religious and spiritual schools of thought and practice. Finding competent instruction in religious studies is not difficult. There are many people with training and expertise in scriptural matters and religious doctrines. The competency required is primarily educational-based. Even in the field of yoga and similar disciplines, which have no shortage of gurus, a teacher's competency is primarily based on intellectual training and experience in the particular field.

According to the writings of past shabd yoga teachers, a teacher of Shabd Yoga, *a true teacher*, has achieved a certain level of spiritual attainment and has been given a commission from the ascended masters to do the work of initiation on the earth plane. How can you possibly know another person's level of spiritual development and whether or not he or she has been given a divine commission to conduct shabd yoga initiation? You can't, at least not with certainty.

> *"Some parrots have become so skilled with the human voice that they could give a brilliant discourse about God and salvation. And a blind man nearby might even begin applauding, thinking that he had just heard priceless jewels fall from a great saint's mouth."*
>
> Hafiz

From the time of Swami Ji's mission in the mid-nineteenth century, the proliferation of schools and teachers offering Shabd Yoga initiation has increased significantly. In 1995, one scholar estimated that there were over two million people in the world at that time practicing shabd yoga. As of the year 2020, some have estimated that as many as ten million people worldwide were practicing some form of shabd yoga.

Throughout history, many masters have chosen to leave only one successor, but that has not always been the case. Even though Jesus may have identified Peter as his primary successor, he actually left at least twelve. Swami Ji left at least a half dozen.

The most common pattern of succession of shabd yoga masters has been one of multiplicity, with a teacher leaving more than a single successor, either by open and outward declaration or by default, resulting from the teacher naming no one publicly to replace him. The model of a teacher publicly naming a single replacement is actually a deviation from the norm.

Swami Ji's own original Radha Soami mission out of Agra, India has splintered into numerous groups with dozens of teachers. Jaimal Singh was one of those teachers who succeeded him. Twenty years after Swami Ji's departure,

Jaimal publicly named Sawan Singh to be his sole replacement.

There is a long-standing controversy over Sawan Singh's intentions with respect to naming or not naming a successor. Notwithstanding, two teachers continued on with Sawan's work. One was Jagat Singh, a Sant who continued to reside in Beas. Jagat Singh took over all responsibilities at Beas, including public discourses and initiation.

Kirpal Singh was given a special commission by Sawan Singh. He relocated to Delhi and with the help of some friends and supporters, obtained a piece of land and established an ashram in Shakti Nagar. From 1949 until his departure in 1974, Kirpal conducted his work from this location in Delhi.

After Kirpal Singh's death, another controversy ensued over the question of spiritual successorship. Again, notwithstanding, many people began teaching Shabd Yoga. It wasn't just two or a few people this time, it was many people. Disciples of Kirpal Singh in North and South America, Europe and India, continued doing Kirpal's important spiritual work. Some of these teachers have subsequently passed on and they too have left living teachers who are now teaching shabd yoga.

Human beings will always have differences of opinion and will argue about everything and anything. The question of successorship of an important spiritual teacher is certainly something that everybody will probably not agree on and will therefore argue about. Looking beyond this unavoidable reality is the tangible benefit that any person can accrue from taking up training in Shabd Yoga and then acting on that training, regardless of who imparts instructions to them. That is, investing the time and attention into the practices and reaping the rewards of that investment through spiritual growth and mystical experience, along with other ancillary benefits related to their mundane life.

However, one question remains. To what extent does the level of spiritual attainment of the shabd yoga teacher go to support the potential benefits that someone can accrue who devotes himself to the prescribed practices? Nearly all previous teachers of shabd yoga have stated that the teacher's level of development is important. This includes historic teachers. Several of the traditional Buddhist sutras allude to the value of being in the personal orbit of the Buddha. The Surangama Sutra suggests that this association alone may be sufficient in attaining Nirvana. Jesus stressed the value of association with him when he said, "No one comes to the Father except the Son, and those to whom the Son reveals". The Sufi mystic poets have written about the value of association with a true spiritual master.

There is a karmic principle behind this value of association. We become attached to those souls and other things that we associate with in our human lives. If our teacher ascends to a high spiritual region, and we are connected to that soul through love, then we will tag along with him.

From the perspective of someone who is new to Shabd Yoga, that person has to use his best judgement. No one can know with certainty what level of spiritual attainment another person has realized. You can read a teacher's writings and you can listen to what other students say about him or her. You can listen to their recorded discourses. You can consult with your own instincts and intuition. You can ask yourself if you believe the teacher is completely committed to the work, or does the teacher have some underlying motive related to attracting personal wealth or notoriety.

Once someone makes a decision on a teacher of shabd yoga, then he or she should proceed wholeheartedly and follow the teacher's instructions with respect to spiritual disciplines and lifestyle recommendations. If the practitioner does not feel he has made sufficient progress after some period of time, the first place to look for a solution is within himself. Is the student following the teacher's advice wholeheartedly? Is the student doing the spiritual practices accurately? Is there some ulterior motive that is driving the student or is he or she sincerely committed to their spiritual growth and development?

Anyone who takes up this practice and applies themselves to it wholeheartedly will derive benefit. The sincerity of the student is paramount. The inner ascended masters will rush to the aid of someone like that. They are attracted to the loving energy of someone with a sincere heart. If in fact that individual has made a wrong choice with respect to their teacher, then eventually they will be guided somewhere else. But it is always best to row on one boat at a time.

Today, there are over a hundred teachers of Shabd Yoga spread throughout the world. In order to help an aspiring student in identifying which one or ones may be fully competent, there are four principal criteria to consider.

1. <u>Level of Attainment</u> – Shabd Yoga Masters are of two kinds: Sat Gurus, who are Sants, and Sadh Gurus. Sants and Param Sants have reached the purely spiritual planes. There may actually be many disciples of a master who have reached these lofty levels. However, their spiritual attainment does not necessarily mean that they are chosen to act as Sat Guru. The reasons why a particular soul is chosen to teach and conduct initiation are known only by the ascended masters. A Sat Guru is likely to lead an ideal worldly life. In his earlier years as a disciple, he very likely had some difficult karmas to work through, but once he commences his spiritual mission and begins conducting initiation, his thoughts, words and deeds are ideal.

   A 'Sadh' or 'Sadhu', is a soul who is firmly established in the third plane and who is an adept in self-knowledge, the art and science of spirit, having experienced himself as pure spirit. He or she now strives for spiritual purification and God realization. A Sadh can also be chosen to act as guru, i.e., Sadh Guru.

Since a Sadh is still engaged in his own spiritual, mental and physical purification, it is possible that his earthly life may not appear to be pure and ideal in some way. These types of teachers can often perform very effectively since they view themselves and their fellow spiritual sojourners as peers.

Regarding the ongoing spiritual revolution, Guru Nanak once remarked that in this age there would be fourteen great Sat Gurus and seventy Sadh Gurus. Any teacher who is duly commissioned by the ascended masters to conduct initiation is a legitimate channel for the God-into-expression-power, regardless of his spiritual level of attainment or personal karmas.

2. <u>Means of Support</u> – A genuine Shabd Yoga teacher will not make his spiritual mission a source of personal income. He has some other means of supporting himself, separate from his spiritual work. He is not the recipient of gifts or favors, but is himself a giver, both materially and spiritually.

An aspirant who requests to receive initiation instructions is never charged any kind of fee. Initiation instructions are always given freely. Spiritual missions, like any other worldly endeavor, do require funding. These funds may come from a variety of sources including donations, and are utilized to pay for transportation, lodging, administrative expenses and a variety of other costs. But the teacher will never use any of these funds for his own personal use.

3. <u>Lifestyle</u> – True masters do not care for showmanship and wear no conspicuous form of dress, preferring instead to adopt the traditions of the culture into which they were born. They are not out for name and fame or celebrity. They are imbued with humility, never taking credit for anything and wish only that their disciples find success with their spiritual endeavors.

They are at peace with all, angry with none, embracing humanity as their own family and will never ask anyone to do anything which may prove to be harmful to themselves or to any other person or animal.

4. <u>Initiation</u> – At the time of initiation, a master will give the aspirant a first-hand experience of the light and sound by opening the inner eye and the inner ear to help him establish a foothold in his meditations. The master does not have to be physically present at the initiation as long as it is conducted by an authorized representative. This criterion, helping souls begin their spiritual journeys by putting them in contact with the inner light and sound, is the gold standard for a Sant Mat teacher. You know a true master the same way you know the mailman or the milkman. They deliver. A true Shabd Yoga master will deliver the light and sound. When you have found a teacher who can initiate your connection to the light and sound, and after following his/her instructions your inner development increases over time, you have made the right connection.

> *"Hafiz, you were a slave to Truth that died like a cut reed and became hollow. You then became a divine instrument that God now lifts to his own mouth, and plays to summon this world to freedom."*

Hafiz

When you meet a master, you meet two teachers; the living teacher, and his teacher. When you meet a true master, you also meet the ascended masters. The living master actually has an easy job. He simply explains the theoretical side of the path and provides instructions. On spiritual levels, everything is facilitated by the ascended masters.

Rai Saligram also wrote on the subject of how to distinguish between a great master, or Sant, and an ordinary religious teacher. In his book, Radha Soami Mat Prakash, he offers the following guidance:

> *"As in these days, there are many who call themselves Sants, Sadhs and guides or leaders of sects and religious societies, etc. It is difficult to distinguish between Sant Sat Guru, or a true Spiritual Guide, and a host of family or ancestral guides and wandering mendicants and religious leaders, except by the means hereafter described:*
>
> 1. *That the True Guide is He who imparts instructions for the practice of Surat Shabd Yoga as prescribed by Radha Soami Faith.*
>
> 2. *That his object in preaching the holy doctrine and giving practical instructions is nothing more than the saving of humanity from perdition and raising the human spirits to the highest and pure spiritual regions from which they originally descended.*
>
> 3. *That He is not actuated to undertake this work from selfish motives or for any personal benefit or aggrandizement.*
>
> 4. *That when envy and jealousy on the part of interested religious parties will try to slander his character and otherwise shower taunts and sneers on Him and His limited congregation, he won't feel ashamed or discouraged by such acts of the ignorant, jealous and worldly people. He will instead go on with His sacred work steadily and determinately with full trust in the Grace and Mercy of His Beloved Father, the True Supreme Being who invariably extends His protection to the sincere lovers of Truth.*

5. *That His discourses, being purely spiritual and full of affection for the Supreme Being, will be heartily attended to by sincere searchers of Truth and true lovers of the Supreme Being, and His instructions sought by them, to practice the mode of devotion, Surat Shabd Yoga, which is formulated to raise the spirit to the Holy and Highest Mansion of the Supreme Father.*

6. *That by acting upon His instructions, sincere lovers of Truth will derive much pleasure in their surat shabd yoga practice, occasionally having internal visions of a supernatural character, and glimpses of higher regions, and also recognize the Grace and Mercy and Protection of the Supreme Father being now and then, extended to them."*

The difficult process of evaluating a potential teacher can be fraught with misconceptions. Faqir Chand rightly explained that spiritual teachers are essentially just like us, in the sense that they live ordinary lives and experience human life much the same way everybody else does. The way in which they differ from others is in their spiritual development, which is invisible to others. For that reason, people judge teachers on the basis of their teachings, their lifestyle and behavior; things which they can see.

People tend to hold spiritual masters up to too strict a standard. We assume that they are perfect beings and that all of their thoughts and actions are likewise perfect. The fallacy inherent here is that the concept of human perfection is purely subjective. One person may see perfection, relative to his idea of what perfect means, while another person may see faults and shortcomings.

One characteristic of any spiritually evolved person, whether they are a teacher or not, is that along with their inner development comes love. They become infused with love and that infusion affects how they live; how they interact and communicate with others. Love, and the qualities and characteristics of love, tends to color all aspects of their human life and overshadow the baser human emotions and instincts that the average person is likely to experience.

Swami Ji provides an excellent case in point. Swami Ji is widely regarded as being a great spiritual master. He played a landmark role in reintroducing and fostering the practice of shabd yoga. When one considers the growth of the movement he spawned, which grew from a few thousand followers to roughly ten million in the span of 160 years, you can't deny the fact that he has had a considerable historical impact and enhanced the spiritual evolution of millions of souls.

Swami Ji essentially lived the life of an ordinary Indian man, residing in a simple house located in a nondescript section of Agra, India. If you were to encounter him out in public somewhere, you wouldn't be able to distinguish him from anybody else. But Swami Ji had some personal habits, which today are viewed by some as being a bit quirky. The best example of this is that he was a tobacco smoker. He was a habitual tobacco smoker. The instructions he drew up for the servants who took care of him included guidelines for how to go about preparing his daily hookah.

The first problem we might encounter when trying to reconcile why and how he became a tobacco smoker is that you can't judge historic events on the basis of today's standards. Today, we know the science behind habitual tobacco smoking and its health risks and related dangers. In the 1860's, they knew none of this. At that particular time, smoking tobacco was considered to be a perfectly normal, healthy habit to engage in for any adult male living in Agra, India. Tobacco was simply part of Swami Ji's diet.

Some contemporary spiritual groups, who for some reason view themselves as rivals to the Radha Soami movement that Swami Ji spawned, take Swami Ji's tobacco smoking as proof positive that he couldn't have possibly been a true spiritual master. Their logic is politically motivated. People who are seeking a competent Shabd Yoga teacher should assume that the teacher they choose will have his own set of personal habits which will prove that, in spite of his spiritual attainment, he is in other respects a regular human being.

Once a student is satisfied that he has made the right choice of a teacher, and that his teacher is competent, then it is up to the student to follow the teacher's instructions which will ultimately lead to success. If a student's efforts do not lead to success, the first question he should ask himself is: "Have I followed my teacher's instructions faithfully?"

Historically speaking, spiritual teachers have primarily manifested in the world in male bodies. It is important to understand that males and females are spiritually identical. They have the same spiritual potential. Females who have ardently taken up the practice of shabd yoga in the past have found the same success as their male counterparts.

The reason that teachers in the past have been males is that the work of guru in this world involves encountering opposing forces. These forces can manifest as intellectual, institutional and even physical and violent opposition. Men, due to their stalwart emotional make-up, have been better suited to endure this kind of strong opposition. However, the world has changed significantly with increased human rights along with religious and spiritual freedom, especially over the past century. Going forward, a Shabd Yoga teacher could be a woman as easily as it could be a man.

Chapter 13

LIFESTYLE

> *"Behold, a sower went forth to sow; and when he sowed, some seeds fell by the way side, and the fowls came and devoured them up; some fell upon stony places, where they had not much earth; and when the sun was up, they were scorched, and they withered away. And some fell among thorns; and the thorns choked them. But others fell on good ground, and brought forth flower and fruit, some a hundredfold, some sixtyfold, and some thirtyfold. He who hath ears to hear, let him hear."*

Matthew 13:3-9

Humans are complex, integrated beings comprised of body, mind and spirit. Our actions, whether they be physical, mental or spiritual, affect us holistically on all three of these levels according to the workings of the law of cause and effect. If you seek success in your spiritual endeavors, it therefore behooves you to be vigilant in all aspects of your life.

> *"Take heed therefore that the light within ye become not darkness."*

Luke 11:35

Your first consideration should be sadachar, or right conduct. Masters encourage their students to lead a simple life, based on the highest principles of ethics and purity. While all masters have laid down their own distinct guidelines in this respect, they all agree that the way an aspirant conducts his life is irrevocably tied to the success he will experience on the spiritual path.

Patanjali, in his Yoga Sutras, stressed the importance of Yamas and Niyamas; the acceptance, cultivation, observance and development of positive virtues, the harboring of good feelings, and absorbing these virtues into one's system; while simultaneously abstaining from vices and from entertaining evil thoughts or accepting any negative impressions which may tend to weaken the mind and the will.

Moses introduced the 'Ten Commandments'; ten fundamental principles of social decorum and personal conduct as a foundation for spirituality.

Zarathustra devised a system of human conduct which was based on the sixteen primary forces established by the creator, Ahura Mazda. The interaction of the eight visible forces with the eight invisible forces produced 64 possible combinations, the sum total of the various types of human interrelations. At the end of each day, his disciples were instructed to consider all 64 possibilities and how they fared in each of those situations.

The ancient Chinese developed the "I Ching", which categorized human interaction into eight trigrams, or combinations of elemental duality. By combining the trigrams together into all possible hexagrams, their system, like Zarathustra's, also resulted in 64 basic types of human interrelations. Confucius developed an even more elaborate system of conduct and ethics, still a part of Chinese consciousness today.

Lord Buddha presented his eight-fold path; right understanding, right thoughts, right speech, right actions, right livelihood, right effort, right mindfulness and right meditation.

In his Sermon on the Mount, Jesus expounded upon the virtues necessary for success in the heavenly realms which have come be known as the 'beatitudes'.

> *"Blessed are those who hunger and thirst for righteousness, for they shall be satisfied."*

Matthew 5:6

Kirpal Singh devised his 'seven paths to perfection', a formula for man-making with these antidotes: non-violence, truthfulness, chastity, universal love, dietary purity, selfless service and meditation.

It has been said that 'cleanliness is next to Godliness'. This is certainly true with respect to our bodies and the quality of our intake of air, water and food, which constitute our primary sources of chi, or life energy. Many masters have stressed the need for a strict lacto-vegetarian diet, one that excludes all forms of meat and eggs. This includes the early Christians. According to Valentinus, Jesus was 'continent', which at the time meant that he abstained from wine, women and meat.[8] Early Christian historians, like St. Epiphanius and Origen, write about the Ebionites, a group formed around the time of Jesus' death. They tell us that this group closely adopted the customs and practices of Jesus, and since the Ebionites were vegetarians, it is believed by some scholars that Jesus was a vegetarian as well.

> *"The 'Gospel According to the Apostles' is a lost gospel which was used by the Ebionites. Herein is found the 'Essene Christ'. He denounces sacrifice and the eating of flesh...The Ebionites refused to partake of flesh or wine, taking as their pattern St. Peter, whose food was bread, olives, and herbs."*

Hastings Encyclopedia on Religion and Ethics

Clement of Alexandria writes that "Matthew lived upon seeds and nuts, fruits and vegetables, without the use of flesh". We find similar references in various Christian literature.

> *"Be not among wine bibbers and among riotous eaters of flesh."*

Proverbs 23:20-21

> *"Do not destroy the work of God for the sake of food! Everything is pure in itself, but it is*

---

[8] Benton Layton, 'The Gnostic Scriptures', 1995, Valentinus, Fragment E

wrong to eat if by eating you cause another to stumble. It is right to abstain from eating meat or drinking wine or from anything else that causes a fellow Christian to stumble."

Romans 14:20-21

"All abstain from eating the meat of quadrupeds."

St. Benedict

"The monks are prohibited from eating meat, according to the ancient custom as attested by St. John Climacus and St. John Crisostomos."

Kormcaia, Chapter 10

Indian Saints have also weighed in on the importance of a pure vegetarian diet.

"Believe me friend, those who eat meat and fish and drink intoxicating drinks will all be rooted out. Like weeds are removed from a fertile field, they will be cast aside into the valley of death."

Kabir

"Kill not thou any living beings, sayeth Ravidas. Living beings veritably are of the family of God."

Ravidas

"When I see men feeding on the coarse and vicious food of animal flesh, it is an ever-recurring grief to me."

Ramalinga

"Eaters of the flesh of beasts,
Are bound by death's chains.
They find the jaws of hell,
Consumed forever."

Tirumoolar (Sundernath), The Tirumantiram

Buddhism resounds the same theme.

"If one is trying to practice dhyana and is still eating meat, he would be like a man closing his ears and shouting loudly and then asserting that he heard nothing. How can a Bhikshu, who hopes to become a deliverer of others, himself be living on the flesh of other sentient beings? They are not true disciples of the Buddha."

Surangama Sutra

Living as a vegetarian in a meat-eating world poses certain challenges. Most of these challenges are related to one's social interaction with others. When someone prepares his own meals, he is in control of what goes into his body and can apply strict guidelines. He can read labels when shopping to check for animal product ingredients.

But in a social setting, when someone else is preparing food, it is always best to inform them in advance of your dietary guidelines and your degree of commitment to the vegetarian diet. If someone adopts a purely vegan diet, which avoids all animal-related foods, including dairy-derived foods, then it is best to supplement the diet with Vitamin B12, since B12 is difficult to obtain through a purely vegan diet. Vegetarians should also consider supplementing their diets with iron, accompanied with vitamin C, and zinc.

Perhaps the most critical area of maintaining a pure diet is the abstention of intoxicants. Since there are a variety of both legal and illicit substances available to people in the twenty-first century, they should be considered separately.

1. <u>Alcohol</u> – Alcohol is a poison. It is poisonous to body, mind, and spirit. It is also addictive for many people. Anyone who drinks alcohol will not make any spiritual progress while intoxicated and for several days thereafter. There are some people who can use alcohol

sparingly, who are not at risk for using it habitually. These people are rare exceptions. Even if you are one of those people, you will suffer several days of retarded progress each time you consume. Alcohol is sometimes present in medicines, like extracts and tinctures. Using alcohol in this way is not harmful unless you are addicted to alcohol, in which case even these small amounts should be avoided.

2. <u>Opiates</u> – Opiates are also poisonous and must be completely avoided, even as prescribed medicines. Opiate resins build up in the body and are very difficult to expel, causing a severe sickness known as 'withdrawal'. Anyone who uses opiates will not make any headway on the spiritual path and should focus all of their attention on cleansing their bodies and keeping them clean. Once sobriety is firmly established, one can resume his spiritual quest.

3. <u>Hard Drugs like Cocaine and Methamphetamine</u> – Hard drugs are poisonous and must be completely avoided. They cause psychological aberrations and block entry into the higher planes. Anyone who uses hard drugs, even on a casual basis, will not find any appreciable success with their meditations.

4. <u>Cannabis</u> – Marijuana is the least harmful of the intoxicants, but it too will stand in the way of an aspirant's spiritual progress. While the cannabis resin is in the body, which can be a week or two after each use, it is not possible to have any of the higher types of spiritual revelations, like samadhi and visionary dreams. Cannabis does help a person still the body, due to its sedative effect, but no significant spiritual development is feasible for a habitual cannabis user.

If you are earnest about your spiritual development and you use intoxicants, continue with your spiritual disciplines. Your meditations may not be fruitful for a time and your development will be retarded, but you will keep your good habit of daily meditation intact and the God-into-expression-power will come to your aid by helping you get back on the right track.

Chapter 14

LIFE ENERGY

Human energy; i.e., life energy, sexual energy, and spiritual energy all spring from the same source: spirit. Life energy (prana or chi) is essential to the maintenance of your health and well-being. Spiritual energy is life energy that you invest in your spiritual development. Sexual energy is life energy that you invest in the regenerative system. What is important to understand about these three applications of life energy is that we only have so much of it and we should be mindful about how we manage it. The less energy required for maintenance of the physical systems, the more you will have to apply to your spiritual disciplines.

The quest toward God realization requires a temple (body) which is at peace, and a body at peace is one which is vital, healthy and fit. Anyone involved in this quest is in training, like an Olympic athlete is in training. The principal difference is that this training is permanent. A body which is under duress is not a temple in which the God-into-expression-power is likely to manifest. The first consideration is diet, and not just abstention from meat and eggs, but the quality of your food and how much of it you eat. You should also keep your body fit and engage in some physical activity on a regular basis which challenges you in a way appropriate to your age and physical capabilities.

The relationship between sexual energy and spiritual energy is an area which has been written, debated and philosophized about for centuries. It is an important subject and deserves an honest and open discussion.

Sexual energy is the most powerful force in nature. Each species of life has developed, through evolution, a reproductive strategy which is many times more efficient than is necessary to ensure that each life form is replaced by one or more new ones. One tree may produce tens of thousands of seeds over the course of its existence. An herbaceous plant may produce a thousand seeds in a single season. Animals respond to sights, sounds, and smells in a way that when it is time to mate, it is time to mate, and nothing, including eating, drinking, and sleeping is going to interfere. This urge to mate is, of course, a very powerful force in humans as well.

If you explore the sexual attitudes and customs of cultures throughout history you will find a striking variation in the way people have viewed human sexuality over the millennia. What is even more remarkable is the degree to which our cultural myths and traditions influence these attitudes and behavioral norms. In the Judaic-Christian world, our myth of Adam and Eve presents sexuality in a negative context, associating it with shame and evil. The Egyptians, on the other hand, viewed sexuality in a favorable, sacred context.

Sexuality is not good, bad, evil, or sacred. It is simply a part of life; a necessary and unavoidable part of life. Some spiritual teachers and religious leaders, past and present, have insisted that chastity, or celibacy, is a necessary component to physical purity and spiritual development. Conserving one's sexual energy and investing it in spiritual disciplines is, in fact, an effective way to facilitate and accelerate spiritual growth. So, these teachers and leaders are not wrong about this energy equation. What is wrong is how many of them have gone about presenting this to spiritual and religious aspirants, and to people in general, by imposing unrealistic expectations on people with respect to their sexual behavior.

For the general population, how much sexual energy a person expends or whether or not someone eats meat or partakes of intoxicants is not such a big issue. Everyone needs to be attentive to their health and wellbeing and judicious about engaging in potentially harmful behaviors in excess. But spiritual aspirants who are earnestly seeking God realization are in training; lifelong training. They need to be especially vigilant in the maintenance of their physical health and life energy.

One of Guru Nanak's goals was to have spirituality incorporated into the lives of ordinary people. This of course meant married people with jobs and families (householders). Nanak was himself married as was Kabir. In fact, most of the Gurus in the 500-year Radha Soami lineage were married men who raised families. So, sexuality is no bar to spirituality as long as these energies are not spent so excessively that the expenditure serves to retard spiritual growth by bankrupting life energy.

Chapter 15

MEDITATION AND DEVELOPMENT

At the time of initiation, an aspirant is given instructions on the two types of meditation practices; simran (light), and bhajan (sound). Masters have prescribed a period of two hours of meditation daily, with an equal amount of time devoted to each. Two hours is approximately one tenth of a day, so this devotion to spiritual disciplines is comparable to a tithe of your worldly time. Actually, due to the physical and psychological benefits reaped from stilling the body for two hours, at least an hour of sleep will be compensated for. So, if an aspirant normally sleeps for seven hours a night, after devoting two hours to accurate meditation he will require only about six hours of sleep. Every aspirant should also try to plan periods of complete solitude, perhaps on retreats or nature expeditions, where he can devote five or more hours per day to meditation for a week or longer.

The most ideal way of structuring one's meditation time is doing it all in one sitting, either in the early morning hours or at night prior to sleep. However, with the fast-paced, unpredictable lives that most people lead, finding two available hours can sometimes be difficult. The best time to meditate is when you have the time at your disposal. Even if it has to be broken up into thirty, or even fifteen-minute blocks, snatch your time whenever you can. What is most important is not the amount of time you devote to the practices but your degree of concentrated attention. Fifteen minutes of fully concentrated attention is worth more than two hours of random, wandering thoughts.

While you may find yourself meditating in many different places, and at many different times throughout your days, it is good to have one special place, preferably in your home, that you devote to meditation. It could be a small room, a closet, or perhaps just a spot on the floor or in a particular chair. This location will develop a charging which will help you focus when you sit. While it is ideal to have a silent, peaceful place to meditate, it is not always feasible to have perfect conditions, especially for those who live in cities. If there is noise and a clamor of activity around you, the light and sound will increase to compensate for it. Even in a brightly lit room, or out in sunlight, the inner light will be visible.

While practicing simran, keep the inner gaze fixed intently, minutely in the middle of the screen before you. This is your inner screen, your window into the beyond. When the mind is led away by some rambling mental chatter, bring it back and refocus your gaze. During light practice, the sound will at times grow loud and its strong presence will assist you in keeping the wandering mind in check.

When you are fully attentive in the eye focus, the guru dev will be there gazing back at you. You may or may not see him but he is there. If you do not see him, he is behind the veil. The guru dev will appear out of a very tiny eye which forms in the middle of the gaze, or he will appear out of a large, glowing ring of purple and gold light which turns into a large eye before the rest of the face is revealed. Finding the guru dev in meditation and keeping your gaze focused on him is your assurance of success because one day he will escort you into the higher spiritual planes.

At the time of initiation, the aspirant is given a five-word mantra. The groups which have evolved out of Swami Ji's original Agra group use a two-word mantra; 'Radha Soami'. Radha Soami is believed to be the true name of the lord. The five words have no special meaning, but are instead like passwords for admittance into the inner planes. These words are charged with spiritual energy and are a vital component to simran, helping the mind to remain focused in the gaze. They are to be repeated slowly, over and over with the tongue of thought. When an aspirant becomes more experienced in his practice, the words can be repeated simply by thinking of them, rather than hearing the mind actually saying them. Sant

Mat is a path of experience and masters do not ask their disciples to take much on faith. But relying on and having faith in the efficacy and benefit of these words, especially in the beginning stages, is an example where the aspirant needs to act on faith. As time goes by, the aspirant will come to appreciate the value of the words through his own first-hand experience. For example, there will be times when some malevolent entities may pester the aspirant during sleep. If the aspirant has the presence of mind to repeat the words in this situation, the entities will vanish instantly like a puff of smoke.

The term 'simran', which means repetition, is also used in a broader context to mean the repetition of the five charged words during waking hours as one goes about his daily activities, such as walking, driving, or preparing foods. Simran is especially beneficial just prior to falling to sleep which will often lead to spiritual dreams.

> *"One should attend to one's simran in the same way as a water carrier girl keeps her attention on the pitcher on her head while she walks on rough, uneven ground conversing with her friends.*
>
> *"One should preserve one's simran in the same way as a miser keeps his money. He never wants to part with it, and is constantly comforted by its presence."*

Kabir

One long-time disciple of Kirpal Singh wrote a book entitled; "Salvation Through Perpetual Simran". If one contemplates the title alone, reading the book really isn't necessary.

Basking in the spiritual power of the Word daily for two hours will accrue benefits to your body and mind. In the case of the body, if you take notice, you will find your over-all health improved and your health care needs and their related costs diminished.

With respect to the mind and consciousness, the aspirant will find a calming effect on the emotions which will help to steady his dealings with people and situations as he navigates through his day-to-day life. When the mind becomes infused with the Word, one's cognitive ability will also benefit with an improved ability to concentrate and enhanced memory.

Another inevitable effect, or side effect, of meditation on the Word is the awakening of some of the mind's latent or 'psychic' abilities. These abilities are natural to the mind but are asleep to most people due to our materialistic tendencies and the karmic dross which envelops the soul on the earth plane. The power of the Word has a cleansing effect on the mind and when the dross is burnt off, the mind is infused with spirit and these natural abilities are revealed.

The development of these abilities can serve to retard spiritual growth because they become like a new toy, and the attention is diverted away from meditation to psychic exploration. Another dilemma develops after an aspirant begins to receive precognitive information, either through visionary dreams or from the spirit voice. The problem which will arise is that the information which is received may not be valid or it may be presented in a way which requires interpretation on the part of the aspirant. Masters who have reached the planes of pure spirit have these abilities, of course, but the information they receive is all valid since it emanates from the highest source. But these abilities begin to dawn in aspirants as they are working their way through the lower planes, and so the information they receive can be from an unreliable source or even a malevolent source. There will be times when there is no doubt that the information comes directly from the master within, and in those cases the aspirant can have full confidence in what he has come to learn. But these cases will be the exception. Most of the psychic information which an aspirant receives as he treads along on his spiritual journey should be considered suspect.

At some point in an aspirant's development, he will begin to hear the sound during waking hours as he goes about his mundane activities. At certain times, the sound will suddenly become louder. When this happens, the aspirant should pay attention, especially to the direction from which the sound originates. If it comes from the left, it is some kind of warning or an acknowledgement that there is some negative energy at work. If, on the other hand, the sound comes from the right, from above, or from all around, this is a positive sign, a message of encouragement and support. This type of spiritual communication can almost always be relied upon, although it often necessitates some degree of interpretation.

The most welcome effect, or side effect of meditation on the Word is the development of love, which is the innate quality of the God-into-expression-power. This gift will manifest in your thoughts, words, and deeds and bless all aspects of your life, including your relationships. You will become a beacon of spiritual light for all those around you to bask in.

PART V

The School of Pranayam

The path and practice of Pranayama is an ancient tradition which has produced many spiritual adepts and practitioners of Shabd Yoga.

Chapter 16

THE SCHOOL OF PRANAYAM

The School of Pranayam is a widely-practiced system of yoga which has evolved out of Indian and Hindu culture, and can be traced to yoga's earliest roots, perhaps predating the Bhagavad Gita and the Vedas. It is well-established in our modern world with thousands of schools and teachers, both in India and worldwide, teaching some form of pranayama.

What distinguishes pranayama from other spiritual disciplines, including Shabd Yoga, is its emphasis on controlling and empowering the pranic energies through the practice of breathing and breath-control sadhanas. These disciplines, when practiced accurately under the guidance of an adept teacher, can accrue many life-supportive benefits to the yogic practitioner. The oxygenation of the blood which takes place, for instance, is healthy as long as it is not overdone. These disciplines can be very rigorous and a teacher will typically prescribe a variety of breathing methods to be used conjointly with each other.

The practice of pranayama has a powerful effect on regulating the flow of life energy through the three primary nadis; the Ida, the Pingala, and the Sushmana, all three of which run up and down the spinal column. Pranayama helps to activate life energy from the base chakra, or guda chakra, and attracts it up the spine to the ajna chakra between and behind the eyebrows. Another outcome of this process is the activation and clearing of the six primary chakras. Pranayama also accrues other benefits, some of which are psychological. Practitioners often experience improved cognitive ability and some heightened intuitive or psychic sensitivities.

Virtually every teacher of pranayama, both historic and modern, includes meditation as a prescribed sadhana. The meditation practices often involve the repetition of a mantra or mantras and sometimes include features related to Hindu culture. But the meditation sadhanas are separate and distinct from the pranayama sadhanas in one important way; the rigorous breathing techniques practiced in pranayama are not utilized in meditation. In the meditation sadhanas, the breathing is quiet and the attention (dharana) is focused on something else. The most common method is focusing the attention in the third eye center, or ajna chakra. It is at this point where Pranayama and Shabd Yoga converge.

If you explore the many past masters and sages who have practiced pranayama successfully, you will find that many of them described their mystical experiences in terms of the light and sound they experienced.

> *"In this world, they conquered death,*
> *And escaped the pangs of birth.*
> *The Siddhas, immersed in the melodious*
> *Shabd,*
> *Found rapture beyond description."*
> *"When the Siddhas went deep within,*
> *They found illumination within the eye.*
> *In silence they saw and listened,*
> *Then opened other's eyes to wisdom."*
> *"Bell, sea, elephant, vina and flute,*
> *Bee, dragon-fly, conch, drum, and lute*
> *Audible, these subtle ten sounds are*
> *By those alone who*
> *Master Dharana's quietude."*

Tirumoolar

> *"When the nadis have been cleansed, the body*
> *becomes lean and radiant. The health is*
> *ideal, the appetite is strong, pranayama can*
> *be performed easily, and the divine sounds*
> *become audible."*

Gorakshnath

So, the successful practice of pranayama should ideally culminate with the practice of Shabd Yoga. What pranayama has afforded, for both ancient and modern yogis, is a preparatory ground for the successful practice of meditation. Pranayama is an excellent preliminary stage; a purification process for all of the bodies - physical, astral, and subtle. The experienced yogi, an adept in pranayama, will find easy access into the inner planes and the mystical revelations accessible through the inner eye and the inner ear. So, the ultimate objectives of pranayama and Dharana Nada are the same: successful meditations culminating in Samadhi.

Shabd Yoga masters teach that the practice of pranayama, while beneficial in its own right, is an unnecessary step in the quest for fruitful meditations leading to Samadhi. All that is required is the development of the inner eye and the inner ear under the guidance of a competent teacher. Pranayama is an arduous discipline which requires a full commitment and a substantial investment of time. There is no inherent conflict between the two practices. Ancient yogis combined them successfully for thousands of years. The only real conflict between the two practices is in the time factor. If one is to achieve the ultimate success with either of these disciplines it requires a serious commitment. With pranayama, a yogi should devote a minimum of one hour per day to his practices if he is to realize his objectives. With Dharana Nada, one should devote a minimum of two hours per day to meditation. In our modern, fast-paced busy lives, how many people have three hours or more per day to devote to their sadhanas? Few, if any. This is the principal reason that teachers of Shabd Yoga recommend that spiritual aspirants forgo the practice of pranayama in favor of devoting all of their time to the development of their inner eye and inner ear.

Historically, perhaps the best example we have of a yogi combining the practice of pranayama with the practice of Shabd Yoga, comes from the seventeenth century, Dara Shukoh. Dara Shukoh was the eldest son of the Indian emperor Shah Jahan and was identified in chapter one as being a practitioner of shabd yoga.

Dara Shukoh was mentored by Sufi mystics, so his methods represent the way shabd yoga was taught and practiced in India in the seventeenth century. Dara Shukoh combined pranayama with simran and bhajan. Not only did he practice all three of these disciplines, he practiced pranayama and listening to the sound together, simultaneously. Shabd yoga is not taught and practiced this way by contemporary teachers and practitioners, nor is there any historic evidence that anyone else practiced it this way, with the exception of these seventeenth century Sufis.

Here is how Dara Shukoh describes his practice in his pamphlet, Compass of Truth:

> *"The method of practice, which has been adopted by this writer and which he has found the best, is the regulation of breath. This is a method without which success cannot be obtained, and so everyone ought to practice this method of control of breath: and it is done in this way.*
>
> *"Sitting in a retired spot, place the elbows of both hands on the two knees, and with the two thumbs, close the hole of the two ears, so that no air may pass out of them. With the two index fingers, shut the two eyes, in such a way, that the upper eyelid may remain steadily fixed on the lower eyelid, but that the fingers should not press the eyeballs.*
>
> *"Place the ring and small fingers on the upper and lower lips, so as to close the mouth. Place the two middle fingers on the two sides of the nose, the right middle finger on the right side, and the left middle finger on the left side. Having assumed this posture, first let him*

firmly close the right nostril with the right middle finger, so that air may not come through it, and the opening the left nostril, let him breathe in slowly through it.

"After this he should close firmly the left nostril also, with the left middle finger, and thus keep the air confined withing the body. Then repeating, he can gradually increase the period of restraining the breath. Then he should throw out the breath, by opening the right nostril, by removing the middle finger from it, and the breath should be thrown out slowly. Let him keep the breath confined so long as he easily can do so without feeling suffocation."

The breathing method he describes is a fairly standard technique, one taught and practiced today by contemporary teachers of pranayama along with other breathing techniques. What is unique about this particular method is that he also plugs the ears at the same time. By plugging the ears, he is doing pranayama and shabd yoga simultaneously. This description provides the best historic evidence we have that some mystics did practice these methods together.

If a person chooses to practice both disciplines, pranayama and shabd yoga, he would be best advised to practice them separately, in distinct sessions. Since pranayama is an active, physical process, the body is not at rest, but rather is in motion. Shabd yoga must be practiced while the body is at rest. Therefore, if someone wants to practice both, he should leave a period of thirty minutes or so of between the two practices, so that the body can more easily adjust between the two opposite states; motion and stillness.

<u>**The Himalayan Tradition**</u>

The long history of the school of Pranayam includes many great yogis and masters who utilized pranayama as a preliminary stage in their quest for self-realization and God realization. There is evidence from their writings that they communed with the nada and had visions of inner light. While it is impossible to know any past sage's level of development, we can take clues from their life stories and especially from their writings, where many of them make references to their mystical experiences of light and sound.

The school of Pranayam is deeply rooted in Indian culture, so when sharing the life stories of these sages, Hindu references are unavoidable. It is also important to remember that the biographical and historic accounts of these yogis are fused with a combination of historical fact, legend, and allegory. The further we go back in time, the less historic accuracy we will find compared to allegory and myth. The yogis and sages referred to here in this collection are by no means a complete list of historic masters of Pranayama, but it does include many important ones.

Many of the ancient teachers of Pranayama were yogis who lived in the Himalayan region. They had high levels of attainment, living the austere life of a yogi, in a community of yogis. Theirs was a simple, rustic lifestyle, close to the land and close to one another. They had a strong sense of community with their neighbors, dependent upon one another for mutual sustenance. Their spiritual practices, of course, were the focal point of their lives.

Hamlets and ashrams were always built near a river, with fresh water being required for survival. Their thatched cottages took many shapes, mostly round and rectangular, engineered with four to six vertical posts inside, over which a sheet of woven branches and grasses was layered. This thick sheet of thatch, rightly constructed, could keep the region's brutal weather out. Building sites were strategically chosen under large stands of trees or against rock facings. Their huts were versatile, allowing for warmth in the harsh winter months, while being cool during the sun-intense summers. The flooring was made from a mixture of earth mixed with cow dung and straw, and was effective in repelling unwelcome insects. Each day the floor was sprinkled with water and buffed to renew the surface.

Those involved in growing food had to terrace the sloping hillsides. They grew a variety of crops, including rice, grains, beans, lentils and root crops. Every home was planted with apple and apricot trees, so fruits were abundant. Families kept bees for honey and wax, cows for milk, and goats for hauling. What little grasslands they had were used for grazing. They crushed oil from mustard seed, which they used for cooking and lamp fuel. The mountains were crisscrossed with a network of trails along which people and commodities traveled to nearby settlements and marketplaces. In some places, the pathways were so narrow that only a single man or goat could pass.

The pastoral lifestyle offered many opportunities for gatherings, especially in the ashrams. These meetings often involved spirited philosophical discussions and debates. The masters, in those days, gave discourses out in the open air, sometimes under the wide canopy of a fiscus tree.

Eager devotees would gather and sit on the ground. There were no books. Knowledge was conveyed orally and committed to memory by disciples. The masters would sometimes sit on short platforms, called pitha, from where they would impart spiritual knowledge and instructions.

Life in the Himalayan uplands was arduous and challenging, but the pure environment was conducive to spiritual pursuits. It was then, and is still today, a sacred region, where many great rishis and siddhas found enlightenment and realization.

Pranayam Lineage of Teachers
Lord Dakshinamurthy

Dakshinamurthy is believed to have lived in South India in antiquity, although he is now revered as a primordial Guru, like Lord Adinath. Dakshinamurthy literally means, 'one who is facing South'. If a person does not have a guru, they are advised to consider Dakshinamurthy as their teacher until they are fortunate enough to meet a living master.

Dakshinamurthy is a powerful avatar of Shiva, and a teacher of yoga, meditation, wisdom, and the arts, like music. He imparts awareness, understanding, and comprehension. He teaches through para vak, a form of divine communication, inaudible to human ears. He resides in the deep recesses of silence. The following ode is attributed to the ancient Rishis;

> *"Salutations to Sri Dakshinamurthy,*
>
> *Whose Exposition through Profound Silence is Awakening the Knowledge of the Supreme Brahman in the Hearts of His Disciples; Who is Himself Youthful ...*

Dakshinamurthy is said to have lived the life of an ascetic, calling the shade of a banyan tree in the deep forest his home. His was a life of physical and spiritual freedom, unconcerned with the affairs of the world. The people of the region claimed that just his mere touch would result in visions of God.

The poet of the king happened to be a disciple of Dakshinamurthy. One day, he arrived at court deeply absorbed in loving remembrance of his master and sang a thousand couplets in praise of him. One of his verses honored him with the term 'bharani', which is a special reference given only to the greatest warriors who had killed hordes of elephants in war. The king was offended by this because he was the only one in the kingdom who had achieved this, and was the only person who was ever referred to as 'bharani'.

The king called the poet before him and asked why he had conferred such an honor to a naked beggar living out under a banyan tree. He demanded that the poet find a way to justify such a claim or the poet would lose his head. The poet calmly admitted that he had no proof to justify such a claim, but that he was not afraid to die since Dakshinamurthy had already granted him spiritual freedom. The poet pleaded to the king that before he carried out the sentence, would he kindly visit the humble saint just once and sit in his presence. The king agreed.

The king gathered his entourage and they trekked into the forest in search of the 'naked beggar'. When they found the saint in a deep state of samadhi, the whole area hummed with an intense vibrating silence. When the king approached the saint with the thought of scolding him, he was suddenly immersed in Dakshinamurthy's powerful aura. The king's mind went blank. The saint opened his eyes and simply nodded to a spot next to him. The king sat. His entourage sat.

They sat in silence. They sat for a day. They sat for two days. After three days, the king's mind had become so purified by being in the physical presence of such a great master that he was intoxicated with compassion and joy. Eventually the king spoke and said, "I believe that my kingdom needs its king back". They had spent days without food, without water, without sleep. But they were neither hungry, thirsty, nor tired. With abundant energy and good spirits, the king got to his feet and asked his poet to accompany him back to the palace. After they returned to the palace, the king asked the poet to continue composing songs in praise of Dakshinamurthy.

__Yogi Nandinath__

Long ago, centuries before the Christian era, in the remote highlands of the Himalayas there lived a great yogi known as Maharishi Nandinath. He was one of those rare gifts from God, an illumined soul, a knower of Shiva whose inner eye was open to the mysteries of the universe. He himself had evolved out of a long line of Sat Gurus whose names and stories have been lost to the winds of time. He was one of the earliest seeds of Light which would one day come to be known as the Nath Sampradaya, or Nath Tradition.

'Natha' means lord, or master, a knower of the Self who has mastered the intricacies of his subtle bodies and levels of consciousness. Through the millennia, Nathas have been embodiments of esoteric knowledge, having attained to Siddhatva. There are many accounts of these Siddhas displaying extraordinary abilities as a result of their acquiring the transcendental powers, or 'siddhis'. Every significant yogic movement which has developed over the last two thousand years can be traced directly back to Nandinath and his disciples.

Nandinath was a 'grandfather guru', being the progenitor of many masters, a teacher of teachers. Amongst his numerous disciples were Sanaka, Sanantana, Sanatana, and Sanatkumara – all bearing the title of Nandi. Besides them were Sundernath (Tirumoolar), Shivayogamuni, Vyaghrapada, and Patanjali. All eight became a spiritual founder of one of the initial Agamic schools and were known as Nathas.

All of Nandinath's disciples, and their subsequent disciples, traveled far and wide teaching yoga, not only through the subcontinent, but as far away as China and beyond. In those times, if a master was to make a connection with sincere seekers, he had to travel. Otherwise, how was anyone to find him, especially if he was living high up in the Himalayan region?

Nandinath's yogi disciples became well-versed in the Siva Sutras, whose aphorisms were regarded as the voice of Shiva himself. These writings are an enigmatic, sophisticated set of fourteen couplets that appear on the surface to be about the Sanskrit alphabet, but on deeper reflection are actually a key to understanding the cosmos, showing how Sanskrit provides a link to the very roots of divinity. The Siva Sutras have been studied and pondered over for centuries, and are still studied today by yogis and scholars, hoping for a deeper understanding of the gross and subtle nature of the universe.

Nandinath's advanced disciples; Sundernath and Patanjali, were able to hear the transcendental sounds of Shiva's drum, but as disciples, were still unable to grasp the core meaning of the aphorisms. When they approached Nandinath for clarification, he was moved by their sincere desire for this rare knowledge, so he revealed to them the true meaning of the writing's essence.

The original Siva Sutras, and Nandinath's Kashika, are intentionally opaque. In those days, the secrets of yoga and higher consciousness were thought to be too precious to be openly expounded. Therefore, they were concealed in a cryptic language so that only those spiritually qualified would be able to access while others would remain confounded. While this method may produce some frustration with today's students of yoga, it gives us a glimpse into the hearts and minds of the ancient progenitors of yoga; the Himalayan masters.

Patanjali

Patanjali was one of Nandinath's most advanced disciples. He is the author of the 'Yoga Sutras', an important component of the Shastras, the six distinct schools of Indian philosophy. While some would like to credit Patanjali as being the creator of yoga, this is not the case, as yoga had been practiced for thousands of years prior to his birth. There are references to yoga in the Vedas, the Upanishads, the Mahabharata and also the Gita. Shiva is considered by many to have been the first yogi, or 'Adiyogi', who transmitted yoga to the Saptarishis many thousands of years ago.

In the Mahabharata, Krishna states that the sun god, Hiranyagarbha, was the original 'knower of yoga'. (The Sanskrit terms Hiranyagarbha and Vivasvan are both found in Hindu literature, used interchangeably to refer to the sun god. Shiva is also associated with the sun in certain Hindu writings.) In the Gita, Krishna states:

> *"The Blessed Lord said: I instructed this imperishable science of yoga to the sun-god, Vivasvan, and Vivasvan instructed it to Manu, the father of mankind, and Manu in turn instructed it to Iksvaku."*

What Patanjali did was to transmit the philosophy of yoga, and the fundamental principles of the practice of yoga, to the world, for all time, in writing. Prior to Patanjali, this had never been done. Patanjali was a realized master, a Siddha, who was also a consummate scholar and master of Sanskrit, a rare combination. His knowledge of human consciousness was complete and his knowledge of the intricacies of yoga was complete. His contribution to yoga and to the spiritual evolution of humanity cannot be overstated. While yoga had existed prior to Patanjali, one could rightly state that he is the progenitor of all of the world's modern systems of yoga.

Patanjali loved music, was an accomplished musician and singer, and composed many ragas. His favorite instrument was the vina. As a young man, he once got into a friendly debate with Vyaghrapada, one of his fellow disciples, over musical composition. Vyaghrapada insisted that under certain restrictions, no one could compose a cohesive, tonal piece of music. Vyaghrapada was right, that these limitations seemed insurmountable, but Patanjali managed to compose an extraordinary raga within the limitations anyway. Such was his great intellect and artistic proficiency.

'Sutra' means thread, a thread that leads us somewhere. It is like a formula or a solution to an equation. The Yoga Sutras are a formula for self-realization. They are brilliantly conceived and written and are one of the most coherent and literary components to be found in ancient Hindu literature. They are a document about life and about us, a formula to open up our inner life and reveal our higher selves.

Patanjali begins his foundational work with a chapter containing only three words.

"And Now Yoga".

He is saying to us, "All right, you have established yourself in the world, your family is provided for, your obligations have been met…now yoga. It is time to fulfill the highest purpose of your human birth."

Patanjali's work is more a complex, but practical set of tools than it is a step-by-step set of guidelines of practice. In fact, he does not expound any comprehensive system of practice. He lets future yogis and teachers of yoga devise their own unique approach. This is just one of his many masterful contributions to future generations of yogis. He does, however, establish a set of benchmarks; a foundational basis upon which yoga can be built. He calls his foundation, 'Ashtanga', or 'eight limbs', the eight universal elements that make up the practice of yoga; all yoga.

Patanjali defines yoga as 'Chitta Vritti Nirodha', meaning the removal of the continual oscillations in the chit, or mind-stuff, leading to ascension over duality and mergence with the Over-self. Therefore, stilling the mind is the direct pathway to self-realization and God-realization. He who conquers the mind, conquers everything. Yoga utilizes meditative and yogic disciplines, or sadhanas, to attain a state of consciousness, free of rambling thought where one's consciousness is distinct of any object or thought external to itself, and becomes aware only of its own pure essence.

<u>The Yoga Sutras</u>

The Yoga Sutras are a collection of 196 sutras (aphorisms) on the theory and practice of yoga. The work is divided into four chapters, or books.

1. <u>Samadhi Pada (51 sutras)</u> – This book gives an introduction to yoga and the nature of its ultimate goal, the attainment of Samadhi. He describes various forms

of Samadhi and defines it as the state of perception where the yogi's self-identity is transmuted into a state of union with the object meditated upon, where the witness, the process of witnessing, and that which is being witnessed becomes one.

2. <u>Sadhana Pada (55 sutras)</u> – He defines sadhana as practice or discipline. Then he outlines two primary forms of yoga, Ashtanga and Kriya. He writes that Kriya is the practice of three of the 'Niyamas' of Ashtanga: austerity, self-discovery, and devotion to God. He then explains the eight components of Ashtanga: (1) Yama, (2) Niyama, (3) Asana, (4) Pranayama, (5) Pratyahara, (6) Dharana, (7) Dhyana, and (8) Samadhi.

3. <u>Vibhuti Pada (56 sutras)</u> – Vibhuti means power or manifestation. In this book, he describes the transcendental powers, or 'siddhis', which can be acquired as an outcome of the practice of yoga. The combined, adept practice of dharana, dhyana, and samadhi can lead to these abilities. He warns that these abilities can easily become an impediment in a yogi's quest for complete spiritual liberation.

4. <u>Kaivalya Pada (34 sutras)</u> – This book describes the process of spiritual liberation and the nature of the realized self.

<u>Ashtanga Yoga</u>

Patanjali's classical system is comprised of eight essential components.

1. <u>Yamas</u> – Yamas are moral imperatives, especially involving the eradication of negative tendencies, and their subsequent replacement with virtues. The five yamas listed by Patanjali are:

    o Ahimsa – non-violence and non-injury to all living beings

o Satya – truthfulness

o Asteya – non-stealing

o Brahmacharya – chastity, including marital fidelity and self-restraint

o Aparigraha – non-greediness, non-possessiveness

2. <u>Niyama</u> – This component includes the cultivation of virtuous habits, behaviors, and observances. The niyamas listed by Patanjali are:

o Shaucha – purity, clearness of mind, speech, and body

o Santosha – contentment, acceptance of others, acceptance of one's circumstances, personal optimism

o Tapas – persistence, perseverance, and austerity

o Svadhyaya – study of scriptures, self-introspection of one's thoughts, words, and actions

o Ishvarapranidhana – contemplation of God

3. <u>Asana</u> – Patanjali discusses the yogi's asana or posture. He describes it as a posture that one can hold for a period of time, while staying relaxed, steady, comfortable and motionless. This combination will lead to the body being still and not quivering. In the Yoga Sutras, he does not recommend any particular asana over another. But in another of Patanjali's writings, the 'Bhasya', a commentary on his Sutras which was most likely written some time later, he suggests twelve seated meditation postures.

o Padmasana (lotus)

o Virasana (hero)

o Bhadrasana (glorious)

o Svastikasana (lucky mark)

o Dandasana (staff)

o Sopasrayasana (supported)
o Paryankasana (bedstead)
o Krauncha-nishadasana (seated heron)
o Hastanishadasana (seated elephant)
o Ushtranishadasana (seated camel)
o Samasansthanasana (evenly balanced)
o Sthirasukhasana (any pleasurable, motionless posture)

Each of the above postures is essentially an adaptation of the 'Lotus posture', sitting cross-legged on the floor or on a platform.

4. <u>Pranayama</u> – Pranayama consists of two Sanskrit words, prana (breath), and ayama (restraining, extending, stretching). Once the desired posture has been achieved, he prescribes the conscious regulation of the breath. He says that this may be done in several ways; inhaling and then suspending exhalation for a period, exhaling and then suspending inhalation for a period, slowing the inhalation and exhalation, and consciously altering the time/length of the breath (deep or short). Pranas are classified into five important categories according to the nature of their functions:

   a. Prana is concerned with the respiratory system.
   b. Apana helps the excretory system.
   c. Samana aids the digestive organs.
   d. Udana is connected with swallowing.
   e. Vyana helps in maintaining the circulatory system throughout the body.

5. <u>Pratyahara</u> – Pratyahara is the combination of two Sanskrit words; prati (against) and ahara (bring or fetch). This is the process of withdrawing the sensory currents from the outside world and all external distractions. It is not just closing one's eyes to the

world outside the body. It is closing the 'mind' to the sensory world outside. It is the process of re-directing one's attention from the magnetic pull from the external world to the inner world of consciousness. Pratyahara marks the transition point in Ashtanga from the outer to the inner.

6. Dharana – In Sanskrit, dharana means concentration, introspective focus, and single-mindedness. It consists of holding the mind's attention at a particular point. This point may be the repetition of a mantra or it could be some outside object, like a statue or a physical place. It could also be a feature of the body, such as the breath, a thought, or a chakra. Fixation of the mind means not wavering from one point of concentration to another.

7. Dhyana – Once Dharana has been established, Dhyana is the ensuing, ongoing stream of experience with the attention fixed, moving forward in time. It is contemplation. It is meditation. Whatever the mind has been fixed on in Dharana, Dhyana is its contemplation. Rightly practiced, it is the focused, uninterrupted train of thought, perception, and flow of awareness.

8. Samadhi – In Sanskrit, samadhi means joining, combining with, union, and a harmonious whole. Samadhi is the achievement of oneness with the object of Dhyana. When fully achieved, there is no distinction between the contemplator and the contemplated. In Samadhi, the consciousness of the yogi loses its identity of individuality. The yogi and his object of contemplation become amalgamated.

<u>Yogi Sundernath (Tirumoolar)</u>

Like his fellow disciple Patanjali, Sundernath became renowned for the wealth of writing he left humanity in the form of hymns; in particular, his collection of over 3000 hymns known as the "Tirumantiram". These writings are a part of the bedrock of Saiva Siddhanta and are considered second in importance only to the Vedas, the Upanishads, and the Agamas. They constitute the most complete and most profound exposition of the esoteric wisdom of Saiva Siddhanta ever written.

Sundernath was born in the Himalayan highlands and became a disciple of Nandinath. 'Sunder' means beautiful, and 'Nath' means divine lord. He devoted himself to his sadhanas and became an advanced yogi, a Siddha, at a young age. As a young man, he enjoyed exploring the solitudes that are to be found in the remote Himalayan wilds. He developed the habit of performing his tapas in a cave near the Badrinath Temple. Anyone who visited him there would experience the powerful vibration of his spiritual radiation.

On one occasion, some young mischief-makers decided to visit the famous yogi in his cave. When they arrived, they found him in deep samadhi. They had never seen anyone in samadhi, so they decided to test Sundernath, to see if he was truly out of his body. They retrieved a burning ember out of the fire and placed it on the yogi's thigh. The coal burned deeply into his skin.

When Sundernath returned to his physical body, he saw what the boys had done. But rather than scold them, he thanked them for allowing him to demonstrate to them, and to himself, his deep absorption in samadhi. After that day, he felt confident that nothing would ever dissuade him from his spiritual quest.

When Nandinath could see that his advanced disciple was fully prepared, he sent him off on his own mission, to teach yoga and establish his own spiritual legacy. He instructed

Sundernath to travel to the south of India, where he was to revive the age-old study and practice of yoga.

His travels took him to Vindhya and Kalahasti. Later, he passed through Tiruvilankadu and Kanchipuram. Then he trekked to Chidambaram, where he stayed for a time. Leaving the little village, he crossed the Kaveri River and reached Tiruvavaduthurai. He was drawn to the area and felt that perhaps he had reached his ultimate destination.

One day, while walking along the banks of the Kaveri, he came upon a herd of cows who were bellowing loudly. He could sense anguish in their cries so he approached them to see what had caused them to make such a clamor. When he neared them, he discovered the dead body of their cowherd in their midst. Sundernath felt compassion for these poor creatures, who were clearly mourning over the loss of their herder, whose name was Mular. He was also concerned for the fate of these poor beasts, who if left out in the open at night, risked attack by wild animals. He devised a plan to remedy the situation.

He searched the area for a place to hide his physical body and found a hollow log. He crawled inside, went into samadhi, and left his body. Then, with his astral body, he returned to the herder and entered his dead body. To the delight of the cows, the herder's body suddenly came back to life. The cows were literally crying tears of joy and began licking the body of Mular. The cows went back to grazing, to the delight and satisfaction of Mular (Sundernath). As evening began to set in, he led the cows back to the village.

Back at Mular's gate, his wife was waiting. She immediately noticed his changed personality and behavior. She reported to her friends and neighbors that her husband was acting strangely. He was not his old self. The villagers came and spoke with Mular. They agreed that he had changed, but it appeared that he had changed for the better. He seemed very spiritual, very wise. They decided to give him a new name, "Tirumoolar", meaning 'holy' Mular.

As soon as he had the chance, Mular returned to the hollow log, but his Sundernath body was gone. It had disappeared!   He searched for days and days, looking everywhere. Finally, he stopped looking and returned to the log. He sat against it and went into samadhi. Nandinath appeared to him in his radiant form and explained to him that now he had a body that was recognized by the local people and while in it, he could speak the local language, Tamil, fluently. This was Shiva's way of facilitating his ability to engage with the local people and begin to teach them. From that day, Sundernath became Tirumoolar and he began his important spiritual work.

Tirumoolar continued with his habit of spending long periods in samadhi. When he returned to his body, he would compose the hymns which would one day be compiled into the "Tirumantiram", his epic work. Within this collection of work, he writes about Ashtanga yoga in numerous places. This body of sacred writings would become the most extensive texts written by the early masters of the Nandiantha Sampradaya (tradition).

Tirumoolar clarified the principals of Ashtanga Yoga and helped erase many of the ideological divisions that had emerged in South India, prior to his arrival. He helped create a more integrated culture in the area and an era of peaceful co-existence. Tirumoolar had seven principal disciples, including his successor, Kalanginath. And from Kalanginath, would spawn the great world teacher, Bhogarnath.

The Tirumantiram

The Tirumantiram has been referred to as a book of Tantra, Mantra, Yantra, and Yoga, a book combining philosophy, prayer, and meditation. Tirumoolar's original title for the book was 'Mantra Malai', which means 'garland of mantras'. The book is a collection of nine 'Tantras', or categories of knowledge. Within these Tantras, he speaks of special mantras for particular applications and expounds extensively on the meaning of the Primal Mantra, Aum, including various ways of intoning it. Literally, 'mantra' is composed of two syllables; Man, or 'mind', and Tra, or 'opening, liberation'. Thus, Mantra is a device for liberating or opening the mind or heart.

The Tirumantiram expounds on the ancient teachings, including the Vedas, and proclaims the oneness of Godhead, and the means to it, being man's mergence with Shiva, the individual Soul in the Oversoul. Each of the nine tantras is devoted to a different aspect of Spirituality. He discusses the acquisition of knowledge, the bliss of true, inner knowledge, the state of cosmic liberation, and the Samadhi of Silence. He also mentions the inner light and sound and meeting the Guru Dev within. His writings include mention of the Ashtanga system, taught to him by his guru, Nandinath, and provide evidence of Tirumoolar's high level of attainment.

During the master's time, there was no paper and pen so writing was accomplished with a stylus. The characters were scratched into a specially-prepared leaf, called an Ola leaf. Many ancient writings were produced in this manner, and amazingly, some ancient writings produced in this way still exist today. The original text was written in a rhyming, metered, lyrical style, cloaked in a mystical code, coaxing the reader to explore the depth of knowledge inherent in the verses. It is based in the science of yoga, showing and explaining how yoga leads to man's knowledge of his true self.

> *The Guru:*
> *"Entangled in the senses,*
> *Consciousness aimlessly drifts,*
> *rudderless.*
> *'Come hither, into the depths',*
> *The guru beckons. He points the way."*

"Guru is none but Shiva,
Shiva they see, but see not.
Guru is your Shiva and guide,
Through him is knowledge beyond speech
and thought."

<u>Siddhas</u>:
"Realized Yogis ascend beyond the
wheel.
With enchanted breath, find perpetual
harmony.
All conscious, yet in the world,
In the body, yet knowing death in life.
The outer and inner become one,
As nectar flows from its source.
Shiva light begets the light of Siddhas,
Their splendor graces my vision."

"The Siddhas testify to the Shiva world,
Knowers of Nada and Nadanta (sound
current),
Established in bliss, pure and eternal,
Have tread the pathway to liberation.
Ascending the celestial steps to freedom,
They reached the ineffable realm of bliss.
Having known Shiva,
Realized, they stay on."

<u>Mortality of Man Body</u>
"With horse and sword and canopy
outspread,

Man fills his futile years with pride of life.
But as the grand cavalcade passes, left and right,
The breath of life expires in all.
Now, the ravens pick at his body,
Now, scorned by the living left behind.
This old bag of leather, now deflated,
Yama blows his conch, and smiles."

"The lamp remains but the flame is out.
Fools, wailing in grief, prolong their debt,
Failing to see night following day.
Immersed in maya, they fall and wail,
Ever sobbing more and more."

Worldly Wealth

"The radiant moon turns to darkness,
The riches of the world find the same fate.
Seek the gold of heaven's King,
And the Lord's bounty will pour from the clouds."

"Foolish those who claim their wealth their own,
Close at hand, yet fleeting as their shadow.
As their very life is but a temporary wayfarer,
They see not its luster, nor its source."

*"The joys of wealth and family, life's
cherished gifts,
Yet fragile and fleeting they be.
The yogi who seeks his treasures within,
Finds Shiva's fortune, and abundant
company."*

Value of Youth
*"The visiting sun counts our days,
Will we ascend to Light,
Or fall in Karma's grip?
Our fate is sealed in our youth."*

Diet
*"Eaters of the flesh of beasts,
Are bound by death's chains.*

*They find the jaws of hell,
Consumed forever."*

Mystic Journey
*"Like ghee, hiding in the milk,
Shiva speaks out of pure silent thought.
Those listeners, fortunate few,
Shed the mortal raiment in blinding
light."*

*"As the sky's torrent rushes down from
the heights,
So does the divine stream flood my being,
Pure, vibrant, crystalline,
It flows boundless from my Master."*

<u>*Ashtanga Yoga*</u>
"Waver not in your quest,
But follow the eight-limbed Yoga.
Those who tread this path
Shall reach the highest,
Shall know Samadhi,
And not suffer rebirth."

"Purity, compassion, frugal food and patience
Forthrightness, truth and steadfastness –
These he ardently cherishes;
Killing, stealing and lusting, He abhors –
The yogi who observes Niyamas,
Stands atop the mountain."

"The Yogi rules the body, battles the senses,
His warrior's steed at the ready.
The steed will carry an adept to the goal,
But throw the frail one off to the side.
The steed is the mastery of dharana."
"Within the undistracted gaze is light.
Gaze on it, mingle, and become one.
The heavenly stream will snatch you,
And pull you up to the infinite void,
Where the Uncreated Being is witnessed."

<u>*Samadhi*</u>
"There is a way to the Lord's realm.

*The Celestial Beings searched, but could
not find.
Trek the mystic path to the mountain's
summit,
For there, the ambrosia flows.
The transcendent reward of Samadhi,
Will take you there."*

*"Earth's Light-bearing visitors, the
Siddhas,
They come and go and come again.
In the world, yet reposed in silent
equipoise.
How can we know? How can we
describe?
Shiva hides. Those who seek in Samadhi,
Indeed, will find him."*

<u>Yogi Kalanginath</u>

Kalanginath was one of Tirumoolar's leading disciples, and he is generally believed to be his 'successor'. He was born in Benares, traveled extensively, and lived in various places throughout his life. In South India, he was known as 'Kanjamalai Siddhar'. Kalanginath is revered by both the Nath tradition of Northern India, and the Siddha tradition of Southern India. During his earlier years, he spent most of his time with his guru, Tirumoolar, traveling throughout the South.

Kalanginath's most important contribution to the world was probably his mentoring of his dearest disciple, Bhogar. In Bhogarnath's writings, he refers to Kalanginath as 'father', showing the closeness of their relationship. They had an ideal guru/disciple exchange, one that fully prepared Bhogar for his important life's work that lay ahead of him.

Kalanginath traveled to China and began teaching yoga to the people there. After a time, he sent a message on the inner planes to his beloved disciple, Bhogar, asking him to join him in his work. Bhogar answered his master's call and traveled to China, where he would spend most of the remainder of his life.

Yogi Bhogarnath

Bhogarnath was a Tamil Siddha, who received initiation from his guru, Kalanginath. He was from a caste of goldsmiths and gained an interest in metallurgy at a young age. He also learned the principals of Siddha medicine from Kalanginath, who had become a proficient herbal healer.

After spending many years together with his young disciple in the South, Kalanginath traveled north to China to spread the knowledge of yoga and traditional Siddha medicine, leaving his dear disciple behind. The separation between guru and disciple was a difficult one for both, for the two had developed a very close relationship, having spent nearly all of their time together for so long. Eventually, the pangs of separation for both became too much to bear. Kalanginath wanted his gifted disciple at his side, to help with the work in China. He transmitted a psychic message to Bhogar, who settled his affairs and began the journey to China by sea route. He located his master in the ancient Lu province, north of the Yangtze River.

Bhogarnath adopted the name 'Bo-Yang', which was derived from "Bhogam", meaning bliss. Master and disciple worked side-by-side, traveling up and down the rivers by boat, and on pathways from village to village, teaching and collecting disciples as they went. Eventually, the time came for Kalanginath to return to Northern India, to his roots. He asked Bhogar to stay on in China to complete the important work they had begun together.

Bhogar experimented with many different herbal formulae for various healing purposes, but his most potent remedy was one for prolonging human life. The formula utilized a total of thirty-five different herbs. He called his medicine, 'kaya kalpa'. After grinding the plants into powders, and preparing them according to a careful process, he pounded them into small tablets. Bhogar describes his special formula in one of his songs.

One day, Bhogar called for his three favorite disciples and his faithful dog, and led them to a nearby mountaintop. He offered a kaya kalpa tablet to the dog. The dog keeled over dead. He then offered his leading disciple, Yu, a tablet. Yu fell over dead. He then offered tablets to his two remaining disciples. They took the tablets, but terrified by what they had seen, they hid them. Then Bhogarnath consumed the remaining tablets and he keeled over. In a state of panic and grief, the two disciples hurried down the mountain to find help to haul the dead bodies down for burial.

When they returned, the bodies were nowhere to be found. They searched, but all they found was a note written by Bhogarnath.

Bhogarnath was a prolific writer. His largest body of work is the "Bhogar Sapta Kandam", a collection of over 7000 hymns. Today the collection is known simply as, "Bhogar's 7000". It is believed that he wrote most of these in the Himalayan highlands near Mt. Kailash.

But Bhogar may be remembered for a much shorter collection of writings; the "Tao Te Ching". The yogis of the Nath Sampradaya claim that when Bhogar was in China, he adopted the name Lao Tzu, and is in fact the author of the Tao Te Ching. The Tao Te Ching has stood the test of time, being cherished by Taoists and Buddhists, and is regarded by religious scholars throughout the world as one of humanity's most important philosophical writings.

Some modern scholars have questioned the link between Bhogarnath and Lao Tzu. However, on close inspection, the possibility that they may have been one in the same person is intriguing.

The Naths argue that the author of the Tao Te Ching writes in one of the chapters that 'Lao Tzu' was not his real name, which is true. A careful examination of the underlying ideas presented in the Tao Te Ching reveals that all of its basic philosophical principles and concepts appear to derive from Vedantic philosophy, or Ashtanga Yoga.

Lao Tzu wrote the Tao Te Ching in the language of the time, Archaic Chinese. The book was written in a lyrical style, using images and metaphors which were commonly understood by the people in China at the time he wrote it. While Lao Tzu doesn't use Indian or Vedantic terms or references, his ideas are all compatible with Hindu philosophy, including yoga.

He writes extensively on the concept of duality. He refers to the body's ten doors and discusses ahimsa. Using his own terminology and imagery, he refers to all of the components of Ashtanga Yoga. He speaks to the importance of yamas and niyamas. While not mentioning the term asana specifically, he talks about the need to be in a still position. He describes fixing the attention and contemplation; dharana and dhyana. He references the process of withdrawing the senses to an inner focal point; pratyahara. He writes extensively about

Samadhi (the return to the 'Always So'), and the way to go about attaining it.

Lao Tzu addresses many aspects of mysticism and the spiritual life, including spiritual seeing (ajna chakra) and hearing (shabd yoga), the importance of stillness and contemplation (dhyana and dharana), cause and effect (karma), duality, the role of the master, and returning to the source of all life.

Chuang Tzu, a Chinese philosopher who followed in Lao Tzu's footsteps a couple of generations later, comments extensively on Lao Tzu's work. He describes Taoist yoga, which appears to be identical to Indian yoga. Chuang Tzu describes the need to travel back through successive layers of consciousness to the state of pure consciousness. He also describes pratyahara, dhyana, and dharana, and the need to sit like a 'corpse'; meaning silent and motionless.

He goes into great lengths describing the practice of pranayama, both theoretically and practically. He describes Chinese yogis doing various breathing exercises, and the state of consciousness which resulted, comparing it to a trance in which some kind of profound metamorphosis had taken place. One yogi he observed replied, "You have put it very well. When you observed me just now, my 'I' had lost its 'me'." Chuang Tzu goes on to describe, 'sitting with a blank mind…slackening the limbs and frame, blotting out the senses of hearing and sight, clearing the mind of outside forms and impressions, and being absorbed into That which Pervades Everything'.

Chuang Tzu writes,

> *"The breathing of the sage is not like that of ordinary men. The sage breathes with every part of himself, right down to his heels. He keeps the great treasure of his life breath in perpetual renewal. He renews with his 'clarified breath', and eliminates his*

contaminated or evil breath. The breathing of the sage (in Samadhi) becomes like that of an infant, or a child in the womb...He who has mastered this breath control becomes immune to epidemics, can charm snakes and tigers, can stop wounds from bleeding, can stay under water or walk on its surface, can endure hunger and thirst, and prolong his lifespan. The beginner draws in a breath through his nose, holds it while he counts mentally up to one hundred twenty, and then expels the breath through his mouth...The counting should gradually increase up to a thousand, at which point the yogi will find himself growing daily younger, instead of older".

Where did this Chinese (Taoist) yoga come from? It almost had to come from an Indian yogi. Did Bhogarnath introduce the Chinese to yoga?

After many years, Bhogarnath, accompanied by his lead disciple Yu, returned to India by land route. He would ultimately spend much of his remaining time on this earth in Sri Lanka. One of his shorter writings, "Initiation into Samadhi", includes the following verses;

"The guru manifests as Truth;
It dispels all darkness.
In the elemental are spaces of vital energy,
The Divine illuminates the darkness.
In these spaces are found the Siddhis
The hub of metamorphosis.
Only Samadhi's Light remains."

"The box is locked, you have the key,
Pry the lid and stir

Bhogarnath's leading disciples were Pulipani and Sattaimuni. He ultimately turned over most of his work on the kala kalpa and healing to Pulipani, but the spiritual work he entrusted to Sattaimuni.

Yogi Sattaimuni

Sattaimuni is a renowned Siddha who was born in Sir Lanka, and lived most of his life in the Southern India Tamil-speaking regions. He was born into a family of poor farm workers but he didn't take to farming. He spent most of his time as a mendicant, outside one of the local temples. He was attracted more to the temple itself, and the activities going on there, than he was to his begging. But the begging gave him a reason to be there.

One day, he encountered an extraordinary sage who was visiting the temple. The sage glowed with the radiance of his spiritual eminence. All of Sattaimuni's attention was riveted on this sage. When the sage left the temple, Sattaimuni followed. As they walked together, he questioned the sage about spiritual matters and was astounded by the man's wisdom. He realized that he had met a very great soul indeed, and continued on with him from that day. The sage's name was Bhogarnath.

During the time he spent with Bhogar, he also had the good fortune of meeting other great spiritual luminaries.

Bhogar mentored him in the Siddha medical arts, especially regarding longevity and rejuvenation. He also became expert in chemistry and anthropology.

In those days, the most important writings, especially esoteric writings, were written in a type of code, which was called 'Sandhya Bhasha'. This code was understood only by the Siddha intellectuals. It was believed that this higher knowledge should remain amongst the elite, and not get into the hands of ordinary people. But Sattaimuni disregarded this approach, believing that knowledge was for everyone and that it should be shared freely. This viewpoint most likely originated from his own humble upbringings.

Sattaimuni's literary contributions include numerous writings on anthropology, medicine and chemistry. His approach to his writing was to always attempt to tie in the subject matter with the quest for the divine. From one of his medical sutras, he writes;

> *"Man is said to be the Microcosm and the Universe is said to be the Macrocosm; because the elements in the universe exist in man too; or in other words, there is nothing in the macrocosm of nature that is not present in man. So, man must be looked upon as an integral part of universal nature and not as anything separate or different from it. This closely follows the Siddhar doctrine. When there is abnormality in the nature of these elements in humans, diseases are caused. Similarly, in nature, when there is a disturbance in the elements, disasters like earthquakes, storms, lightening, and torrential rainfalls resulting in floods are caused."*

Regarding the quest for self-realization, he composed the following verse;

"By ascending above the five lower chakras to the sixth,
With silence and support,
And with the 'Mantra of the Beloved as the Essence',
Like a thread out of hand,
You too will cross time, birth, and death."

Nath Tradition (Sampradaya)

The Nath Tradition first became recognized as an organized body of yogis around the beginning of the seventeenth century. Their origins are primarily tied to the Himalayan regions of Northern India and Tibet. But these yogis traveled far and wide. Their missions took them throughout all of Southern Asia and as far north as China. Most modern historians trace their direct lineage of gurus to a much earlier time, around the ninth century, with the appearances of Gorakshnath and Machendranath. However, the tradition of great yogis which we know of today as the Naths can truly be traced all the way back to Nandinath and his disciples, Sundernath and Patanjali.

The Nath Sampradaya today comprises an order of renunciate ascetics and an order of householders. Gorakshnath and Machendranath are considered to be the original founders of the ascetic branch. The householder branch originally evolved out of Nath ascetics who were unable to keep their vows of celibacy. Today, the householder branch is comprised of a large group of Naths who live throughout India and Nepal.

The name 'Nath' was originally a surname, or a suffix attached to one's name, which denoted their adherence to yogic practices and disciplines. Its definition is 'lord'. Not all the yogis and masters in the long Nath tradition used the term as part of their name. The use of 'Nath' to identify a group of yogis is fairly recent, historically. Prior to the eighteenth century, they were simply known as 'yogis.

<u>**The Nav Nath Saints**</u>

According to the Mahabharata, the Nath mission was originally established by Lord Krishna when he called a meeting of the celestial beings and announced to them how he would go about spreading his message throughout the world during the coming age. Krishna said that he would spread his own light through the missions of nine saints, and their subsequent eighty-four disciples. These saints would travel far and wide throughout the known world to spread the message of love, and to facilitate the unification of individual souls with God. He added that, only the souls of the most-worthy could be helped.

The appearance of these nine saints begins with Gorakshnath and Machendranath. These nine masters were Siddhas, with very high levels of spiritual attainment, resulting from their mastery of pranayama, leading to mastery of Dharana Nada. Today, these nine saints are associated with various groups, including Hindu, Shaivist, Buddhist, Nath, and even Sufi. However, while they were alive, working in the world, they did not see themselves as being associated with any group or sect outside of their own master, their spiritual brothers, and their disciples. They were not the monopoly of any sect. They were spiritual emissaries who had been commissioned by God to elevate the consciousness of humanity through the practice of yoga.

While it is not always possible to pinpoint specific historic details concerning the lives of these great Siddhas, we do have many stories about them which have been passed down from generation to generation through oral traditions. Written accounts are more scarce. One reason for this is that great masters normally don't like to draw attention to themselves. They are, at heart, humble beings who are focused on the work of helping and uplifting humanity. They themselves, in their youths, had undergone the process of renouncing the world, in favor of a life of renunciation. They had passed out of their early lives and been 'reborn' (initiated) into their new lives as yogis, becoming totally immersed in their sadhanas and service to the guru.

The names of the masters who are the Nav Nath Saints are:

1. Machendranath
2. Gorakshnath
3. Jalandharnath
4. Kanipanath
5. Gahininath
6. Charpatnath
7. Bhartairinath
8. Revananath
9. Nageshnath

Yogi Machendranath

"Praise to the venerable guru, the embodiment of the supreme bliss, who grants the experience of Eternal Self, by association with, the body becomes transcendent, and mind becomes purified."

"To that yogi who being steadily fixed inside on his soul's light, through yoga, sing praises to him. And sing praises to the True Principle, the cause of time and the ages.

To that holy Mina Natha, the great ocean of knowledge and joy, beyond existence and non-existence, where Adinath himself has merged in continuous Samadhi, worship continuously."

Machendranath

There are many stories associated with this great Siddha, originating in India, Nepal, and Tibet, which describe his transcendental abilities (siddhis). He is often associated with Shiva in the Nath Tradition and with Avalokitesvara in Buddhism. One of these siddhis allowed him to live in his own body, while entering the bodies of other people, and remain there for prolonged periods, even permanently.

Machendranath's origins appear to begin in Bengal, Assam, and Nepal, but his travels took him as far as Mangalore of Karnataka. He was born in eastern India and was a fisherman by caste. His name means 'born of fishes'. The famous exponent of Kashmiri Shivaism, Abhinava Gupta, has mentioned Machendranath in his writings. Since Gupta's work was composed at the end of the tenth century C.E., we can assume that Machendranath most like lived in the tenth century. He and Gorakshnath were contemporaries, with Gorakshnath most likely being his disciple.

Most of the stories associated with Machendranath are allegorical in nature, written with some instructive, underlying purpose. The most famous one has him being consumed into the belly of a giant fish, after preparing his net with a large bait. He remained inside the fish for twelve years. The only thing that he could do in this situation was apply himself to his sadhanas. Ultimately, another fisherman caught the fish and dragged it to his home. It was so heavy, the fisherman thought, "perhaps it has something valuable inside". He cut the fish open and was stunned to find Machendranath inside, glowing radiantly from his long period of meditation.

Yogi Gorakshnath

Guru Gorakshnath is one of history's most revered masters. His praises were sung by the likes of the famous mystical poet Kabir, and in the hymns of Guru Nanak. He has been immortalized in the Puranas, and in numerous stories, mystic tales, and legends. The Naths refer to him as Siva Goraksha. Others have referred to him as Mahayogi, Mahaguru, Adinath, Siddha Yogiraj, and so on. Gorakshnath is viewed as the progenitor of the Nath tradition. Even today, there is still a large following of his devotees to be found at Ahmednagar in Maharashtra. There are numerous caves throughout India where he is thought to have meditated, some of which now have shrines atop them.

Historical accounts imply that he was originally influenced by Buddhism, along with his master, Machendranath, but ultimately took to Sivaism and yoga and the Advaita Vedanta interpretation of the Upanishads. He thought that dualist and non-dualist philosophies were both impractical. He believed instead that self-realization was the conscious choice of the yogi; that it was a practical path of self-discipline, leading ultimately to a state of Samadhi and Universal Consciousness.

He traveled widely throughout the Indian subcontinent, with records showing him in Nepal, Punjab, Sindh, Uttar Pradesh, Uttarakhand, Bengal, Karnataka, and as far south as Sri Lanka. While the Nath tradition had existed for centuries prior to Gorakshnath, it was under his leadership and guidance that it grew and expanded widely during his lifetime. Many consider him to be greatest of all the Nav Nath Saints.

> *"The nine Naths and 84 Siddhas are all human forms, created as yogic manifestations to spread the message of yoga and meditation to the world. It is they who will reveal samadhi to mankind".*

He was a prolific writer, the author of numerous books on yoga, including; "Goraksha Samhita", "Goraksha Gita", and "Yoga Chintamani". He is considered to be the developer of Hatha Yoga as we know it today, which his book, "Siddha Siddhanta Paddhati", is devoted to. He describes the state of the liberated yogi, and explains that the yogi sees himself in all human beings and all beings within himself, with Atman existing within Brahman, and Brahman existing within Atman.

> *"The four castes are integrated in the human form; i.e., Brahmana in sadachar (righteous conduct), Ksatriya in Saurya (valor and*

Goraksh literally means, 'one who has mastered his five senses'. He taught that God existed within us, through the five elements, and that these elements transmute into divine energy through proper conduct and meditation. His teachings are timeless for the aspiring yogi, as relevant today as they were when he was alive.

"The ajna chakra is also called uddiyana and the jinna-lotus. It is situated between, and just behind the two eyebrows, and consists of two white petals. The ajna is the seat of buddhi, pure mind, and has command over all sensory and motor functions in their subtle state. Here sits Paramasiva."

The Goraksh Bani

"Speak not in haste, without understanding. Walk not in haste, without knowing the path. Take slow, cautious steps. Let not pride overtake you and lead a simple life, says Gorakshnath."

"Gorakshnath says, one who remains steadfast in observing his sadhana, who is true to his spiritual practices, who maintains strict eating and sleeping habits, under strict yogic disciplines, will neither grow old nor die."

"He who chants the name of God in meditation vocally or mentally (japa – ajapa), controls the five senses, and he who burns his body in dhyana brahmagni, finds Mahadeva."

"The mind is the abode of both good and evil. One has the choice to allow the good to prevail, or to allow lower instincts to inhabit. The mind becomes pure and pious when the good is allowed to prosper. If it contemplates evil thoughts, it will become impure and impious. Yogamarga is the means by which mind can be trained to promote and sustain good instincts and tendencies."

"O Yogi die; die to the world. Such a death is sweet. Die in the manner of Goraksh who

'died' (to the world) and then saw the Invisible."

<u>Yogi Jalandharnath</u>

Jalandharnath was a mahasiddha yogi, who some say was a direct disciple of Shiva. He is revered by a number of traditions, including Tibetan Buddhism, and the Shaiva Nath tradition, and is known by various names. He was the author of several books, including "Suddhivajra Pradip", and "Hevajra-Sadhana". He was an ardent practitioner of pranayam, and through its mastery, developed various siddhis.

According to Tibetan tradition, he was born is a small village named Nagarghog into a Brahmin family. From a young age, he became disinterested in the affairs of the world. Rather than getting involved with a worldly duty, he preferred to trek through the mountain trails, contemplating the non-permanence of life. One day he had a vision of a Dakini, who instructed him that he must be vigilant with his mode of living and thinking and remain pure and clean. The spirit gave him initial instructions in yoga and directed him to travel south, where she would guide him to a great master.

He traveled to Bengal where he met Gorakshnath and received initiation instructions into the practice of yoga. One of Gorakshnath's disciples was Queen Mayanamati, mother of the ruler of Bengal. The master asked the queen to please have her son, Raja Gopicandra, become initiated and accept Jalandharnath as his guru. When the queen mother proposed the idea to her son, he resisted. So Gorakshnath put the queen mother through some very difficult tests. But by chanting her guru's name, "Siva Goraksha", she was able to pass through each one. Raja Gopicandra was so impressed by this that he renounced his throne and became a disciple of Jalandharnath.

<u>Raja Bhartarinath</u>

King Bhartarinath was one of the most educated people of his time and authored numerous writings. Three of his books have become standards of ancient Indian literature. "Vairagya Sataka" is a hundred verses on renunciation. "Srngara Sataka" is a hundred verses on beauty and love. "Niti Sataka" is a hundred verses on the art of politics.

The story of King Bhartarinath is legendary throughout India; the tale of a king who renounces the world, and abdicates his throne in favor of his younger brother. He then becomes an ascetic and takes up the spiritual path. Bhartair, having been first-born, had succeeded his father, King Gandharva-Sena as Raja of Ujjain.

As a king, Bhartair would have come into contact with all of the spiritual luminaries of his time, especially in his region of India. He most likely received spiritual mentoring from one or more of these individuals, including instructions in the practice of yoga. Bhartarinath was the type of soul who comes into the world with a high level of spiritual development, and for a soul like him, a little bit of guidance and training can be all that is needed.

There are a number of variations on the story of what prompted Bhartair to renounce his kingship and become a renunciate, but there is one common theme in all of them. He was heartbroken over the infidelity of his favorite queen, Pingala Rani.

Bhartair had many wives, but he was still unsatisfied and decided to take on another, named Pingala. She was young and very beautiful and Bhartair became very attached to her. He doted on her with gifts and favors, letting her have anything she asked for. But Pingala wasn't as beautiful on the inside as she was on the outside. She was very cunning and took advantage of the king's adoration of her and began causing mischief, including meddling in the affairs of state. The king's devoted younger brother, Vikram, could see what she was up to and went to Bhartair to complain. He also suggested that she may not be loyal to him. But the king sided with Pingala and exiled his brother from the kingdom.

One day, Raja Bhartair was visited by a great Rishi. The king showed the holy man great respect and began serving him in various ways. The Rishi was very moved by the king's sincere gestures and offered him a special fruit, which he claimed could bestow perfect health, longevity, and even immortality. The king felt that such a valuable gift should not go to him, but should go to his beloved Pingala, so he presented her with the fruit.

Pingala had a paramour, who was the lead charioteer in the king's army. The two of them liked to sneak off alone together for chariot rides. Pingala offered the fruit to her lover. Pingala thought that the charioteer was devoted to her, but he had a courtesan who he had pledged his heart to. Later, when he met with his courtesan lover, the charioteer offered the fruit to her. Now, the courtesan felt that she was not worthy or deserving of such a magnificent gift, so she offered it back to the king, who she admired more than any other man in the world.

When the king received the fruit from the courtesan, he wondered how it could have gotten into her hands. He investigated the matter, and in the process, learned of his beloved Pingala's infidelity. Suddenly his whole world was shattered. His belief that he and Pingala were devoted to each other was a sham. He had sided with this deceitful, disingenuous woman and had ordered his loving and loyal brother, banished. He saw that no one was truthful and no one was loyal to their friends and family. He felt extreme disgust for the world and its trappings. So, he gave up his throne, donned a loin cloth, and moved into the forests to live the life of a sannyasin.

Vairagya Sataka

> *"I am content to wear tree-bark for clothes, and you with your rich garments; but the satisfaction is alike, and the differences not*

significant. He whose desires are numerous; he is indeed poor. If the mind finds contentment, then who is rich and who is poor?"

"Winning the approval of others is difficult. Why, then, does your heart seek to appease them? With inward tranquility and simple living, wise thought arises spontaneously. Should you wish for anything, what will you not acquire?"

"As long as this body is healthy and free of infirmity; as long as senility is at a distance; as long as our faculties are vigorous; as long as we are not disabled; until then, the wise ones should make great efforts to reach the supreme goal of life. For what is the use of digging a well when the house is already on fire?"

"Surviving on alms, not needing the company of people, moving about with total freedom, disengaged with the exchange of wealth; such a one is a true ascetic. Wearing worn-out rags thrown in the streets, using a discarded blanket for a seat, without pride or selfishness, the ascetic seeks only the satisfaction of the mind controlled."

" 'Is this person an outcast?' 'Perhaps he is twice-born.' 'Maybe he's a shudra or a renunciate.' 'Could he be some master-yogi, filled with philosophical jewels?' When the yogi hears this prattle coming from the mouths of the people around him, doubting and debating, he walks away, neither angry nor amused."

<u>**Kanipanath**</u>

Kanipanath was a great Siddha yogi, and a remarkable personality, who is today revered in the Yoga traditions of India and Tibet. He was the chief disciple of Jalandharnath, and became a great Nath yogi and teacher with thousands of disciples. He is also recognized as an important master in the Vajrayana Mahasiddha Buddhist tradition. He is associated with a prophecy made by the Buddha, that there would one day be a great saint born near Bengal, and throughout all of India, there would be no yogi equal to him. He would have many disciples, but six of them would become great Siddha yogis in their own right. The prophecy even included a version of Kanipanath's name.

Kanip was born into a Brahmin caste of clerks and first became a monk at Somapuri Vihara in Bengal. He was initiated into yoga by Jalandharnath and lived amongst the Nath Yogis. He practiced his sadhanas earnestly for twelve years in the mountains of Rajasthan, before achieving self-realization.

Kanipanath authored many books on tantric yoga and both he and his master, Jalandharnath, are highly respected in the Tibetan tantric traditions. His writing includes a combination of traditional tantric ideas mixed with Saiva themes. His collected works include at least six writings on philosophy and seventy-four on tantric subjects. He is also popularly known for his devotional hymns.

> *"Taking three refugees in a boat, I captured eight.*
>
> *In my body resides compassion, and the chamber is empty.*
>
> *I crossed the river of existence like a dream.*
>
> *In mid-river I came to know the waves.*
>
> *I used five tathagatas as oars.*
>
> *Kanip rows the boat like a dream.*
>
> *Smelling, touching and tasting as they are*

Kanipanath developed a number of transcendental abilities, by virtue of his acquisition of certain siddhis. But by using them inappropriately for a time, his guru, Jalandharnath, withdrew them. After learning his lesson, the siddhis were restored.

Gahininath

Gahininath was a disciple of Gorakshnath. He liked to spend his time meditating in caves in the hills of Western India, living for many years at Brahmagiri, now located in Maharashtra. One day, a young boy named Nivritti accidentally entered a cave where Gahininath was practicing his sadhanas. Gahininath believed that the boy's sudden presence must be Shiva's work, so he instructed the boy in yoga and provided him with full initiation instructions. Nivritti became an adept yogi and went on to initiate his entire family and many more people in his region.

Revananath and Nageshnath

Revananath was a great Siddha of ancient India, born near the banks of the Narmada River and raised in a farmer's family. Revananath became self-realized at an early age and received siddhis, after being blessed by Lord Dattatreya, who recognized him as an avatar. After receiving Datta's blessing, the boy's family was blessed with an abundance of foods and grains from that time onward. Machendranath visited the boy's village and warned Revananath about misusing his transcendental gifts. He counseled him, telling him to focus on his further inner development and to work for the welfare of the hungry and needy.

There is an allegorical story about Revananath, which informs us about his transcendental attainments, and how he was involved in the birth of Nageshnath, another great Nav Nath Saint. In his province, there lived a woman, known as a 'maiee', who liked to cause trouble for all of the saintly people, especially Revananath. His disciple, Marul, requested his guru to put an end to the maiee's nuisance. Revananath accepted his disciple's plea and converted the woman into a musical instrument, which he kept as one of his possessions and played for the remainder of his life. After this, the people in the area referred to him as 'Kada Siddha'.

Revananath liked to travel around to the local villages, blessing the people with his wisdom and kindness. Once, while on a pilgrimage, he arrived at a village in Maharashtra, and was invited into the home of a local Brahmin who was conducting a ceremony to name his newly born son. He stayed over with the family and the following morning the family discovered that the child had died. The family was overcome with grief. The Brahmin took Revananath aside and spoke to him, telling him that his family was cursed. This was the seventh son who had died. Revananath knew that he must have some special duties to perform for this family. He prayed to Shiva to return the souls of the seven children to the Brahmin, and Lord Shiva reinstated all seven children to the parents, alive. All seven boys ultimately became disciples of Revananath.

The eldest son of the Brahmin was named Nageshnath. As the boy grew up, he and his friends used to play at the local temple, pretending to feed the deities there. One day Lord Datta appeared to the boy and asked, "I am a guest here. May I also have food?" The other boys were reluctant, but Nageshnath pretended to serve him food. Lord Datta immediately recognized the boy as an incarnation. He was so pleased with the boy's generous spirit that he told him, "Henceforth, whenever you want or need food, it will appear instantly in front of you. You will be able to serve these children and anyone else who is hungry."

Nageshnath later learned that Lord Dattatreya was living in a village to the South. He traveled there and searched for the great saint but could not find him. Then he went to the temple priest with a plan. He said he would create a giant feast for the entire village, in hopes that Datta would hear of the feast and attend. The priest agreed and the feast was a big success. To the delight of Nageshnath, Lord Dattatreya did attend and the two enjoyed a heartfelt reunion

Charpatinath

Charpatinath is one of the most distinguished Siddhas of the Nath Sampradaya, and was a disciple of Gorakshnath. He is recognized by many later writers, including Guru Nanak in Sidh Gosti, a portion of the Guru Granth Sahib. He was the brother of Mayanamati, who was the mother of the ruler of Bengal, Gopicandra. By virtue of this relationship, he was introduced to Gorakshnath and received initiation. Later in life, he was occasionally referred to as 'Raja', due to his royal bloodline.

Charpatinath became the 'Raj Guru' to Raja Sahil Varman in the Himalayan mountain kingdom of Chamba, which made him the king's spiritual advisor and closest administrator. He was involved in most of the important decisions involving the kingdom, including the relocation of the capital to the site where the city of Chamba is today. The king benefitted greatly from his close association with the master, and during his last years, he abdicated his throne in favor of his eldest son and moved into Charpatinath's ashram. As a result of Charpatinath's powerful spiritual influence on the fate of this family, the same dynasty of kings still administers Chamba today.

There are some important literary works attributed to Charpatinath. His main book, "Carpatanatha Sataka", is an important work in the Nath tradition. It is a practical book, aimed at the individual yogi, with motivational counseling and common-sense wisdom.

Carpatanatha Sataka

> *"After making obeisance to Gorakshnath,*
> *Who is supported by the gods and goddesses,*
> *The delusion in my words vanished,*
> *Replaced by the master's wisdom."*

> *"If you are after realization, renounce anger forever.*
> *Even a moment of wrath,*
> *Can burn up the benefit of*
> *Countless years of penances."*

> *"He who knows that his wealth, house, and son, belongs not to him,*
> *He is the wise one.*
> *The illusion of 'yours and mine', perverts the mind,*
> *And must be forsaken."*

> *"His limbs become feeble,*
> *His twisted long hairs gray.*
> *Without teeth,*
> *He supports himself with a stick.*
> *But even then, the old man,*
> *Holds to his hopes of never-ending life."*

> *"Oh mother, after seeing me take to the path of yoga,*

Contain your affection.
Oh father, don't grieve a lost son.
Oh brother, cry not over shared memories.

We all live our own karmas,
And never those of another."

"Like the chameleon, some may change
their garments,
And outwardly renounce the world.
But if mind and heart are not changed,
If he is mired in lethargy,
How can the yogi progress?"

"Who am I and who are you?
Who is father and who is mother?
From where did this misery come?
The yogi contemplates and questions,
And recognizes the world as a passing
dream."

"Determined to clean the body, he cleans
and cleans.
Outwardly he shines, but inside is still
soiled.
He performs the required rituals,
But has left his soul polluted with maya."

Part VI
The Spiritual Revolution

Chapter 17

THE SPIRITUAL REVOLUTION

"So, Springtime is upon us now; there will be more fragrant Saints, I would say now, who will come up and give us, through the grace of God, a contact with the God-into-expression-power. And this is the revolution, the spiritual revolution, which is coming up – an awakening all around."

Kirpal Singh, 'The Coming Spiritual Revolution'

Shabd Yoga has been practiced all over the world throughout the course of human history by mystics and sages from every ethnic and religious background. It is a natural process, available to everyone. The ability to contact and commune with the harmonic current of life is built into the make-up of human consciousness, and there are various ways a person can be introduced to it.

Over the millennia, some saints have discovered it spontaneously. During periods of prayer or repose, their inner eyes opened to visions of the higher planes and their inner ears heard the sound current. Once they became established in this process, they continued to utilize their inner eyes and ears without any guidance from a teacher. Others received instructions from a teacher, who provided essential information and facilitated the development of their ability to see and hear within. We have the records of the lives and teachings of the past masters in the form of our sacred literature. These writings attest to the timeless and universal nature of communion with the light and sound by these past saints. Religious and spiritual diversity is humanity's great jewel.

Many of the great yogis who practiced and taught pranayama over the centuries traveled extensively, teaching yoga and inspiring thousands of souls to seek self-realization. Many of them also became adept in the practice of communing with the nada, resulting from their austere lifestyles and yogic disciplines. Shabd Yoga utilizes Patanjali's Ashtanga Yoga is a blueprint for successful practice, with one added feature; in Dharana, the concentrated attention is focused on seeing with the inner eye (ajna chakra), and/or listening to the sound current. Every other aspect of the two yogas are essentially the same.

Today, the world has become a much smaller place with modern transportation, communication, and world trade. Any person who wants to explore the religious or mystical teachings of a particular teacher or tradition can easily do so. In the West, there is a growing curiosity about Eastern ideas and traditions. In the East, many social and technological advances which originated in the West have been embraced and integrated into everyday life. These social and ideological exchanges serve to facilitate the evolution of human consciousness and the fostering of integration and brotherhood.

The cornerstone of Guru Nanak's mission was to export spirituality throughout the subcontinent, across the Himalayas to the north, and all the way west to the Mediterranean. He did so on the backs of donkeys and on foot. Even so, he reached thousands of sincere seekers with his resolute efforts, and in doing so, he planted the seeds of a spiritual revolution. Five centuries layer, Kirpal Singh traveled tens of thousands of miles as he crisscrossed the globe, sowing the seeds of spirituality on five continents. Since the departure of Swami Ji, hundreds of teachers of shabd yoga have joined Kirpal in spreading the message and methods of Radha Soami far and wide.

Today, with over a hundred teachers teaching Shabd Yoga methods throughout the world, millions of people are now practicing the yoga of light and sound. As a result, the spiritual consciousness of these millions of people is evolving, because shabd yoga is a valid, effective means of awakening and developing a person's consciousness and spiritual awareness. Ultimately, this will have an aggregate effect on the conscious evolution of humanity on the whole.

The rapid rate of growth of Radha Soami as a global religious/spiritual movement is unprecedented in the history of the development of religious and ideological institutions. All of these millions of practitioners have received their training from a contemporary group, tied either directly or indirectly to the nineteenth-century spiritual mission of Swami Shiv Dayal Singh Ji in Agra, India. Some scholars estimate that by the year 2020, as many as ten million people worldwide may have been practicing some form of Shabd Yoga. If this rate of growth continues, Radha Soami will one day be counted as one of the world's leading religions.

God realization is, and has always been, available to every human being who has come into the world. Looking ahead, teachers who provide humanity with training into the principles and practices of Sant Mat will continue to help foster this inevitable, ongoing spiritual revolution.

Bibliography

Attridge, Harold W., "Anchor Bible Dictionary Vol. VI", Doubleday Books, 1992

Barks, Coleman, "The Essential Rumi", Castle Books, 1997

Brooke, John Hedley, "Science and Religion: Some Historical Perspectives", Cambridge University

Cameron, Ron, "Anchor Bible Dictionary Vol. VI", Doubleday Books, 1992

Campenhausen, H. von, "The Formation of the Christian Bible", Fortress, 1972

Capra, Fritjof, "The Tao of Physics", Shambhala, 2000

Chan, Wing-Tsit, "A Source Book in Chinese Philosophy", Princeton University Press, 1963

Ehrman, Bart D., "The Orthodox Corruption of Scriptures", Oxford University Press

Ewing, Upton Clary, "The Prophet and the Dead Sea Scrolls", Tree of Life Publications, 1993

Ezekiel, Isaac A., "Kabir The Great Mystic", Radha Soami Satsang Beas, 1992

Finocchiaro, Maurice, "The Galileo Affair", University of California Press, 1989

Goddard, Dwight, "A Buddhist Bible", Beacon Press, 1994

Golb, Norman, "Who Wrote the Dead Sea Scrolls?", Simon & Schuster, 1995

Grant, Robert M., "Jesus After the Gospels: The Christ of the Second Century", Westminster/John Knox, 1990

Khan, Hazrat Inayat, "The Mysticism of Sound", Sufi Movement, Geneva, 1979

Klijn, A. F. J., "Jewish Christian Gospel Tradition", Leiden: E. J. Brill, 1992

Ladinsky, Daniel, "The Gift – Poems by Hafiz, The Great Sufi Master", Penguin Compass, 2000

Ladinsky, Daniel, "Love Poems From God", Penguin Compass, 2002

Lane, David, "Shabd Yoga - Esoterica from the East", 2018

Lane, David, "The Radhasoami Tradition", 2015

Lane, David, "Rai Salig Ram", 2018

Lane, David, "The Unknowing Sage, The Life and Work of Baba Faqir Chand", 2014

Lane, David, "Prince Dara Shukoh's Compass of Truth", 2020

Layton, Bentley, "The Gnostic Scriptures", Doubleday, 1987

Lindberg, David C. and Numbers, Ronald L., "God and Nature: Historical Essays on the Encounter Between Christianity and Science", 1986

Miller, Robert J., "The Complete Gospels", Polebridge Press

Muller, Max, "Rai Saligram Sahib Bahadur", 1898

Osler, Margaret, "Science and Religion in Early Modern Europe", 1998

Puri, J. R., "Guru Nanak, His Mystic Teachings", Radha Soami Satsang Beas, 1993

Puri, J. R., and Sethi, V. K., "Saint Namdev", Radha Soami Satsang Beas, 1978

Puri, J. R., and Sethi, V. K., "Tulsi Sahib, Saint of Hathras", Radha Soami Satsang Beas, 1978

Puri, J. R., and Shangari, T. R., "Bulleh Shah", Radha Soami Satsang Beas, 1986

Robinson, James M., "The Nag Hammadi Library in English", Harper & Row, 1988

Saligram, Rai, "Radha Soami Mat Prakash", 1896

Singh, Jaimal, "Spiritual Letters", Radha Soami Satsang Beas, 1976

Singh, Kirpal, "A Great Saint, Baba Jaimal Singh", Sat Sandesh Books, 1973

Singh, Kirpal, "Godman", Ruhani Satsang, 2002

Singh, Kirpal, "Jap Ji, The Message of Guru Nanak", Ruhani Satsang, 2002

Singh, Kirpal, "Naam or Word", Sat Sandesh Books, 1972

Singh, Kirpal, "The Crown of Life", Sat Sandesh Books, 1974

Singh, Kirpal, "The Teachings of Kirpal Singh", Ruhani Satsang, 1981

Singh, Kirpal, "The Way of the Saints", Sant Bani Press, 1976

Singh, Sawan, "Spiritual Gems", Radha Soami Satsang Beas, 1980

Singh, Swami Ji Shiv Dayal, "Sar Bachan", Radha Soami Satsang Beas, 1978

Szekely, Edmond B., "The Zend Avesta of Zarathustra", International Biogenic Society, 1990

Tagore, Rabindranath, "Songs of Kabir", Dover Publications, 2004

Trumpp, Ernest, "The Adi Granth, or The Holy Scriptures of the Sikhs", Munshiram Manoharlal Publishers, 1978

Upadhyaya, K. N., "Dadu, The Compassionate Mystic", Radha Soami Satsang Beas, 1980

Upadhyaya, K. N., "Guru Ravidas, Life and Teachings", Radha Soami Satsang Beas, 1982

Waley, Arthur, "The Way and its Power", Grover Press, 1958

Wallace, B. Alan, "Hidden Dimensions, The Unification of Physics and Consciousness", Columbia University Press, 2007

Watson, Burton, "The Lotus Sutra", Columbia University Press, 1993

Welch, Holmes, "Taoism, The Parting of the Way", Beacon Press, 1966

Wigg, Eileen and Narendra, Devinder, "Love, Light, and Life", 2010

NOTES

* 9 7 9 8 9 8 9 4 8 7 1 4 1 *